The return of the housewife

Manchester University Press

The return of the housewife

Why women are still cleaning up

Emma Casey

MANCHESTER UNIVERSITY PRESS

Published by Manchester University Press
Oxford Road, Manchester, M13 9PL

www.manchesteruniversitypress.co.uk

British Library Cataloguing-in-Publication Data
A catalogue record for this book is available from the British Library

ISBN   978 1 5261 7097 2   hardback

First published 2025

The publisher has no responsibility for the persistence or accuracy of URLs for any external or third-party internet websites referred to in this book, and does not guarantee that any content on such websites is, or will remain, accurate or appropriate.

EU authorised representative for GPSR:
Easy Access System Europe, Mustamäe tee 50, 10621 Tallinn, Estonia
gpsr.requests@easproject.com

Typeset
by New Best-set Typesetters Ltd

Contents

Introduction: Why are women still cleaning up?

It is September 2022 and social media is awash with images and posts about the end of summer and the autumnal chill in the air. Pictures of beaches and sunsets are slowly replaced with fireplaces, candles, blankets and pumpkin-themed decor. At the same time, social media influencers are turning their attention to preparing their homes, clothes and families for winter. The seasonal change is palpable, with scents, textures, food and home decor all shifting in line with the colder months to come. For the social media cleaning influencers – the 'cleanfluencers' – each change in season is critical. It's not just the weather that matters, it is also a time to mark the seasonal changes through the visual representation of the home. There is a renewed focus on the repositioning of household objects; a shift in soft furnishings to include more faux fur, fleece and blankets; changes in food preparation, bringing out the slow cooker and making hot chocolate; back-to-school organisation and planning; even beginning to prepare for Christmas. And for the cleaning influencers, autumn marks a key time for notable changes in cleaning practices. Gone are the breezy, floral scents of summer and lines of washing drying on the line outside, to be replaced with more earthy autumnal scents such as pumpkin and blackberry that will soon move on to more Christmassy scents of cinnamon and orange. The seasonal change is a big moment for the cleaning influencer; it is a chance to persuade followers of the need to *change*, to try something new, to feather the nest of home in a way that exudes cosiness, organisation, comfort, cleanliness, calm and order. These

1

moments of change represented in the display, planning, organising and preparing of domestic spaces are an opportunity to rearticulate the home and one's position in it.

At the same time, in autumn 2022, the UK's most popular and well-known social media cleaning celebrity, Mrs Hinch,[1] has embraced the end of summer and the beginning of autumn with the launch of a new range of 'Mrs Hinch' branded Procter & Gamble cleaning products. There is Fairy washing up liquid, Flash floor cleaner, surface spray, dishwasher tablets, laundry detergent, fabric conditioner and 'scent booster' powder. All are conspicuously branded with the Mrs Hinch logo and are scented with the new 'Frosted Eucalyptus' fragrance. There is a dramatic online build-up to the launch on Instagram, with the Joy of Clean Instagram page posting 'hints' to their followers that there is something big afoot; a 'big announcement' is on its way. The build-up continues in the days before the launch with a picture of Mrs Hinch sitting behind some bunches of eucalyptus sprigs. The Joy of Clean promises that 'something very exciting (like new-level, never-done-before kind of exciting) is on its way ... we can't wait to tell you. We know you're going to love it!!!' Then, forty-eight hours later, the big product launch alongside a hashtag especially created for the occasion – #HinchAlyptus – which shoppers can use to tag themselves buying the products that are, for now, exclusively available at the British discount shop Home Bargains. In a 'reveal' story posted to her Instagram page and shared to her four million followers, Mrs Hinch creates a dramatic launch of the new cleaning range. Shot to look like she is creating the film herself on her own phone, the camera moves through her immaculately clean and stylish kitchen towards the under-sink cupboard. The door is slowly opened to reveal a perfectly clean space decorated with more eucalyptus leaves below which bottles, containers, boxes and bags of her new Procter & Gamble Frosted Eucalyptus cleaning products sit. In a combination of humour ('yes, I decorate my under-sink cupboard!'), excitement and gratitude, Mrs Hinch directly addresses her followers – the people most likely to buy the products. In her launch post she writes, 'I can't believe the day is here!' and 'Can't wait to see what you make of it', before directly thanking her followers with a 'Thank you' message surrounded by hearts.

Almost instantly, the products appear in other social media cleaning accounts all over Instagram, Facebook and TikTok. Videos are uploaded into stories of shoppers thrilled and excited at the new product: 'I'm just so excited!'; 'I've waited so long for this!'; 'Honestly it smells amazing!' The products are shown laid out on kitchen worktops, in cupboards, in shopping trolleys, in shopping bags and even in excited selfies of shoppers holding their coveted bottles of Mrs Hinch Frosted Eucalyptus products. The next post on the Mrs Hinch Instagram page shows a montage reel of seemingly endless Instagram posts of the new cleaning products. Played against the 2021 single 'Summer 91 (Looking Back)' by Noizu, the lyric 'I just can't stop looking back until it's a memory' reminds us of the message behind influencer culture. It is presented as an intimate journey of discovery and joyful personal betterment; a reflection of how far you've come, but always remembering and humbly reflecting on your roots; 'Thank you: all of your tags, posts, stories, reels are incredible. I'm a bit speechless if I'm honest.' Narratives like this one are of course key to the success of the advertisement. *Cleaning must be seen as absolutely more than simply cleaning.* Selling cleaning products today is not just about buying the right product to do the job well; rather, cleaning is entwined with popular notions of positive mindsets, personal fulfilment, excitement and enhancing your sense of self; a type of sentimental reflection of *who you are*.

Switching to slower-tempo piano music, the next post shows Mrs Hinch sitting serenely in a beautiful late summer field, sun low in the sky, occupied with her baby son and surrounded by grazing animals. It's a picture that perfectly captures contemporary ideals of home and domestic labour; love, happiness, serenity and calm from the chaos are all achievable to those who adopt the right mindset, who conform to gendered norms of domesticity – and of course, to those who are savvy enough to buy the right cleaning products. Mrs Hinch again thanks her followers: 'Thank you so much for today. It really blows my mind to think how our home and cleaning community on here changes lives … lots of love to every single one of you.' It is a reminder again, not only of the promise of the transformative potential of cleaning, but also that her new products have been created with a type of altruism in mind – with an illusion of *love* and *care* for the people buying them.

What happened? How did the seemingly mundane activities of cleaning and tidying become such a hyper-visible and prominent feature of contemporary popular culture? How did the new online cleaning cultures become so integral to the multi-billion dollar global giants of the domestic cleaning industry? Moreover, why does it matter and what can the so-called cleanfluencing phenomenon tell us about ourselves? To what extent is cleanfluencing a reworking of the age-old stereotype of the happy and willing woman who finds joy and satisfaction in mundane housewifely chores and who excitedly awaits the next product or device supposedly designed to lighten the load of domestic drudgery? In this book I address these questions. I explore the phenomenon of making housework 'glamorous', noting that although popular images of the immaculately presented housewife, smiling as she effortlessly performs household labour, is nothing new, within contemporary media cultures housework is repositioned as an integral part of the 'self' – a key feature of *who we are*; as a route to aspiration; as something attractive, appealing and exciting. In other words, I explore what I term the 'reglamourisation' of housework. In many ways this offers a reproduction of the old gendered stereotypes surrounding cleaning, while at the same time suggesting a modern and 'glamorous' version of the housewife that is seemingly more palatable to today's postfeminist audiences and consumers. Indeed, we only ever see Mrs Hinch in an apron with curlers in her hair, her face distorted using a social media filter into a cartoonish horror version of the 1950s housewife when she wants to 'complain' – either about the mess in her house or the lack of support she gets from her husband in keeping the house clean and tidy. It serves as a timely reminder that the 'complaining' and protesting housewife is a relic of a bygone age: a grotesque parody of the woman who says no – who isn't willingly compliant in her domestic role.

Of course, Mrs Hinch is just one example of the seemingly infinite number of social media accounts dedicated to offering new, glamorous retellings of the chores associated with housework and to curating digital images of the perfect, immaculately clean and well-ordered home. It might strike the reader as odd that in an age of widespread feminist activism and a supposedly enlightened attitude towards gender equality, so many women have actively embraced the seemingly hyper-normative, even conservative world of digital housework. In this book I attempt to make sense of this apparent contradiction. Namely, how it is that in spite of the feminist ideal of women being freed up for creativity and independence, a hyper-visible, highly popular and thoroughly ubiquitous digital media trend has materialised; one which appears to be dedicated to enabling their overwhelmingly women followers to micro-plan, organise and account for every minute of their lives.

Who are the cleanfluencers? And what is cleanfluencing?

This is a book about the digital housewife or 'cleanfluencer'. It focuses primarily on cleanfluencing within the UK context. This is in part because the British cleanfluencer, although often lumped together with other depictions of the housewife, such as the 'tradwife' in the US, is a product of the extraordinary British economic and political landscape of recent years, which has resulted in cultural shifts from which the cleanfluencer has emerged. In particular, cleanfluencing emerged against the backdrop of the COVID-19 pandemic and the ensuing shifts in domesticity and digital cultures during this time. In the UK, the pandemic triggered a retreat in recent advancements towards gender inequality, particularly within the domestic sphere.[2] Moreover, cleanfluencing occurs alongside the economic impacts of British austerity politics, a worsening of living standards and the decline in health and social care provision.

Alongside these social and political shifts, recent years have witnessed an upsurge in online digital 'influencers', particularly on social media sites such as Instagram and TikTok. The influencer boom, alongside a renewed post-pandemic focus on keeping homes clean, germ-free and 'safe' – not only from bacteria but also from the ravages of economic insecurity – has culminated in the burgeoning popularity of the cleanfluencers, an online reconfiguration of the white woman housewife responsible for curating digital images of the perfect home. The book explores the ways in which the reglamourising of housework in contemporary digital media has helped to distort the wider processes that ensure the continued exploitation of women's unpaid labour.

The 1959 Disney film version of *Sleeping Beauty* features a famous 'cleaning-up' scene where Sleeping Beauty's three fairy godmothers retrieve their magic wands from the attic and use them to magically clean up the mess in their kitchen. Against a catchy song made famous by the film, they dance and smile as plates, bowls and cups fly effortlessly to their rightful position on the dresser. Drawers open by magic as cutlery flies into place, and a mop dances across the floor on its own. Using magic to transform cleaning up from drudgery and toil to joyful and fun is a recurring theme throughout Disney princess films. The song 'A Spoonful of Sugar' in the 1964 film *Mary Poppins* depicts cleaning as 'a lark, a spree' so long as it is performed with the right attitude. Mary clicks her fingers and beds are magically made, folded clothes fly into drawers and toys jump back into their boxes. More recently, the 2007 film *Enchanted* features the 'Happy Working Song' where Princess Giselle in her ball gown summons animals to help her clean her apartment. Everything is magical, sparkling, effortless and, in the end, *perfect*. Some sixty-five years after the cinema release of *Sleeping Beauty*, the appeal of watching magical, *impossible* depictions of housework as easy, effortless and speedy have resurfaced. One of the most popular trends within cleanfluencing is the accelerated video reel where multiple cleaning and tidying activities are condensed into thirty seconds. Some cleanfluencers even use songs from Disney princess films in their videos. We rarely see the effort and energy that goes into housework – just a quick click of the fingers and in an instant everything is back in its place, immaculate, shining, ordered.

In order to make sense of the new popular appeal of social media depictions of housework, the book explores how the contemporary phenomenon of cleaning influencing or 'cleanfluencing' has become one of today's most popular social media trends, especially on the digital platforms Instagram and TikTok. As a widespread popular cultural phenomenon, cleanfluencing gained particular prominence during the COVID-19 pandemic alongside the wider 'influencer boom'. The first use of the word 'cleanfluencer' that I can find was in a 2019 article by the *Guardian* journalist Arwa Mahdawi,[3] who used the term to refer to an apparently new generation of previously unknown or 'ordinary' women who become famous (often spectacularly so, as is the case with Mrs Hinch) via their highly visible social media presence through sharing myriad cleaning and household 'survival' tips with their followers. Many of these tips – spraying and wiping surfaces, using a shower head to clean the bath, pouring toilet cleaner round the rim of the toilet bowl – are by no means new, but the *digital* format (generally self-filmed video footage alongside either uplifting or moving popular music) has proved a huge success. Hashtags such as #cleantok, #shinenotshame, #cleaninginspo and #instaclean, and multiple individual cleanfluencing accounts, regularly gain hundreds of thousands, and sometimes millions (as with Mrs Hinch), of followers.

How can we make sense of this and why is it important that we do? Why did watching seemingly mundane domestic activities and household cleaning practices up close and in this new glamourised way become appealing? What *is* the appeal? Who does it appeal to, why and why now? Moreover, what does it matter?

Historically situating the white woman housewife

In order to begin to make sense of the contemporary digital cleanfluencer, we might consider her visual portrayal alongside previous historical representations of the 'housewife'. What we see is that the popular image of the white woman housewife is nothing new. She is at once both the same as and different from what came before, with the contemporary cleanfluencer just one in a long line of popular, often sexist, racist and classist, representations of housewives.

In *Imperial Leather*, Anne McClintock traces the emergence throughout the nineteenth century of a 'cult of domesticity', whereby the expansion of empire coincided with the rise of advertising and sale of domestic cleaning products.[4] During this time, the domestic space became increasingly commodified in a way which reflected the racist imperialistic fantasies of 'racial hygiene and imperial progress' that became popularised in the nineteenth-century Pears soap advertisements.[5] By the end of the nineteenth century, the home had become a place for the display of status and civilised respectability. This process of 'domestic colonialism' relied on the removal of any visible remnant or trace of female labour, with femininity instead becoming a spectacle symbolised by gleamingly clean surfaces, spotless, streak free shine and dazzlingly white laundry.[6]

In the 1980s, the feminist scholar Maria Mies coined the term 'housewifization' to refer to the conscious creation of the increasingly popularised figure of the white woman housewife, whose growth paralleled colonial and industrial histories and processes.[7] Variously depicted and mainstreamed within colonial cultures as the epitome of 'purity', 'heroism' and 'civility', Mies describes how the expansion of colonialism and imperialism occurred in tandem with the rise of the 'housewife' in Europe and the United States. The creation of the almost saintly figure of the housewife was depicted as long ago as the seventeenth century by Dutch masters whose paintings imagined a 'virtuous' and 'ideal' housewife, serenely sewing, cooking, sweeping and child-rearing, always in spotlessly clean homes (Figure 1). Often a Bible was visible too, representing morality and piety of thought; a sense of 'dignity and moral vigour' within the most mundane of domestic scenes.[8]

This new reworking and reinvention of domestic interiors and women's central place within them was part of an intentional and calculated global process that was ultimately effective in creating a casual female labour force of unpaid domestic workers, represented as willing, content and actively choosing housework as their vocation. The 'good' and virtuous domestic woman was placed at the very

1 *The Virtuous Woman*, Nicolaes Maes c.1655. Reproduced with permission from the Wallace Collection.

centre of capitalism and colonialism, with privatised arenas of 'home', 'family' and 'love' increasingly separated, both physically and symbolically, from the public realms of production and accumulation. Housewifisation was thus the process of 'civilising' women across the colonial world in the art of 'cleanliness, punctuality, obedience and industriousness'.[9] Bourgeois laws around marriage and the family were also extended to the proletarian, who himself became 'civilised', acquiring his own mini-colony and domesticated housewife. House-work thus acquired a new function central to 'capitalist accumula-tion', with the unpaid domestic labour of women increasingly being seen as a 'natural resource, freely available like air and water'.[10] More recently, Gargi Bhattacharyya has described how racial capital-ism is sustained via reproductive labour.[11]

In this book, I describe how, in order to make sense of popular representations of housework today, we must also consider the legacies of the colonial roots of women as housewives. I argue that housework is a potent form of *capitalist accumulation*. What I mean by this is, first, that in their role as unpaid domestic worker, women have long conducted the invisible labour, caring and childcare that props up capitalist economies; and second, that housework itself has increasingly become intensively commodified. All of this relies on and centres around the expectation of women as willing and natural arbiters of domestic labour and the home, which are just as intrinsic to popular representations of housework today as they were in the past. The solemn and unrelenting commitment to creating a clean, ordered home as a sanctuary from the ravages of the public spheres of production, depicted as far back as the seventeenth century, *lingers*, finding its contemporary expression in twenty-first-century digital representations of housework.

And yet, at the heart of the long-popularised image of the happy, serene and naturally competent housewife lies a contradiction that often rumbles but is rarely directly addressed. Noting this contradic-tion, the scholar and activist Angela Davis describes the plight of the white housewife who is expected to willingly expend her labour free of charge for the benefit of personal and familial respectability and wellbeing; in their relegation to the domestic sphere, women became appendages to men, even servants to their husbands.[12] In such an unequal setting, Davis argues that there was always 'bound to be resistance'. By appropriating the language of abolition towards an account of their subordination within the home, and channelling this into their own participation in the campaign for abolition that offered 'an exciting alternative to their domestic lives',[13] white women housewives were able to publicly resist the 'passive' housewife role.

Recent history too is littered with examples of opposition to and protest at the expectation that women will compliantly carry the bulk of unpaid domestic drudgery. Underpinning the book is the conundrum of why the sort of hyper-visible, mainstreamed and highly normative images of women as happy and willing housewives persist in spite of centuries of feminist activism and protest. Many of these protests have been enormously high profile, helping to illuminate the gender inequalities at the heart of domestic labour. For example, in Iceland in 1975, 90 per cent of Icelandic women participated in a day of strike action nicknamed the 'Women's Day Off'; a twenty-four hour walk-out from housework. Newspapers reported on the ensuing chaos, as men took their children to work, shops sold out of sausages – the cheap and easy to cook 'fast food' of the day – and, as the *Boston Globe* reported, dishes were left unwashed and beds unmade.[14]

Almost fifty years have passed since the women of Iceland took their day of strike action and since Silvia Federici wrote her seminal essay *Wages Against Housework*, in which she described the 'occupational diseases of the housewife'.[15] It is also half a century since the American feminist and activist Selma James founded the Wages for Housework campaign. And yet, gendered inequalities around domestic labour remain stubbornly persistent. Rather than *working less*, as James had demanded in her address to the 1972 National Conference of Women in Manchester, women in particular face a raft of new and intensified domestic demands.[16]

Alongside the intensification of the unequal distribution of housework, the COVID-19 pandemic also saw more women making regular use of social media, especially Instagram and TikTok, where the widespread use of housework-themed memes became popular as a humorous response to unprecedented circumstances. The health crisis of the COVID-19 pandemic was notably accompanied by a sharp increase, particularly for women, in unpaid domestic labour. 'Glad the weekend is here, I can wash the dishes, mop floors, dust the furniture, and do the laundry!' read one popular meme against an image of a smiling woman, cloth in hand. 'Me after following the cleaning accounts on Insta for a few days!' read another against an image of a stack of Amazon parcels on a doorstep. These witty and ironic rebuttals often appear among pages and pages of posts uncritically offering 'hacks, motivation and inspo' to keep homes clean, tidy and well organised.

The COVID-19 'lockdown' transformed the usual taken-for-granted rhythms of everyday life. In particular, it coincided with new ideas and meanings of 'home' and what we mean by 'domestic life'. During this time, homes were being repurposed as simultaneously places for paid work, educating children, leisure and shopping. In many ways, this was entirely at odds with the rigid demarcation between home and work that developed during the expansion of industrial societies discussed earlier. And yet, *home* and the idea of the 'ideal' home as a sanctuary, a safe space of calm and order away from the chaos and disorder of the outside world, became even more entrenched during this time, with an explosion of soothing adjectives to describe the home, which became increasingly curated to create a 'cosy', 'comfy', 'happy place'.

A decade ago, the home-furnishing trend 'shabby chic' promised a thrifty, make-do-and-mend aesthetic that coincided with the economic recession and austerity politics. Similarly, today an explosion in popularity of the Swedish concept of *hygge* offers a domestic alternative to the crisis; a safe and cosy retreat from the chaos of an outside world made all the more dangerous by an unprecedented health pandemic. Both aesthetics quickly became heavily commercialised, for example by the Kath Kidston range of 'vintage' printed homeware, through to the proliferation of branded *hygge*-themed homeware. Yet what we saw in evidence, particularly during the COVID-19 lockdown, was the intensification of social media, in particular Instagram and TikTok, as a means of *promoting, marketing* and *selling* products.

In recent years, new, highly conspicuous ways of managing and displaying the home have become a way of creating a space of order and calm away from the chaos of crisis capitalism, with women disproportionately bearing the burden of achieving this. Early research findings in the immediate aftermath of the pandemic showed that it was women who were doing the lion's share of extra Covid-related unpaid labour in addition to the housework they had been doing anyway.[17] The pandemic bore a renewed focus on and intensified fear of 'germs' and bacteria, and this, alongside a generally heightened health fear, coincided with an increased vigilance in keeping homes clean and sanitised. This intensified concern with domestic cleanliness meant that inevitably the domestic load became significantly bigger, including advice to wipe down individual items of shopping and regularly sanitising surfaces and door handles. The usual tasks of tidying, washing and cooking became endless as families congregated at home, while empty supermarket shelves caused by stockpiling and supply chain problems necessitated more regular trips for food shopping and endless food and meal planning. Alongside these intensified domestic demands, the almost total collapse of childcare during the pandemic and the sudden, unprecedented shift to mass home-schooling meant that the effective functioning of domestic life was nearly impossible without the permanent presence of someone at home. I argue that what became visible during and after the pandemic was a *bolstering* of the expectation that this labour is performed by women. It was an expectation centuries in the making that has become galvanised rather than challenged in recent years, finding its visual expression on digital social media.

We know that substantially more women than men have not returned to their paid work following the pandemic and that women have disproportionately taken responsibility for managing the home, have continued to work part-time more often than men and have abandoned their plans to change jobs or apply for promotions.[18] In her book *Heading Home*, Shani Orgad shows that the pattern of highly educated professional women leaving the workplace once they have children is in part explained by the powerful expectation to maintain high standards of home order and childcare that still falls primarily to women.[19] These expectations – the popular assumption that women will bear the brunt of domestic chores and that women are blessed with the financial and career privilege to stay at home – remain overwhelmingly unchallenged. In a hastily pulled, ill-advised lockdown Home Office campaign, 'Stay Home Save Lives', four cartoon images of homes depicted women ironing, home-schooling children and sweeping floors. Only one of the images featured a man (relaxing on the sofa). Around the same time, the then chancellor Rishi Sunak made a point of 'thanking mums everywhere' for their lockdown contribution, again compounding the idea of women's rightful role as chief arbiters of the home and as managers of the domestic sphere, and also echoing the centuries-old rhetoric around 'heroic' mums whose duty it is to step forwards to save the day in times of crisis. The campaign, compounded with Sunak's tribute to mums, also betrayed an almost total lack of awareness that staying at home at all during lockdown was a privilege bestowed on those who were financially secure and working in the right sorts of jobs. During the pandemic, many poorer women continued to go to work during lockdown, shouldering what must have felt like an unbearable quadruple burden of domestic work, childcare, home-schooling and paid work.

It is particularly interesting that this dramatic and sudden influx of extra domestic demands and work during the COVID-19 lockdown coincided with a notable exacerbation of intense digital visual images, not only of the perfect, immaculately clean and tidy home, but also the intense proliferation of *women* performing the bulk of this labour. How can we make sense of this? One might imagine that in an age of supposed 'kindness', empathy and equality this would be a good time for pressures to ease. The fact that the opposite appears to have happened is a key theme of the book. Although often shrouded in assurances that 'my house is really messy', 'I have a storage room like Monica's!'[20] and 'life's too short for housework!', we never see any evidence in the cleanfluencing accounts of the mess, dirt, clutter or exhaustion; in other words, of any representation of the gritty reality of housework. Why is this? What purpose does the 'ideal home' narrative serve, particularly in times of crisis? And why does there seem to be so little resistance?

Social media has become the central space for creating, sharing and engaging with the daily realities of housework. Today, it is awash with groups, accounts, hashtags, video reels and stories that offer followers an abundance of online content related to housework, along with unbridled access to links that take you to websites where you can purchase the commodities that promise to help you recreate the same within your own home. One of the most ubiquitous online cleanfluencing genres is the accelerated video reel consisting of a montage of short multi-frames featuring close-ups of mundane cleaning activities around the home. Cleanfluencers have become adept at using social media apps to produce their own self-filmed video reels, which have become possibly the most recognisable and ubiquitous feature of contemporary social media. The video reels are short (Instagram increased the maximum length of their video reels from sixty to ninety seconds in July 2022), so multiple video extracts are remixed and edited together to create breathtakingly fast-paced, quick and easy to watch footage. A *single* thirty-second reel might include: a plastic bin being rinsed with a shower head; a kettle being filled with white vinegar, boiled and rinsed; a vacuum cleaner being pushed in neat lines up and down a carpet; a smaller handheld vacuum sucking up dirt from the corners of a room; a bright pink liquid being poured round the rim of the toilet; and a scented candle being lit. The videos feel almost hypnotic in their pace, backed by catchy music, often with uplifting lyrics – 'I'm a survivor', 'I wouldn't have it any other way', 'When love takes over' – that mask the ordinary sounds of housework, their brevity followed seamlessly by another, similar video. For a follower of the contem-porary world of digital housework, one becomes caught in the seemingly never-ending, unlimited loop of speeded-up video reels, drawing the viewer into a highly sensory saturation of multiple images and sounds. The montages seem to emphasise speed, energy and efficiency, almost in the style of an exercise video, with creators regularly using their new-found digital fame to become product 'ambassadors', 'influencers' and representatives for domestic cleaning companies. They are uplifting, fun, entertaining and illuminated with the promise of satisfaction, serenity and wellbeing that, it is promised, are the chief rewards for the labour that goes into cleaning and ordering your home.

This hyper-accelerated representation of cleaning is a central feature of the cleanfluencing genre and an interesting reversal of the repetitive mundanity and plodding drudgery of housework. The latter was famously depicted in the slow cinema feminist classic *Jeanne Dielman*, a 1975 film directed by Chantal Akeman.[21] The film depicts in almost real time (the film is long at 3.5 hours long) the daily domestic routines and rituals of Jeanne, a widowed mother who is variously shown dusting ornaments, peeling potatoes, polishing her son's shoes, grinding coffee and making beds. Jeanne is also a sex worker, and her visits from men are woven into her almost obsessive everyday housework routines. The film is unusual in its centring of the female perspective and particularly of its depiction of domestic labour and sex work. Ultimately Jeanne has nothing for herself – her life is structured around servicing men, including her teenage son – and her underlying anguish slowly builds throughout the film.

The contradictions inherent in the rampant inequalities of domestic labour that Angela Davis once described, and the patriarchal expectations placed on women depicted in the slow cinema of *Jeanne Dielman*, are thrown into stark relief in the contemporary world of the cleanfluencer, where inequalities are repackaged as offering glamour, security and a quick-fire route to calm, order, personal betterment and status. This book draws on examples of some of the most well-known 'celebrity' cleanfluencers such as Mrs Hinch, discussed earlier, but also on the seeming accessibility of cleanfluencing – exploring the possibility that part of its appeal lies in the idea that anyone with a smartphone can achieve the same dizzy heights of fame and fortune. In addition, as 'ordinary' celebrities, the most popular cleanfluencers are also the ones who *appear* to be most like us – with the same humble beginnings and reluctant attitude to 'fame' – and who present their stories in a way that directly speaks to the everyday stresses, anxieties and longings of their followers: 'I'm really just like you!'

I argue in this book that the glamourising of housework makes it very difficult to challenge. Why would we refuse something so appealing, something that we are repeatedly promised will make us feel good? At the root of contemporary consumer culture is the idea that happiness and satisfaction can be found *within*; that it is accessible via the products we purchase and our lifestyle choices. Against a backdrop of multiple and overlapping crises where inequalities appear to be as unbridled as ever, women are discouraged from saying no, resisting, making a fuss or 'overthinking'. The solution is to use commerce, surrounding ourselves with the right type of domestic aesthetic, self-help books and products that will make our lives easier, and of course to use social media to spread the word to others. Importantly, as others have noted, social media itself has in recent years, particularly following the pandemic, become a key mode of shopping; from the algorithm-driven direct marketing of products through to the celebrity influencer who shrouds her sales pitches behind witty and friendly intimacy with followers.

The most successful cleanfluencers are adept at producing social media content that directly addresses the 'problem' – the mess, the dirt, the never-ending admin, the clutter, the absence of any help with the chores – and then proposes a solution that often boils down to women working on themselves to find joy and satisfaction in housework and working more efficiently. This is all achieved with the support of a range of products that promise to make housework a more joyful and streamlined experience, and a raft of social media accounts that are dedicated to helping overwhelmingly women followers to micro-plan, organise and account for every minute of their time; to *work smart, not hard!* This, of course, is far removed from the feminist ideal of women being freed from the shackles of domestic drudgery; however, by reinventing housework, cleanfluencers promise a 'helping hand', a 'fun' alternative to the old-fashioned toil of housework and the promise of happiness, calm and order to those who capitulate. Cleanfluencing accounts are packed with tips designed to persuade followers that the well-organised housewife has an enjoyable and happy life. The Mrs Hinch-branded 'list-book' is a bestseller on Amazon and is regularly tagged in cleaning and tidying accounts across digital media. The book is a type of diary where cleaning, tidying and motivational 'ta-da!' lists relating to domestic labour chores can be made: make beds – tick!; put a load of washing on – tick!; polish door knobs – tick!; clean kitchen floor – tick!; clean inside microwave – tick!

Perhaps the most well-known cleanfluencer globally is Marie Kondo, a decluttering and tidying expert from Japan, who founded the 'KonMari' or 'sparking joy' approach to housework, particularly folding, tidying and organising. Kondo's popular Instagram account is accompanied by a Netflix show, *Tidying Up*, a range of bestselling books and an online shop selling all the items you might need to replicate Kondo's method in your own home. These include storage boxes and baskets, drawer dividers, glass jars with cork lids and handbag organisers, all promoted against an ultra-minimalist, perfectly tidy ideal. In the UK, Gemma Bray, 'The Organised Mum' blogger, also has a bestselling book, this time offering housework time-management tips, print-off worksheets for housework planning, a housework 'bootcamp' and a popular app that promises it will help to wipe cleaning 'from your mental load'. An accompanying playlist series, 'Rock the Housework', offers uplifting, energising tunes to make the job easier.

And so what is new? How do these contemporary representations of housework differ to what came before? For example, in Mrs Beeton's 1861 *Book of Household Management* and her early veneration of the 'intelligent and thorough' housewife who embraces housework as a vocation, with the same zeal and enterprise as the 'commander of an army'. In this book, I describe the cleanfluencers as the latest in a long line of public figures made famous for imparting their rules around and knowledge of housework to their followers. I show how new representations of housework as fun and a type of self-expression add an extra layer to the long-standing myth that, done properly, housework has a kind of magical ability to transform homes, lives and families. Feminists have long argued that the unequal division of domestic labour not only hinders women's ability to fully participate in public life but also that the drudgery associated with the never-ending demands of housework as a set of soul-destroying, repetitive tasks is fraught with anxiety and compulsiveness. And yet, as I explore in this book, one of the most enduring myths of the last century is that of the happy, content housewife.

It is a myth which, as we shall see, finds its most recent incarnation in the twenty-first-century digital housewife who ascribes her happiness to a clean, tidy and well-organised home, finding solace and order in domestic cleaning rituals and processes.

Organisation of the book

The book is structured around five key aims. The first is to offer a novel account of the reglamourisation of the white woman housewife as a 'cleanfluencer' in contemporary digital cultures and to explore where she came from and her role within the supply chains of global capitalism. Second, the book aims to make sense of the sheer persistence of gendered inequalities around housework. Despite decades of feminist action and intervention, these inequalities remain seemingly undisturbed, particularly following the COVID-19 pandemic.[22] The book explores the role of the cleanfluencer in reproducing these inequalities. Third, I account for the dramatic recent popular appeal of the cleanfluencer as a heavily commodified contemporary depiction of the housewife rooted in ideals of aspiration, glamour and desirability. This connects to the fourth aim, which is to examine the relationships between housework, self-realisation and the positive-thinking movement and to ask: is it possible to clean and tidy your way to happiness? Finally, the book considers radical alternatives to current inequalities of housework by identifying cleanfluencing as part of the highly individualistic and commercial structures of late capitalism.

Each chapter explores themes that help to address these five aims. In Chapter 1, '"I really wanted to share this with you all!": The commercial success of the cleanfluencer', I explore the relationship between the cleanfluencers and the celebrity housewives that came before. It examines the meteoric rise of digital media to help explore today's representations of the housewife. I begin by focusing on the idea of the 'celebrity housewife', describing how the celebrity housewives of the past were essentially educationalists, with their tips for cleaning, tidying and cooking doubling up as a type of public service often facilitated by the BBC. With their cut-glass accents and rather patronising teacher-like tone, their appeal lay in providing an education for women in housework, home management and home economics.

The celebrity housewives today use their platforms on social media to share cleaning and tidying tips and strategies in much the same way as their predecessors did. But, in contrast to the homemaking educationalists, this new generation of celebrity housewives are presented as 'ordinary', accessible, friendly, down to earth and relatable. Cleaning and tidying tips, and advertisements for associated consumer products, are shared with followers as an act of kindness and as a show of solidarity with their followers or 'Insta-family'. Followers are actively encouraged to avoid overthinking or looking outwards into the world too much and to instead to focus on *self*-improvement. I show that there has been a revival of earlier ideals around the housewife as responsible for *displaying* a particular version of her home exacerbated by the hyper-visible world of Instagram and TikTok. Even social media accounts that are not about housework per se regularly feature immaculately clean, tidy and fashionable high-spec homes, especially kitchens, in the background of posts about yoga, cookery and fashion for example.

In our new digital worlds, housework has become increasingly bound up with how individuals define themselves. In the ultra-curated social media universe, homes are more carefully presented and displayed than ever. Moreover, the actual work of housework is either rendered invisible or else tasks such as mopping the floor or folding washing are filmed alongside uplifting music and made to look effortless, relaxing, rewarding and satisfying.

Chapter 2, 'Housework turned inwards: Cleanfluencing and the self', delves further into the cultural phenomenon of the cleanfluencer, situating her within wider historical and cultural contexts. It asks: where did the cleanfluencer come from? How and why does her image feature so prominently in the popular cultural imagination? Who follows her and why? In order to answer these questions, in this chapter I describe a process of 'turning inwards' whereby housework becomes more than simply a set of tasks to be completed or a calling for women to work heroically towards the greater good, as earlier ramifications of housework had been. Instead, housework became part of a personal project of the self; an act of self-realisation. I describe the series of events through which housework began to be associated with a 'feminine *self*', leading ultimately to the emergence of the digital cleanfluencer. In the chapter I argue that in order to understand the contemporary figure of the cleanfluencer, we also need to consider how she is located within wider twentieth-century developments of 'selfhood'. To do this, the chapter explores how the housewife and her contemporary reinvention via cleanfluencing accounts is a direct product of wider processes of consumer capitalism, postcolonialism and patriarchy. She is often worshipped and venerated, seen as heroic, stoic in times of crisis and the heart and soul of the family and home. And yet her work – the *tasks* of housework – is rarely celebrated. These tasks are either invisible or else devalued and outsourced as low-paid labour, often to the poorest women in society.

The relationship between cleaning and selfhood is developed in detail in Chapter 3, '"I'm broken and it's beautiful": Digital housework and the promise of happiness'. Housework within cleanfluencing accounts often promises to 'spark joy' and influencers sell the notion that it is possible to clean and tidy yourself happy. In this chapter, I consider where these narratives came from by situating cleanfluencing within the burgeoning positive-thinking and self-help movement. Cleanfluencers often structure their content around an enthusiastic portrayal of the supposed mental health benefits of cleaning and tidying. Stories are regularly intercepted with reels featuring cleanfluencers taking antidepressants and describing their experiences of anxiety and stress in candid detail.

The idea that housework might be reframed as a form of self-help is particularly fascinating given that feminists have long pointed out the opposite – that housework triggers negative emotions of boredom, loneliness and unfulfilment. I consider how it is that housework today came to be bound up with positive thinking and self-care. In order to do this, I look at online housework cultures in light of the broader, highly popular positive-thinking and self-care movement. The search for happiness and wellbeing, while nothing new, is increasingly played out on social media in novel ways. Within the digital self-care movement, the secret to alleviating negative feelings of anxiety, depression and personal struggle is thought to be through a personal search for happiness; a process of 'looking within' and working on yourself to be a better person. Happiness and personal satisfaction are increasingly seen as achievable through positive thinking, kindness, gratitude and joyful 'energy'. The chapter shows how distracting yourself through housework and counting your blessings are presented as key to happiness and personal satisfaction. Within cleanfluencing accounts, positive affirmations abound – 'You've got this!', 'You are enough as you are!', 'Just be you!' – and regularly appear alongside endless adverts for cleaning products and homeware. The message is clear – you *are* enough, *but* you should still buy this scented candle, tea towel, surface cleaner, etc.

The entrenchment of the self-help and positivity movements within cleanfluencing are further explored in Chapter 4, '"Laughter can get you through the hard days": The cultural politics of housework. In this chapter, I examine the ways that cleanfluencers embrace positive-thinking discourses and mindsets by closely integrating them into their own content. The repeated use and popular appeal of hashtags such as #ShineNotShame echo the recent focus on the supposed association between cleaning and mental health. Cleanfluencers often describe their content as destigmatising mental health, but I argue in this chapter that their content also contributes to a concerning normalisation of psychological suffering. These discourses, alongside increasingly conservative representations of women frantically cleaning and tidying their homes, abound on social media where a type of intensive consumer culture is celebrated alongside the mantra that true happiness comes from 'within'. In the new digital worlds of the online celebrity housewife, even the most 'ordinary' person with access to a smartphone can achieve her dreams, happiness and personal satisfaction. The chapter also addresses the absence of any discussion of politics or how the stubborn inequalities around housework might be challenged. Followers are repeatedly warned against the harms of 'overthinking' and of 'trying to change things you can't'. The result is that inequalities are either ignored entirely or alluded to via humorous references to male incompetence around housework.

Chapter 6, 'The return of the housewife: Housework in the aftermath of crisis', is the last substantive chapter in the book. In it, I describe how over the years, women have, in various ways, been promised that housework will bring them freedom and pleasure. This promise is rarely realised. Digital media and cleanfluencing accounts offer new sites whereby inequalities are sometimes confronted, but mostly they are reproduced and almost always tolerated. In the chapter I show how the digital image of the cleanfluencer represents the housewife as always flexible to the continuing and contradictory demands of neoliberalism. Chapter 6 concludes by suggesting some radical alternatives to today's highly unequal, commercialised and digitised versions of housework. I discuss ideas of 'collective joy' and 'radical happiness',[23] which stand in contrast to individual and competitive searches for happiness and personal betterment that are reflected in the cleanfluencing accounts that I explore throughout the book.

What is housework and why does it matter?

I normally try to avoid starting with excuses, explanations and excessive justifications, finding it frustrating that some aspects of social life – often those that are associated with women and the domestic – are seen to lack importance or scholarly relevance. However, given the historical dismissal and chronic invisibility of housework, both culturally and scholarly, I want to spend a bit of time highlighting how crucial a focus on domestic labour is for social science research. The domestic sphere has long been overlooked and positioned as the 'poor relation' to modernity.[24] This has often been accompanied with an absence of scholarly studies into the processes and practices of domestic life, with domestic labour in particular labelled unimportant and irrelevant, even negatable, and regularly invisible. Scholarly absences often mirror cultural ones,[25] and nowhere is this truer than for the study of domestic labour, which is habitually glossed over as 'reproductive' work: the hidden, monumentally unimportant sibling to paid labour, which is the place where *real*, meaningful exploitation and inequalities occur.

The evolution of the commercialisation of domestic life echoes the unfolding of modernity and wider cultural changes to women's lives. Historically, feminist scholarship has tended to overlook the mid-century retreat to the home and return to domestic life for women, save to critique the depressing homemaker role from which women are supposedly powerless to resist.[26] Rachel Mosely highlights the need to avoid reducing women's post-war lives to a simple 'shift' from the public to private, and instead shows that this was an important period for the renegotiation of feminine identities. The domestic, and the processes and practices within it, she argues, were highly significant 'responses to the modern'.[27]

Historically, 'deep thinking' around the family, domestic life and especially housework has been sidestepped. For Friedrich Engels,[28] the silencing of women's domestic lives was in part what made capitalism and women's subordinate position within systems of production hold strong. In addition, the stubborn silence and absence of women's lives reflects the privilege of philosophers who generally had the burden of housework removed from them.[29]

Late modern industrial societies still rest on an outdated model of heterosexual nuclear families. Workplaces, even post-pandemic, remain broadly inflexible with the physical presence of workers still assumed to be 'right and proper' and a deep sense of suspiciousness of remote working.[30] As the recent 'Pregnant then Screwed' campaign reminds us,[31] there are infinite stories and examples of workplace inflexibility leading to crippling levels of stress and anxiety for those who are effectively expected to – often literally – be in two places at once. Women, and especially poorer women and women of colour who are more likely to work in jobs without any flexibility, are the most likely to suffer this.[32]

So I make no apologies for the topic of this book and want only to reiterate its relevance. Any comprehensive understanding of life in late capitalist societies, which are rife with injustices, inequalities, precarity, fear and judgement, is incomplete without a discussion of the everyday and mundane routines and practices of the domestic sphere. Of course, as I explore in the chapters that follow, one of the most fascinating facets of cleanfluencing culture is the way in which something that has long been deemed *too* ordinary, mundane and basic to warrant academic attention is transformed into something bright, seductive, entertaining and even, to borrow from Ien Ang,[33] pleasurably melodramatic. I argue in this book that this popular digital reframing of housework serves a dual purpose. First, it reproduces the entrenchment of cleaning and tidying dialogues within women's everyday lives – and notably also their digital lives – reminding us of its importance and of women's role in the *doing* of it. Second, it offers up a version of domestic labour that is playful, joyful and in various ways *revalues* domestic unpaid labour that has historically been routinely ignored, unseen and unvalued.

Housework has long been perceived as disappointingly conformist, apolitical, boring and the preserve of people who aren't interesting or important. And yet, as I explore on the pages of this book, housework offers a unique insight into the everyday, domestic articulation of some of society's most entrenched and taken-for-granted inequalities.

The discussion of housework and its peculiar role and meaning within the lives of women is present but often buried away within the literature and academic scholarship. It is often euphemistically alluded to within wider accounts of societal expectations of women as unpaid labourers within domestic spaces. Carol Shields, in *The Republic of Love*,[34] for example, writes about the monotonous, repetitive practices of housework as a type of embodied practice of the stresses, strains and limiting disappointments of middle-aged womanhood.

Of course, housework is *supposed* to be invisible, tucked away from public life and something that women are expected to get on with without complaint. And yet, today housework is far from hidden. Digital social media is flooded with images of women performing domestic labour. These have become so ubiquitous, colourful, fun and seemingly joyful and effortless that the most popular and successful cleanfluencers have become household names and celebrities in their own right. And yet I argue in this book that cleanfluencing is the latest embodiment of a highly influential form of popular culture. Cleanfluencing not only helps to reinforce centuries-old gender stereotypes around who is responsible for the housework and the promise of gaining 'joy' from domestic labour but also facilitates a rigid acceptance of pre-existing inequalities, making it a core part of a broader global system of capitalist reproduction and often chronic exploitation. In a world riddled with inequalities and lack of opportunity and precarity, but where the promise of meritocracy continues unfettered, it is no surprise that so many women look to ways of finding satisfaction and value in their domestic labour. It is also unsurprising to see how digital social media, in its absolute accessibility and seeming open opportunity for anyone to create and curate their own content, has been seized on as an opportunity for seeking value and success where there are so few alternative opportunities available, especially for working-class and lower-income women. The focus of this book, then, is *inequality*. As a cog in the system of capitalist reproduction, it is particularly effective because it simultaneously reinforces the 'rightful' position of women as arbiters of the domestic sphere and the 'natural' unpaid labour on which capitalist society has long depended.

This book explores how the new digital narratives of domestic labour are entwined with multiple commercial opportunities. These are presented as a favour – a 'gift' – to followers with cleanfluencers careful to ensure that the pact of friendly intimacy with their followers remains intact. The book tells the story of what happens when the false promise of 'domestic bliss', and neoliberal striving towards self-realisation via housework, is combined with the meteoric and unbridled success of social media. It explores the onslaught of heavily commercialised social media content which is saturated with images of women as competent and happy homemakers who find personal contentment and satisfaction in their housework. In doing so, I describe how the global exploitation of women and the broader socio-economic dynamics of the white woman housewife are obscured and mystified by digital media.

Introduction: Why are women still cleaning up?

The return of the housewife describes the march towards increasingly impossible-to-achieve ideals of housework and the cleanfluencer's role in perpetuating these. It explores the ever-evolving ways in which contemporary digital culture has contributed to the adage that housework is after all *women's work*. I now turn to an exploration of this unique, glamorised digital reinvention of housework.

'I really wanted to share this with you all!': The commercial success of the cleanfluencer

> Hello lovely people, I'm Laura also known as @cleaning_at83 on TikTok. My journey began during lockdown after I had my daughter and I was stuck at home with 2 kids, on maternity leave and also home learning. With nowhere to go and very little people to see, I filled my free time creating content. I've always loved a clean, tidy and decluttered home but with 2 kids in a small house it was becoming a difficult task, but I love showing everyone my reality and that's what it's all about.[1]

It's October 2022 and the Clean & Tidy Home Show at the ExCeL centre in London is in full swing. The show, the first of its kind in the UK, promised visitors an 'inclusive and accessible event' that would provide the 'tips, tricks, tools and motivation you need to clean, organise and take control of your home, regardless of size or budget'. In a departure from the much older and more established Ideal Home Show,[2] the Clean & Tidy Home Show centred on social media influencing throughout, promising to 'celebrate the home influencer community's success in keeping Britain's homes sparkling'.[3] Earlier home improvement exhibitions, such as the Ideal Home Show, have a long history of inviting celebrities to give talks, host events and even just make an exciting celebrity 'appearance'.[4] However, the central focus of much of the marketing and promotional material for the Clean & Tidy Home Show on cleanfluencers is a notable new trend. The first thing that a ticket to the Clean & Tidy Home Show promises is an opportunity to 'meet your favourite cleanfluencers and learn their latest hacks, hear from expert organisers and see them in action, then shop the aisles with the latest products on offer at discounted show prices'.[5] In this chapter I explore the palpable association between cleanfluencing and shopping in more detail. I explore how 'ordinary' women have become adept at making use of social media as a way of seeking their own opportunities for entrepreneurship, via cleaning and tidying.

The hashtags #shinenotshame and #ShineSquad feature heavily on the Clean & Tidy Home Show webpages and have amassed hundreds of thousands of followers on Instagram. Following the hashtags leads one to multiple cleanfluencing accounts featuring uplifting and lively video streams of speeded-up montages of cleaning and tidying. The mood is excitable, energising, colourful and fun. Cleaning is presented as satisfying and something that will make you feel great: a perfect activity for creating both a tidy mind *and* home. Some of the associated accounts have only a small following, others have amassed a large number of followers, sometimes (as with Mrs Hinch) extending into millions, resulting in lucrative promotional deals with big cleaning brands. The Clean & Tidy Home Show is keen to focus on both established celebrity clean-fluencers and those who are just starting out. There is a big focus on 'celebrity', on bringing in the 'big names' in cleanfluencing, but this is offset by the central profiling of early career cleanfluencers. The homepage for the show includes a special feature on Laura Mountford (@lauracleanaholic), who is invited to share her 'Shine Squad' story and tell readers why she started her TikTok account. In the quotation from Laura at the beginning of the chapter, we hear a familiar story of the stresses involved in balancing domestic and cleaning responsibilities with paid work, and – during COVID-19 – the demands of home-schooling, all while looking after (it appears single-handedly) two very young children. From Laura's quote, it appears that loneliness, exhaustion and an inescapable pressure to present a clean and tidy home conspired to present cleanfluencing as a realistic option in a situation where few alternatives existed. The interview has the effect of positioning Laura as the ideal neoliberal citizen. She is relatable and able to clearly articulate a familiar set of anxieties that are symptomatic of contemporary capitalist societies. But she is also resilient, independent and always able to cope; she holds it all together against the odds with ease and without external support:

Interviewer: Do you ever feel overwhelmed? How do you cope?

Laura: ABSOLUTELY! I have high expectations of myself when it comes to my home. I like things to look a certain way before bed and when I leave the house. Lowering those expectations and being kinder to myself helps me cope and realise it doesn't have to be that way! I love a list, writing lists is my go to when I'm feeling overwhelmed and spreading everything out over 7 days instead of cramming it into 1 definitely helps to relieve the pressure.[6]

As others have also pointed out,[7] social media acquired a fresh allure during the COVID-19 lockdown. Being stuck at home meant that social media played a fresh role in creating a space for entertainment, socialising, community, seeking advice (particularly around health and wellbeing) and of course *shopping*. As Laura explains, for women staying at home with young children, often alongside paid work, social media promises an easily accessible solution; all you need is a smartphone to bring you unlimited access to a world of community, where people share struggles, feelings and emotions that are similar to your own, and importantly where people will *understand*. During lockdown, social media facilitated a new way of communicating with others who not only appear to cope with a raft of conflicting demands but also find ways of making it fun *and* find value, alongside an opportunity for a type of fame, respect and the possibility of making some money in the process. All of this within your own time schedule and without having to leave the home.

Back at the Clean & Tidy Home Show, the UK's most famous cleanfluencers, Mrs Hinch and Stacey Solomon,[8] have arrived to much fanfare. Swanked by security guards, they greet crowds of fans with friendly hugs, exchange pleasantries, sign autographs and pose for selfies. The Clean & Tidy Home Show is also a space to promote a raft of consumer goods, and the cleanfluencers' branded merchandise and product partners such as Minky, Zoflora and Lenor are conspicuously displayed throughout. Mrs Hinch and Stacey Solomon pose with two other cleanfluencers holding a sign surrounded with hearts that reads: 'You Are Enough'. Their legions of fans, or social media 'followers', crowd around, jostling for a better view and responding to the sight of the famous cleanfluencers with all the delight of fans meeting their favourite movie star. The 'meet and greet' cleanfluencing sessions are followed by an outpouring of star-struck devotion and excitement on social media, with many of the smaller cleanfluencing accounts posting pictures of themselves meeting their cleanfluencing heroines, describing their delight: 'This was such a special moment', 'I can't believe I met Mrs Hinch – a dream come true', 'A moment I will never forget', 'What a moment! I didn't know where to look! Sophie on one side and Stacey on the other!' And for those who couldn't attend, a sense of palpable disappointment: 'Oh wow, so gutted I couldn't make it, that would have made my year to meet them both.'

As the meet and greet event at the Clean & Tidy Home Show illustrates, 'celebrity' plays a central role in today's commercialisation of housework. The most popular and original cleanfluencers, such as Mrs Hinch, Gemma Bray (founder of the 'Organised Mum Method') and the decluttering expert Marie Kondo, have steadily become household names. These new celebrities are not the 'untouchable' demi-god Hollywood film actors or pop stars, with a talent and success that feels far beyond reach; rather, they are *relatable* – their lives a sort of reflected, idealised version of our own, where joy and happiness is available from the most mundane of domestic activities. They cook meals, give birth, squabble with their families, go shopping, flop in front of the TV, get married, do the school run, clean their homes, tidy out cupboards, make hot chocolate and share their baby scan photos. Their commercial success, their wealth, their happiness and their *celebrity* is not elusive; rather, we are promised, it is within the reach of anyone who has a home and access to a smartphone. The 'cleanfluencers' are thus the latest in the recent rise of the 'ordinary' or, as Graeme Turner describes, 'demotic' celebrity.[9] 'Famous for being famous', demotic celebrities are seen as regular people like you or I who have nevertheless acquired a level of economic and cultural success that is accessible to all. They don't have a particular skill or talent, and are often vocal about this, but they are loved, respected and venerated by their fans nonetheless, with their lives lived out in hyper-visible public detail.

This palpable sense of 'ordinariness', of *just being you*, of sharing experiences, feelings and anxieties between cleanfluencer and follower, is central to cleanfluencing. The most successful cleanfluencers are adept at this, weaving their stories and posts around a curated version of their ordinariness and the mundaneness of their patterns and rhythms of everyday life. In common with the social media accounts of influencers more generally, cleanfluencing accounts are full of affirmations of being 'real'.

With relatability at its core, social media enables us to see an idealised version of ourselves reflected back at us. The firm emphasis on being 'real' and 'relatable' is crucial and reminds us that those aspirational, perfect, improved versions of our ideal selves might just be within reach. As Mrs Hinch writes in her book *Hinch Yourself Happy*: 'We all have to do what suits us, and not anyone else, because sadly we do live in a world where a lot of people live their lives trying to be like someone else. *Please don't! please be you!*'[10] Despite affirmations of being real, a contradiction here lies in the fact that influencer culture is of course built on aspirational lifestyling whereby followers are endlessly encouraged to be themselves while also being continually reminded of the importance of striving towards a better, more improved version of *you*:

> I don't know why but watching that made me so emotional, I don't know you personally but the pride I have for you right now is immense. You are such a breath of fresh air to watch on Instagram, *so real and raw*. You have helped me in more ways than I can explain so from the bottom of my heart – thank you. Thank you for being brave enough to share the real you on a platform that can be so cruel, thank you for sharing your good days and bad, thank you for showing us that above all else love, kindness and family are the main things in life.[11]

Cleanfluencing accounts thus present a palpable digital version of reality; a seemingly endless set of images of what might be possible. Lefebvre described this as the 'myth of the new life';[12] a promise that is embedded into modernity of a 'new life' which is supposedly only just around the corner.[13] Being 'real' and relatable to one's followers is core to the seductive allure of cleanfluencing social media accounts. As one of Mrs Hinch's followers remarks:

> It's funny feeling proud of someone you don't even know isn't it? ... The respect and I guess sort of bond I feel with you after reading your book and being able to resonate with some things you wrote about is crazy and it brings me so much joy seeing you enjoying times in life like this tonight.

Spending time following cleanfluencing accounts and creating cleanfluencing content is, by any measure, highly individualised labour. People, for the most, are at home engaging with content alone on social media. Yet phrases such as 'teamwork', 'teamspirit' and 'Insta-family' are used repeatedly in cleanfluencing accounts, creating and cementing collective norms around consumption that are decades in the making.[14] Underpinning these discourses of collectivity is, conversely, a highly *individualised* narrative of optimistic aspiration; of believing in your dreams, of never giving up and of submitting yourself to the life-changing potential of consumerism and, of course, the apparently 'natural' logic of unequal domestic labour practices. Jo Littler argues that one of the reasons why individuals remain committed to and invested in exploitative, precarious and unequal capitalist consumer societies is because of an entrenched popular belief in meritocratic folklore;[15] of the 'rags-to-riches' success story – the fabled individual a bit 'like me' who makes it against the odds through sheer hard work and perseverance. For Lauren Berlant,[16] the seductive lure of endless popular representations of 'achievable' fantasies of the 'good life' that are always within reach and there for the taking is simply a 'cruel optimism' – one which has long bolstered the supply chains of global capitalist reproduction.

Within popular media cultures, heavily personalised, individual success stories have become the norm. They serve to deflect focus from the structural inequalities underpinning domestic labour, offering instead a renewed focus on personal and familial aspiration. The most popular and successful cleanfluencers sometimes describe feeling 'blessed', regularly and humbly thanking followers for their support. But the meritocratic mantra of not giving up – that following your dreams, working hard or simply *being you* is enough for anyone to achieve similar success – is never challenged, and cleanfluencers stop short of saying that they have been 'lucky'. We can see how powerful this parable is by the vast number of similar, smaller cleanfluencing accounts that mimic the most popular and lucrative cleanfluencers. The celebrity cleanfluencers have become a blueprint for the thousands of other home-grown cleanfluencing accounts that continue to multiply on social media.

Celebrities: Being 'ordinary', being *real*, being *me*

The hyper-visibility of 'ordinary' people as celebrities was first popularised within the reality television genre and has found its most recent incarnation in the contemporary world of the celebrity cleanfluencer. This new type of 'democratised' culture presents the status of celebrity as achievable to all regardless of talent, status or privilege. Turner notes the 'increasing visibility of the "ordinary person" as they turn themselves into media content'.[17] Writing at the height of the reality television genre of the mid-2000s, Turner notes the increased demand for 'ordinary people desiring celebrification'.[18] This goes hand in hand with an increased desire for the 'confessional' whereby people gain exposure by revealing details of their everyday lives. Today, this expectation of confessional content also extends to those who are already celebrities. The Hollywood actress Jennifer Garner, for example, has a popular Instagram account that often includes pictures and video reels of her laundry room. In one post, she sits on the floor dressed casually in jeans and a T-shirt in front of her washing machine and writes: 'I don't know why I thought you needed this.'

Cleanfluencers frequently capitalise on their 'ordinariness', with regular references to their supposedly non-spectacular, unflashy, profane and 'humble' domestic lives. Often they emphasise their discomfort with celebrity sparkle, insisting that they prefer the ordinary comfort of the domestic sphere. Being 'ordinary', or holding what Turner calls a 'demotic ordinariness', is key to the relatability that is central to being a successful influencer.[19] This friendly relatability is harnessed within cleanfluencing culture as a means of persuading followers to engage in the multitude of opportunities to consume. Most cleanfluencing accounts feature numerous ads, links to products and discount codes which are presented as a 'gift' to followers. The most popular cleanfluencers are those who can most successfully relate to their followers while simultaneously selling cleaning products. Usually the most highly commercialised accounts with the largest numbers of followers are couched in the friendly, relatable language of friendship, kindness, support and generosity – 'I really wanted to share this with you!' and 'I bloody love you lot!' Followers are habitually referred to as 'Insta-family' rather than followers or consumers.

This type of friendly intimacy combined with constant references to the 'ordinary' are core components of the popular success of the cleanfluencer. Often this relatability is enhanced with reminders that 'I'm just like you!' Cleanfluencers regularly share written (but rarely visual) accounts of domestic mess, clutter, dirt, disorder, familial strife, etc. The recent 'Insta vs Reality' trend is a good example of this, whereby images of immaculately clean homes are occasionally intercepted with an image featuring 'mess'. The mess is always quickly swept away but its appearance in the first place is part of an attempt at relatability – at 'keeping it real'. The Irish cleanfluencer Ellen O'Keeffe, for example, dubbed the 'Irish Mrs Hinch', uses her Instagram account to allude to the chaos, disorder and precarity of everyday life, with frequent references to the COVID-19 pandemic, her lack of sleep, home-schooling, her 'messy' children and husband, and her distress over her skin condition. As with other cleanfluencers, O'Keeffe offers a friendly relatability with her followers, providing a type of emotional support and access to an online community of women experiencing similar issues. As O'Keeffe says: 'I don't have a show home and my house is always messy, I own the dirtiest children in Ireland and my partner is unbelievably accident prone. I'm just a normal person trying to keep on top of the housework.'[20]

Cleanfluencing is a contemporary manifestation of the mainstreaming of the 'confessional'. As confessional societies advance, people become *both* the 'promoters of commodities' and the 'commodities they promote'.[21] This shift towards the conscious personal creation of confessional selves is epitomised and embraced throughout social media as users utilise their digital profiles to create idealised virtual versions of themselves and their homes, making oneself 'a notable, noticed and coveted community ... In a society of consumers, turning into a desirable and desired commodity is the stuff of which dreams and fairy tales are made.'[22] This confessional hyper-sharing of the ordinary, intimate, personal and domestic increases digital traffic and the number of followers who can relate.

Arguably, this escalation of the popularity of the 'ordinary' social media celebrity would not have been possible without the social media app Instagram. During the pandemic, Instagram became especially popular as a way of socialising, communicating with friends, marketing, shopping and providing access to support services, such as home-schooling resources, domestic violence advice and debt support. Women in particular, including older women and mothers who might not have previously used social media, became avid Instagram users during the COVID-19 'lockdown' as other, more physical spaces for support were withdrawn. As I discussed in the Introduction, COVID-19 was thus a moment where digital cultures thrived. The exacerbation of inequalities in managing the intensification of the domestic load, which included new routines of hygiene, home-schooling, meal planning and preparation, accompanied a new, hyper-visible digital retelling and curating of the home. Instagram was seized on as a highly accessible method of photo and video sharing, communicating, building online communities and socialising during a real point of crisis. It was also regularly used as a way of sharing a good-humoured protest via memes that offered a witty backlash to the crisis. But Instagram also, in the absence of visitors to the home, proliferated a new type of lifestyle culture, with people habitually sharing multiple images and stories related to homes, relationships and domestic life. As they grew in popularity, cleanfluencing accounts frequently began to offer tips for surviving the intensified domestic burden. The cleanfluencer Gemma Bray, for example, launched her popular 'Organised Mum Method', positioned as offering a helping hand during lockdown and accompanied by a podcast and bestselling book. 'Repeat after me', she reminds her followers concerned about the demands of food preparation for the family in the run-up to Christmas Day, 'it's only a roast dinner'.

The hyper-real aesthetics of heavily curated homes and bodies and the future-oriented aspiration of followers is Instagram's raison d'être and core to its relevance and success. In common with other influencer content, cleanfluencers offer up a 'relatable' self which is as recognisable as possible, an idealised version of *you* that is always just out of reach but which cleanfluencers persuade followers to aspire towards. The ubiquitousness of Instagram today makes it difficult to remember what life was like without it, but it is of course relatively new. Launched in 2010 as a photo-sharing app, the original Instagram logo was an image of an analogue camera. In contrast to earlier social media apps such as Facebook, Instagram's initial focus was on enabling users to create and share their own visual representations of the day. By sharing increasingly posed, curated and filtered photos, users quickly became adept at reproducing a type of future-oriented aspirational tone rather than, as with Facebook, an archive – a record – of the past. This was reinforced following the decision in 2016 to launch a 'stories' feature on Instagram and the launch of the Instagram Television feature in 2018. Whereas most cleanfluencing accounts feature a 'grid' of a selection of photos and some videos, updated only occasionally, the majority of cleanfluencers make frequent and regular use of 'stories' which disappear after twenty-four hours. Many of the most popular influencers update their stories multiple times a day, perhaps – using the language of paid work – taking a 'day off' on Sunday.

Because stories are only temporarily visible, they create a lure to check in regularly before content disappears for good. This mirrors the early appeal of television soap operas. Feminist researchers in the 1980s described the ways that the short, tri-weekly and generally unrepeated episodes meant that tuning in regularly was essential to keep abreast of storylines.[23] Moreover, multiple storylines packed into each episode meant that a type of fragmented viewing was possible, which was compatible with the frequent distractions of domestic life. Some forty years later, the popular success of social media apps such as Instagram rest on a similar premise: the lure of regularly checking the app according to the viewer's own routines and schedule. The unique appeal of Instagram is thus its ephemerality. As Jill Walker Rettberg notes, Instagram offers a 'conversation, not an archive';[24] an aspirational pull towards idealised selves and of course the opportunity to purchase an endless stream of consumer durables to help you achieve them.

In tandem with the increasing popularity of Instagram is the seemingly never-ending search for 'Insta-worthy' content. Instagram uniquely offers a liminal space, which fuses everyday routines and rituals, objects, observations and acts with the *visual*. In effect, Instagram has meant that *anything* – any object, any action – has the potential to be worthy of sharing with followers who may or may not be people who you know in real life. For the cleanfluencers, Instagram has facilitated a space where anyone who possesses a smartphone and a home can share their own content. Domestic life thus becomes ubiquitously visible, and in the confessional society we see an abundance of access to 'free' social media to share it on. This is reflected in the appeal of the hyper-visual sharing of the most everyday and mundane of domestic routines, from making beds, to cleaning ovens, to lighting candles, to cleaning sinks, to mopping floors, to making neat vacuum machine lines in the carpet.

Cleanfluencing demonstrates in the most omnipresent way how the normalisation of sharing intimate, domestic content on Instagram has paved the way for 'a new class of content creators'.[25] This is certainly the case for the cleanfluencers, with a raft of new accounts appearing daily across social media. The launch of Instagram advertising tools in 2015 and the paid partnership tag in 2017, alongside the new logo, represented a move away from Instagram simply being an app for photo sharing: it rapidly became a space where communication and commerce overlap. This overlap was consolidated during the pandemic when Instagram stood out as a virtual communication tool drawing in followers seeking communities and a space to share experiences and survival tips alongside an entrepreneurial opportunity via digital content creation.

In contrast to earlier social media apps, Instagram also allowed users to create multiple different accounts with the intention of empowering users to share different 'sides' of themselves. The idea that there is no single 'authentic' *you* is embraced by the most successful cleanfluencers, many of whom have both a 'business' (public) *and* a personal (private, for a small group of select friends and family only) account. The notion that it is possible to present and curate different versions of yourself is interesting: first, because it flies in the face of the mantra of 'just being *you*' that is so heavily reproduced on Instagram; and second, because it lends itself to the idea that Instagram isn't just an archive of your life – it is also utilised to create *and* curate identities, lifestyles and idealised, aspirational versions of multiple selves, homes and bodies. The extent to which the grit, mess, tears and dirt of everyday life is rendered invisible on Instagram is palpable.

'Just a normal girl living her best life': The importance of 'relatability'

Relatability in advertising is of course nothing new. Companies have long recognised the importance of customers being able to relate to the protagonists in adverts and that maximising relatability can translate into sales.

In order to illustrate this, I want to take you back to the winter of 2012. The British supermarket chain Asda has just aired its new Christmas television commercial. Instagram has only recently been launched as a photo-sharing app and it is another five years until the birth of the cleanfluencers. The commercial features a harried and harassed woman single-handedly preparing the house for Christmas. She is depicted as pressured, exhausted and on-edge, but also smiling, uncomplaining and wholeheartedly in control of the multitude of festive preparations. In the space of the minute-long commercial, we see her choosing and decorating the Christmas tree, writing and addressing a vast pile of cards with a wriggling baby in her lap, supervising children as they messily assist with baking the Christmas cake, shopping for Christmas gifts, untangling an interminable set of fairy lights, wrestling an unruly shopping trolley crammed with food through the supermarket and car park, a haggle of excited children in tow, changing sheets and inflating guest beds, frenziedly vacuuming up pine needles with a baby balanced on one arm, and preparing and serving Christmas dinner to a table full of people who, in a brief moment of appreciation, applause as she surveys the scene in front of her: the family relaxed, happy and well-fed, gathered as they watch Christmas Day television. Throughout, her hapless husband is nowhere to be seen, save for the final scene where he chirpily asks, 'What's for tea love?' The commercial ends with the slogan: 'Behind every great Christmas there's mum, and behind every mum there's Asda.'[26]

The woman depicted in the Asda commercial is just one in a long line of popular representations of the white woman housewife. These earlier representations are important because they show how cleanfluencing is the latest stage in a long historical process of persuading women of their rightful role as purveyors of the domestic sphere. Historically, women have been denied the opportunity to refuse these rigid categories that define them as ultra-competent, happy homemakers and managers, as challenges to the prevailing orthodoxies around the unequal gendered division of domestic labour are quickly shut down. The history of downplaying the social inequalities of domestic labour and ideals of the willing, happy and cheerfully exhausted heroic housewife is a long one. Within cleanfluencing cultures, these same narratives are woven into contemporary articulations of digital housework but with a new focus on the autonomous individual who uses cleanfluencing as a type of entrepreneurialism, opening up multiple opportunities for sophisticated marketing techniques.

The Asda advert represents a key moment in the commercialisation of housework, whereby new cultures of 'relatability' to the everyday experiences of consumers are on peak display. The routines, practices and processes of the ordinariness and mundanity of housework are played out in careful detail, and the taken-for-granted nuances of housework replayed in glorious Technicolor are used ultimately to sell Asda grocery shopping to women who 'relate'. In the wake of the Asda commercial, the Advertising Standards Association (ASA) received a record number of complaints concerning its uncritical and conformist replaying of the old adage that housework and the multitude of domestic labour tasks associated with it, especially during holidays such as Christmas, are unquestionably women's work.[27] The exhaustion might be plain to see but so is a familiar portrayal of womanly willing acquiescence.

In the end, Asda was cleared by ASA of producing offensive advertising. In its statement following the ruling, Asda pointed to their focus group research that had preceded the airing of the commercial, citing consumer feedback which showed that 'eight out of ten mothers … believed the ad reflected common experience, rather than outdated stereotypes'. In other words, Asda saw their role as enabling consumers to *relate to* rather than challenge the unequal experiences of domestic labour depicted in the commercial. It is interesting that unlike the 2012 Asda commercial, we rarely see any meaningful backlash to cleanfluencing cultures. This feels odd given that they often adopt the same reproduction of gendered caricatures of the white woman housewife. Perhaps it is because the women in the cleanfluencing accounts appear in control of their destinies. They are portrayed as making their own judgements, with housework depicted as a *free* choice made by autonomous individuals who gain joy from sharing their content online. Cleanfluencing provides a fresh articulation of these same unequal structures of housework that makes them increasingly difficult to critique.

This commercialisation of relatability that is so familiar in digital culture today has its roots in the much earlier commercial cultures of the 1950s and 1960s, where we see some of the first examples of 'relatable' advertising featuring a female protagonist communicating and relating directly to viewers/consumers. The notion of relatable content that speaks directly to the tired, worn-out housewife is certainly not new. A 1960s commercial for the Hoover vacuum cleaner, for example, depicts a woman slumped in an armchair, aproned, broom still in hand, with a tired and fed-up expression on her face. Speaking directly to the imagined other women viewing the commercial, a speech bubble from her mouth reads: 'It's so silly to go on wearing myself out ... when I can have a maid at 4D a day' – the 'maid' being the new Hoover model. The language used, including that of the product itself – 'the maid' – is an early type of relatability, offering a commercial solution to the slog of housework that we see in abundance in digital cultures of housework today. What is missing, though, is the allure and romantic attraction attributed to housework that is so visible in contemporary cleanfluencing accounts. The message, as with that depicted in the Asda commercial, is that *we know*, we understand, we see you *and* here is a product that can make things easier.

Thus the commercial personalisation of housework is nothing new. What *is* new is the personal relatability of cleanfluencers, many of whom share intimate details of their lives. We know them by name; we know who they are married to and who their children are; we are familiar with seeing them in their pyjamas, drying their hair and lying in bed. The protagonists of housework commercials of the past, such as the 'Hoover for Happier Homes' advertising campaigns of the 1950s and the Asda harassed mother of 2012, were relatable but they were also anonymous. New notions of celebrity mean that relatability is enhanced not only by the idea that we can relate to the actor playing the housewife but also via a carefully curated sense that we *literally* know them; that we are friends rather than consumers. This is a type of friendly intimacy we have never seen before and is thus fostered via cleanfluencing accounts to great commercial effect.

The route from 'ordinary person', to reality television celebrity, to influencing, and to cleanfluencing more specifically, is an increasingly common one, with many celebrities making Instagram their main public profile. One-time *X Factor* finalist Stacey Solomon, for example, who went on to launch a successful cleanfluencing account, neatly epitomises this career route. With almost six million followers, her account skilfully combines picture-perfect images of her home, children and crafting projects. Montages of immaculately organised drawers, storage jars, decanting videos, folding, organising, preparing snacks for her children and creating elaborate front door decorations at her home, 'Pickle Cottage', are all played alongside moving, uplifting music. The most intimate of domestic spaces are cleaned, tidied, filmed and organised, with nothing out of place, and a careful, lovingly curated snapshot of 'everyday' ordinariness is created. The montages, the perfection, the endless, smiling joy, the way everything – quite literally – slots so neatly and perfectly together and into place makes for seductive viewing. We watch and smile. Stacey is witty, kind and personable, adopting a chatty, conversational tone while talking directly into the camera; her luscious, perfectly blow-dried hair, immaculate make-up and mani-cured nails are always centre stage. She is only occasionally inter-rupted by her five children, and although they sometimes present childcare 'problems', the solutions are breezily straightforward: 'He can help me with work!', 'She will just have to come to the pho-toshoot with me!' In short, what is on offer is a type of aspirational lifestyle where everything happily works out in the end, nothing falls out of place and the smiling perfection is never interrupted. It is part of a cartoonish fantasy where a Disney-esque version of the domestic sphere and the work that goes into creating and curating it overrides any notion that home might be anything less than effortless joy.

The lifestyle that is created is one of heavy and unrepentant aspiration. There is an unspoken rule among followers of cleanfluenc-ing accounts that privilege, luck or fantasy don't come into the popular success of the accounts. Stacey is repeatedly described by her followers as 'real', 'authentic', 'kind' and deserving of her success and privilege. The shift from the idealised digital vision of domestic bliss bleeds seamlessly into a raft of heavily commodified content. In the manner of a friend offering kind advice or a helping hand, Stacey directly addresses her camera and followers. 'I've been think-ing', she says, 'I've had so many messages about this ... I'm actually really excited about this because it's something so many of you have asked about', and 'so, for the first time ever, they've given a discount code that isn't just for new customers.'

Doing the digital housework for free

We have seen some examples of the ways in which the marketing of domestic cleaning products crept into the home with increasing intensity, through, for example, magazines, television and advertising. Today, mainstream marketing approaches are complemented by women creating their own digital content, not only via algorithmic gossip – liking, sharing, commenting or tagging – but also by spending more time curating their own *digital* representations of the home, family life, bodies and objects than ever before.

By creating their own content that showcases the use of cleaning products, cleanfluencers provide marketing and advertising for brands, and in doing so they perform a type of 'digital labour' or, as Kylie Jarrett terms it, 'digital housework'.[28] Previously, billboards, television advertising and magazine space would have provided the key format for increasing the visibility and promotion of products and making key brands such as Fairy, Mr Muscle and Flash ubiquitous household names. In the new digital age, cleanfluencing offers a relatively cheap, often free way in which predominantly women create their own stories, posts and content that show products being used, reviewed and discussed. By resharing and tagging content, hashtags such as #joyofclean, #ShineSquad and #HinchArmy, which are often originally created by highly lucrative cleaning brands, ensure cleanfluencers gain wider visibility and more exposure on social media. This means that they are also doing effective branding work by increasing the digital visibility of products. A good example of this is the Mrs Hinch Winter Wonderland range of Procter & Gamble products released during Christmas 2021. Like the Frosted Eucalyptus range launched a year later, discussed in the Introduction, moments after the products were officially launched on the Mrs Hinch and 'Joy of Clean' (Procter & Gamble) Instagram accounts, they simultaneously appeared on numerous accounts all over social media.

Digital labour means that in addition to doing the unpaid domestic labour of the home, women are also often working for free in creating and curating the content of their homes and cleaning practices. As Laura's description of her TikTok account explains, cleanfluencing has for many become an entrepreneurial means of seeking paid work via partnerships, or becoming a brand ambassador, where few alternative options are available, especially for women combining the demands of the home with paid work and young children. Women in particular have long been adept at finding spaces for the pursuit of status external to the home and ways of seeking opportunities for paid work that might be compatible with the demands of the home and children. Given the collapse of childcare during the COVID-19 pandemic and its huge financial cost today, combined with the failure of many companies to offer family-friendly working practices, the popular success of cleanfluencing – as a form of highly flexible labour that can always be performed at home, where you are your own boss and there is the possibility of recognition and maybe even payment for the domestic labour that has historically been rendered almost completely invisible – is unsurprising.[29]

An early example of the sort of commercialisation of domestic life that is so heavily on display in contemporary cleanfluencing accounts can be seen in the rise in popularity of Tupperware in the 1950s. Despite being a particularly mundane product, Tupperware was rendered 'magical', technologically innovative, fun and exciting. Alison Clarke describes the post-war cultural and economic shifts that accompanied the return of ideals around women's 'rightful' place within the domestic sphere,[30] alongside a renewed post-war affluence, the dramatic rise of Hollywood glamour and the commercialisation of aspiration, daydreams and desire bound up with the increasing abundance of new consumer durables. Women who could afford to were often pushed back into the domestic sphere during this time, and a permanent presence and embedding in the domestic took on a new signifier of respectable femininity and middle-class privilege. Middle-class women often sought ways of carving out spaces within the domestic realm for *paid* work and for a space to pursue entrepreneurial endeavours. Tupperware businesses thus cut across ideals of aspiration, familial health, hygiene and wellbeing; the rise in enterprise and entrepreneurialism as increasingly celebrated personal traits and values clashed with the simultaneous reglamourisation of women's position within the domestic sphere. Tupperware parties also offered new networks or 'communities' of consumption. Black-and-white photos of suburban North American women gathered excitedly around mountainous displays of plastic storage containers, listening to a presentation while enjoying drinks and snacks provided by the hostess in her own home, is a fascinating precursor to the #ShineSquad digital online housework communities that similarly promise a respectable (domestic) space for women to be entrepreneurial and valued, and to acquire some fame, all the while bolstering already huge profits in the process.

As modernity advances, we see new technologies and new cultures evolve, but often they are ones that find ways of *responding to* rather than challenging prevailing inequalities.[31] For Clarke, Tupperware represented a key moment when traditional modernist divisions of, for example, domesticity/commerce, work/leisure, friend/colleague, consumer/employee and thrift/excess were bridged. It is a process which finds its contemporary expression in the digital world of cleanfluencing, where commerce becomes deeply and intricately interwoven into the most intimate of domestic spaces, where labour bleeds into a promise of pleasure and leisure, where consumers become friends and where a type of savvy thrift masks the burgeoning excesses of consumer capitalism.

Over time, managing the domestic sphere and transforming it into a solace of safety, calm, order and comfort became an *enterprise* and a commercial endeavour.[32] Over the course of the twentieth century, the instrumental purchasing of domestic cleaning products increasingly came to be seen as a way of providing and facilitating certainty in an increasingly unpredictable and precarious world. The commercial representation of cleaning products, especially within popular culture and advertising, changed during this time, mirroring wider popular narratives and discourses about the housewife. Mid-century representations of cleaning and tidying centred around popular ideals of women housewives as heroic – distinguishable by a uniformity of purpose and pride in housework and by patriotic post-war virtues of homemaking that were extolled within British and American war-time propaganda. Celebratory images of the thrifty housewife whose skills as a resourceful homemaker were promoted and revered, and mass-produced images of the thrifty and economical housewife who is also well-educated in her housewifely skills became core to the new burgeoning post-war advertising. This resonates with a range of feminist scholarship that has identified the ways in which love and care increasingly came to be associated with responding to the likes and dislikes of the family and with careful home management.[33] Alongside this, what we also see during this time is an increased emphasis on the surveillance of women in terms of their ability to do their homemaking work 'well' and an intensification of demand within the confines of often very limited household budgets. This early version of domestic aspiration tended to be bound up with demonstrating an ability to provide 'good care' via hygiene, health, warmth and comfort to the family. The emphasis on *display* and on housework as route to 'self-fulfilment' was yet to come, but the evolution of what Jan Pahl calls a 'caring self' was positioned as synonymous with the selfless and 'proud' act of homemaking.[34] Many domestic educational resources emerged during this time to assist women in the art of attaining ideal home-making skills, often on a tight budget, at a time when in the UK rationing was still widespread. A black-and-white recipe booklet given out free of charge by the BeRo flour company at homemaking exhibitions extolled the exciting new benefits of self-raising flour and offers an early example of popular, mass-produced and *commercial* imagery of the thrifty, economical, proud housewife whose homemaking skills preserve the health and wellbeing of the whole family:

> There's no more pleasing sight than that of a happy family around a well-stocked tea table, all enjoying their food; and the mother who is responsible for the good cooking, and who has prepared it with her own hands, *has every right* to survey the results of her culinary skills with *pride and satisfaction*.[35]

In contemporary digital media cultures, the legacy of the endless search for a perfect standard of homemaking persists, albeit in new, heavily commercialised ways, as cleanfluencers demonstrate to followers in endless reels, videos and photo montages, presenting an image of effortless ease. In one, a pink lunchbox with separate compartments is lovingly packed in a specially created video reel. Snacks are neatly decanted into little pots while a Disney film plays on a flat screen TV above a roaring fire. All is cosy, immaculately clean, tidy and warm. Spinning plates for sure, but doing so with joy and ease.

Cleanfluencing reels are carefully curated to depict care and warmth, where objects easily and pleasurably fall into place. Like the BeRo self-raising flour recipe booklets, the domestic tasks are situated within scenes of effortless calm, within tales of love, pride and satisfaction echoing the homemaking narratives popularised decades earlier.

Of course, the mass consumption of rapidly produced and distributed global mass products, the mountains of plastic, the endless replacement of objects required to even begin to replicate the freshly opened, unused, gleaming products on display, seem worlds away from the relatively austere, homespun and minimal consumer cultures of the 1950s, particularly for lower-income women. Yet much of the language around pride, satisfaction and saving money as part of the package of providing care to the family remains tightly in place, often presented alongside ostentatious and highly conspicuous recommendations to consume.

The hyper-commercialisation of domestic products and practices is perhaps best illustrated via the annual 'Black Friday' event; a day when companies promise the lowest possible prices in order to clear excess stock by offering discounts. Black Friday is embraced in influencer culture, with cleanfluencers devoting their accounts to multiple promotions of discounted goods, mainly via product partners. The popular criticisms of Black Friday as a type of ruthless hyper-consumerism triggered by the creation of new desires and false needs, and as part of an intensified pressure to *spend*, are entrenched, with the cleanfluencers anticipating and addressing these head-on. Thus, cleanfluencers directly address followers with heartfelt promises to only provide links to products 'I *genuinely* use myself and *believe* in'.

Consumption is repackaged as being *part of* rather than contrary to good housekeeping. Black Friday events are hailed as kind and inclusive and, crucially, followers are promised the opportunity to find something for *themselves* not just for their families. As we shall see in Chapter 2, contemporary domestic life is characterised by a decades-old aspirational desire not only to provide care, sanctuary and comfort for the family but also to centre one's own pleasures and 'self-care'. Mrs Hinch, for example, describes the Black Friday sales as a treat to yourself, a 'buzz' of personal pleasure and a fleeting moment within which you can supposedly 'centre' and care for yourself:

> The best thing about Black Friday is obviously the bargains and the deals, but when the products that you buy religiously yourself anyway go in the sale, it's like a little buzz. Do you know what I mean? Like when you get a scratchcard and you scratch it off and you've won a couple of quid. It's that sort of feeling.

The lure and promise of aspirational lifestyles locks followers into an endless and fruitless search for the 'good life'; the age-old promise of perfect homes, bodies and relationships, all presented as achievable via the acquisition of consumer goods. Of course, this isn't new. The 1960s witnessed the consolidation of mass consumption and the hyper-visible and increasingly commodified world of housework.[36] What *is* new is the extent to which individuals not only follow and engage with social media cleaning accounts but also create their own cleanfluencing content.

Popular accounts of housework have fused with many of the core features of reality television to create a unique, never-seen-before representation of an entrepreneurial, aspirational and glamorous housewife. As she creates and scripts her own content, she is deemed to be in control of her own image – something notably different from the heavily edited and scripted reality television shows that are frequently populated by working-class participants, with middle-class producers wielding power over content and representation.

In *What a Girl Wants*, Diane Negra notes the rise of popular cultural representations of a new, flourishing individual choice feminism that is infused with high-consuming ideals.[37] Within this, she identifies the emergence of a type of 'postfeminist homemaking' and a sort of 'luxury' homemaking, such as Nigella Lawson's popular television show and recipe book *How to be a Domestic Goddess*, which stands in contrast to the 'failing' working-class women of reality television shows such as *Wife Swap* and *You Are What You Eat*. Negra's earlier depiction of a new type of female selfhood and the growth of a set of highly conservative – even anti-feminist – ideologies pre-empted the cleanfluencing boom a decade later.

Cleanfluencing culture thus rides the wave of success of the reality television genre. The hyper-visibility and centring of the 'ordinary' celebrity who makes creative use of social media (especially Instagram) to retell the familiar meritocratic 'rags-to-riches' fable was first popularised by reality television. Reality television contestants tended to be working class, while producers and the media pundits commenting tended to be middle class, with the judgement and surveillance of contestants 'behaving badly' becoming a central theme. As the sociologists Bev Skeggs, Nancy Thumin and Helen Wood point out in their study of so-called self-improvement reality television shows – such as *Supernanny*, *What Not to Wear*, *How Clean Is Your House* and *Wife Swap*, which were heavily promoted in the early 2000s – women, especially working-class women, were subjected to a new type of public ridicule and judgement under the guise of self-improvement.[38] Audiences were invited to judge and observe those who were seen to be lacking, in terms of motherhood, fashion, marriage and housework. This public judgement was enabled by the parallel rise in gossip magazines, radio and TV talk shows, tabloid culture and user-generated web content.[39]

Throughout cleanfluencing culture, normative feminine beauty norms prevail, with young, slim, white, able-bodied femme women gaining the most exposure.[40] Cleanfluencing accounts draw on the demand for details of the most intimate, mundane details of everyday life, and celebrate the confessional in the way that reality television had done previously. This time, though, the conflict scenarios that have become familiar in reality television are replaced with 'failure narratives' whereby anxieties around 'mess' are resolved and replaced with calm, order and rigidly enforced practices of cleaning and tidying. Like reality television, cleanfluencing content is almost always politics free – with individual rather than collective action celebrated.

In tandem with a type of 'confessional talk', people increasingly expose intimate details of their everyday lives publically, with the confessional details of the most intimate details of 'private' lives becoming commodities. The commodities for sale are thus people *themselves*.[41] In the contemporary world of social media influencing, the influencer herself, alongside the products she promotes, becomes the commodity: 'simultaneously, *promoters of commodities* and the *commodities they promote*. They are, at the same time, the merchandise and the marketing agents, the goods and their travelling salespeople.'[42]

In confessional societies within which the cleanfluencers are firmly fixed, a desire to be both noticed and coveted is set against the backdrop of societies marked by entrenched inequalities, crisis and infinite, indistinguishable commodities. 'Standing out' against this gloomy backdrop underpins the emergence of contemporary digital cleanfluencer culture, whereby individuals market themselves as desirable and aspirational commodities in their own right. As Zygmunt Bauman notes, in confessional societies that are flooded with mass-produced consumer goods, individuals dream of turning *themselves* into commodities that are 'impossible to overlook' or dismiss.[43] Cleanfluencers are adept at harnessing the appeal of the confessional in order to share multiple details of their domestic lives in order to galvanise interest, intensify desire, increase followers and ultimately enhance consumption of their 'brand'. It is a business model that, from the outside, appears accessible and achievable and has been imitated with varying degrees of success by millions of other social media users.

The pervasiveness of cleanfluencing is such that promotions for cleaning products are increasingly interwoven into paid partnerships across a wide variety of influencer accounts. Often the links to cleaning are tenuous, such as the *Guardian* food critic Grace Dent who used her Instagram account to promote Flash, Fairy and other Procter & Gamble products. Importantly, effective relatability needs to be curated to look like products are being offered in a fun and friendly way, rather than treating followers more obviously as customers in the more traditional, impersonal and direct way of selling. Ideally, the account needs to show that the product on show is simply a prop in the fabric of the usual activities of the influencer. Thus, all over social media, we see accounts that were originally dedicated to a 'non-cleaning' topic being used to promote cleaning products. One example of this is Gemma Bird, otherwise known as @MoneyMumOfficial, who uses her popular Instagram account to share household management and budget advice. In one story – a paid partnership with Hoover – we see her radiant in a blue ball gown on her way to the National Television Awards.[44] She thanks Hoover for the invitation before posting an ad for two new vacuum cleaners. Housework and so-called labour-saving devices are thus increasingly associated with the new ultra-glamour of the digital influencer. Most influencing accounts have a 'theme' – a feature that makes them novel and appealing. And even where this isn't cleaning, cleanfluencing often ends up being part of the commodified content on offer.

A cup of tea and a chat

In this chapter, I have considered the 'success' of the cleanfluencer. As someone offering housework tips and advice to followers, this is nothing new. Yet today's brand of hyper-visible digital cleanfluencer offers a new type of heavily commercialised content and new ways of communicating with followers. The celebrity housewives that came before tended to present themselves as educationalists specialising in disgust and horror at the mess and dirt, for example the popular BBC television show *How Clean Is Your House?* presented by Kim Woodburn and Aggie Mackenzie that ran for six seasons between 2003 and 2009. These television housewives were often depicted as matronly, middle-aged, posh and bossy as opposed to the young and femme contemporary cleanfluencers who tie their love of cleaning to kindness, empathy and a friendly and accessible intimacy with followers and who talk with rather than at their followers. *I get it! And I get it because I am just like you!*

In this chapter I have argued that in order to make sense of the popular success and appeal of the cleanfluencers, we need to consider the historical legacies of housework and the routes that have led us to the hyper-commercialisation of domestic cleaning products and practices. As others have also noted, much of the success of the most popular social media platforms such as Instagram and TikTok is centred around the creation of algorithmic gossip; the endless engagement via follows, shares, tags, likes and views. Any intrinsic value that the vast array of cleaning products might hold is blurred by the constant reproduction of images, videos, slogans and brands that work to intensify interest, engagement and ultimately sales, simultaneously creating a special type of meaning behind the products. Cleaning products – once seen as the most mundane, domestic and utilitarian of consumer goods – acquire a magical status that transcends their intrinsic value. They are seemingly joyful, fun, pleasurable, satisfying and – as I argue in later chapters – a legitimate route to good mental wellbeing and personal happiness.

From the 1960s onwards, we witnessed the intensification of new Technicolor images of domestic life, particularly of homes and food. Today, we see a dazzling fusion of the hyper-visual alongside an intense commercialisation of domestic goods, all bolstered by digital celebrity culture. The popular success of cleanfluencing depends both on the endless creation of new needs and desires and the increased hyper-visualisation of homes and domestic cleaning products positioned within them. In Chapter 2, I describe how the so-called age of individualism and a decline in collective action has meant that cleanfluencing is increasingly bound up with the pursuit of a new, highly individualised consumer selfhood. I explore in more detail the appeal for followers, and situate this within wider social and political economic structures, in order to further understand the meteoric success of the relatively new digital media platforms in successfully tapping into the glamourised cleaning zeitgeist.

'I really wanted to share this with you' has become an almost ubiquitous social media mantra accompanying the familiar pose of the influencer who addresses followers as she speaks directly to the camera, often chin in hand and nursing a cup of tea. Watching the videos has the effect of a supportive conversation with a friend, offering an image of friendly and cosy intimacy. It is a cyber-replica of the timeless 'cup of tea and a chat' that stands in direct contrast to the supposedly distant and impersonal world of production, marketing and selling. There are no invasive, aggressive sales techniques; rather, selling is presented as an act of kindness, a sort of generous gift to followers who are 'friends' and 'Insta-family' rather than consumers and customers.

The ultra-curated world of cleanfluencing has evolved in such a way that it is almost entirely dislocated from the gritty reality of cleaning. In Chapter 2, I consider how cleanfluencing, as a form of digital culture fastidiously harnessed by global corporations, is interwoven with fresh narratives of consumer 'selfhood', whereby housework becomes less a thing that we *do* and more something that we *are*.

2

Housework turned inwards: Cleanfluencing and the self

You deserve the absolute world even if right now you don't think you do. You are enough, and you CAN change your life and make a fresh start if you want it. I did it and so can you![1]

Why does 'Occupation: housewife' require such insistent glamorising year after year?[2]

This chapter tells the story of how housework became a personification – a form of unpaid labour entwined with the self and with the creation of a particular type of feminine identity. Throughout the twentieth century, domestic labour became increasingly commodified and sold to women as a practice of selfhood bound up with personal wellbeing, resilience and betterment rather than simply a list of tasks and responsibilities to be performed. This chapter describes how, in the latter part of the twentieth century, an increasingly fetishised and *glamorous* version of housework emerged, and how the twenty-first-century cleanfluencers have positioned themselves as its most recent, hyper-visible incarnation. I unpick the ways in which the unfolding practice of housework as 'selfhood' paved the way for the cleanfluencers. In doing so, I show how cleanfluencing is about far more than simply keeping a clean and tidy home.

Housework and the 'half-lived' life

When feminist scholars have written about housework, it is often to note the soul-destroying, crippling loneliness, anxiety and regret regarding a life half-lived. In *Matrescence*, Lucy Jones bursts the myth of the 'pastel-hued dream' of pregnancy, childbirth and motherhood, noting that these moments of transition in women's lives are where the tug of responsibility and 'respectable' domestic motherhood become the most intense.[3] These are also moments where women are most ruthlessly abandoned by a patriarchal capitalist system that puts profits before wellbeing and maternal care. Jones writes:

> We have to see the structures we've inherited in order to tear them down. So many women believe their struggles with matrescence are the result of their own weakness and moral failing. This is a lie and it inhibits honest talk and social change. *The difficulties of modern matrescence in neoliberal Western societies are structural and systematic.*[4]

Like the institution of motherhood, housework has presented domestic tasks as heroic, satisfying, caring and central to creating a happy, healthy home and family, a serious business of creating domestic order into which young women – and traditionally not men and boys – were educated.

Throughout the twentieth century, feminist scholars argued that rigid expectations of women as domestic, respectable and godly creatures entrenched their 'rightful' and 'natural' role as the purveyors, curators and managers of the domestic sphere. They also argued that the thankless, exhausting and valueless status of domestic labour *hindered* the emergence of a complete, autonomous, freethinking and liberated self. In *Memoirs of a Dutiful Daughter*, Simone de Beauvoir describes the horrifying consequences of a self stunted by the crippling demands of bourgeois domestic femininity, describing her escape and freedom from the 'revolting fate' that had laid before her and her conflicted feelings for those who had not been so lucky.[5]

De Beauvoir's seminal feminist text, *The Second Sex*, took aim at the peculiar pressures and demands of housework felt almost universally by women tasked with the impossible struggle for 'victory over the dirt'. For de Beauvoir, housework reinforces the infantilised position of women, arranging them primarily as vulnerable and submissive. By fixing women to the domestic sphere, locked in the never-ending cycle of the 'endless struggle without victory' over housework, where satisfaction is never achieved, women are also prevented from mastering a sense of self or any freedom over their own destiny. In seeking to find meaning and some 'social justification' in their housework, de Beauvoir describes the ways in which women seek pleasure and an 'occupation' in their housewifely tasks. She describes the temporary 'satisfaction' to be gained from 'shining stoves, clean clothes, bright copper, polished furniture'.[6] Yet within these mundane, domestic acts there is ultimately 'no escape from immanence and little affirmation of individuality'. She writes:

> Few tasks are more like the torture of Sisyphus than housework with its endless repetition: the clean becomes soiled, the soiled is made clean, over and over, day after day. The housewife wears herself out marking-time: she makes nothing, simply perpetuates the present. Eating, sleeping, cleaning – the years no longer rise up towards heaven, they lie spread out ahead, grey and identical. The battle against dust and dirt is never won.[7]

Of course, cleanfluencing culture reminds us that, over seventy years since Simone de Beauvoir first wrote of housework as a flight from self, women today still seek temporary satisfaction in the most everyday of domestic cleaning tasks and rituals. One of the cornerstones of cleanfluencing is the bright, uplifting video reels of surfaces being wiped, windows shined, floors mopped and carpets vacuumed leaving lines in the fabric. All of which are played back to followers in super-accelerated, edited montages against motivating pop music – neat, happy and easy – often ending with a dish cloth playfully thrown across the room into the sink. Interestingly, the word 'satisfaction' as used by de Beauvoir is also regularly deployed by the cleanfluencers. Cleaning is described not just as joyful, relaxing and stress-busting but also, in an echo of de Beauvoir's stinging critique of housework, as *satisfying*. The job is thus positioned as rewarding, pleasurable and worthwhile *because* of the clean, tidy and shining homes and objects that come to represent the fruits of one's labour.

And yet, as de Beauvoir argues, attempts to make housework into an identity, or to find personal fulfilment and satisfaction through housework, are doomed to failure. The pull of housework as a womanly duty towards eliminating disorder, even sometimes presented as a battle against 'evil',[8] is betrayed by its torturous repetition, mundanity and sameness. Developing a psychoanalytic stance in *The Second Sex*, de Beauvoir suggests that housework might be more appropriately seen as a form of sadomasochism, a flight from self or even compensation for an erotic lack or absence.[9]

More recently, feminist scholars took aim at the irony of the popular notion of the home as a space of rest, calm and tranquillity, given the significant labour, stress and anxiety that goes into attempting to construct this. In *Women's Consciousness, Man's World*, first published in 1973 at the height of the British Women's Liberation Movement, the socialist feminist writer Sheila Rowbotham described housework as an unrecognised form of labour. The *unpaid* facet of housework – the fact that it was lacking in *monetary* value – meant that housework did not share the same association with power, value and independence that men's work and labour enjoys within capitalist societies. Women who were 'housewives' were frequently described as not working at all. For Rowbotham, although women have long found ways to assert their *moral* worth and resist devaluation as housewives, the exclusion of housework from capitalist economic accounts of 'value' has historically meant that the labour performed is rendered invisible and not taken seriously at all, particularly by those who don't have to do it. The consequence of this is that over time, rather than housewives acquiring the identity of worker, housework developed into a form of 'personhood'. The sameness of each day, combined with the monotony of the work and the ways that each achievement – each clean surface, cleared floor, empty kitchen sink, tidied cupboard – disappears almost instantly the moment it is accomplished, adds to the lack of recognition of housework as 'real' work, since 'women receive no wage and do work which is barely recognized as work, in which productivity can't be measured and nothing is ever ultimately accomplished'.[10]

In a society that places so much emphasis on monetised notions of value achievable through capitalist commodity production, the search for personal value and achieving a sense of 'worthiness' might be curtailed for those for whom the products of their labour carry little or no economic value. As Rowbotham notes, for the early 1970s housewife, the search for self and individual identity was limited for those who were locked out of the paid labour market. The painful reality of relinquishing your own selfhood and identity for the benefit of others can be agonising and accompanied by chronic experiences of invisibility or, as Rowbotham contests, 'a terrifying feeling that you are no longer there'.[11] Women, she argued, were often sinking themselves so far into the needs of others that there was simply no space left for the emergence of their own selves. A popular second-wave feminist slogan printed on tea towels as well as protest banners read, 'First you sink into his arms, then your arms end up in his sink', a witty but terrifying reminder of the rapid shift for many young women from romantic love to housewifery (Figure 2). This painful invisibility is vividly portrayed in the 1988

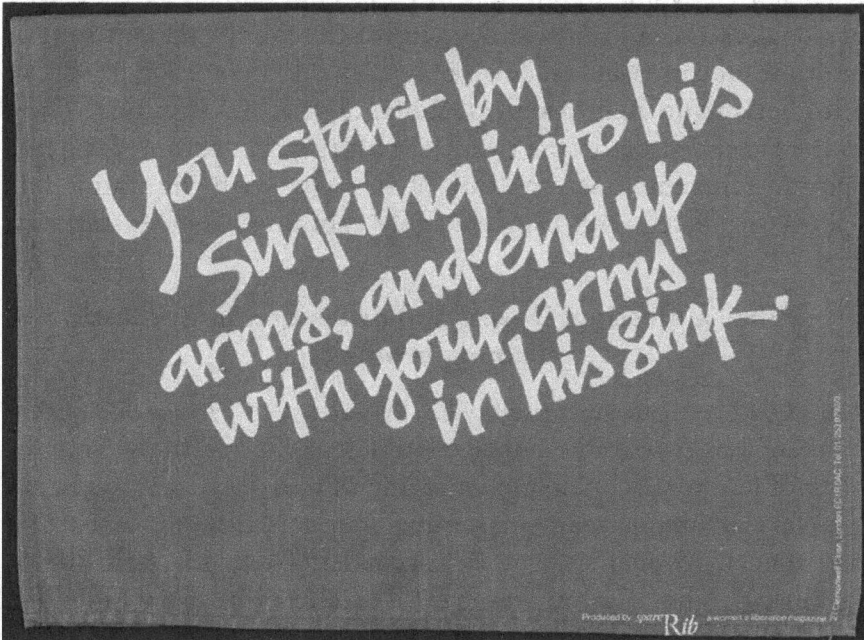

2 Tea towel designed by Pat Kahn and produced by Spare Rib. Reproduced with permission from Marsha Rowe.

Willy Russell play *Shirley Valentine* about a Liverpudlian housewife who – slowly suffocating under a never-ending list of thankless, unappreciated and unpaid domestic tasks – has simply lost her identity and resorts to talking to the walls. She asks sadly, 'why get feelings and dreams and hope that can't ever be used?'

Women have long been tasked with absorbing all of the residue, scraps, stress and pain left over from the ravages of unfettered capitalism;[12] from absorbing and seeking solutions, to the exhaustion and stress of family members, to juggling a complex and limited household budget, all the while labouring to create a sanctuary of love, calm and order away from the chaos. Rowbotham writes: 'The family under capitalism carries an intolerable weight: all the rags and bones and bits of old iron the capitalist commodity system can't use. Within the family women are carrying the preposterous contradiction of love in a loveless world.'[13]

The proliferation of contemporary cleanfluencing cultures makes it clear that women continue to carry this burden as they seek personal value and self-identity within the home and family. The multiple processes and practices of housework become a type of craft with 'fetishistic qualities' in cleaning, tidying and shining.[14] Thus, in the latter decades of the twentieth century, housework gradually became reinvented as a culture of its own, with the norms and values associated with it increasingly communicated collectively.

What a blessing! Desire and aspiration in domestic cleaning products

Ann Oakley's classic study *The Sociology of Housework*, first published in 1974, represents a central contribution to the growing body of feminist scholarship emerging in the 1970s and 1980s as a backlash to mainstream masculine sociological approaches that had tended to dismiss women's experiences of domestic life as lacking in scholarly importance.[15] Revealing the social isolation, undervaluation and invisibility of housework, Oakley's study and the more mass market form of the book *Housewife*, which went on to become a bestseller, dovetailed with the women's movement and in particular the fresh emphasis on disrupting the long-established principle of women as the natural purveyors and managers of the domestic sphere. In a 2018 essay reflecting on the original study, Oakley recalls the broadly dismissive response to the idea of a scholarly study of housework from publishers and also from the wider academic community, at a time when the concealment of women's lives and experiences was commonplace throughout the social sciences.[16] However, this early scepticism was tempered by the political feminist climate of the 1970s, which often centred on demands to re-evaluate housework and in particular to examine why women are so persistently manoeuvred into doing 'dirty work'. Oakley notes the stubborn persistence of the 'working mother' diktat that implied that only labour performed outside the home counts as 'real' economically valuable labour. She also notes the dissonance between housework as an occupation – available as an occupational category on census forms for example – and women's acute awareness of the way that housework as an occupation is so routinely devalued.

In a particularly memorable passage, Oakley recalls one woman's weekly practice of washing all the curtains in her house. Rather than dismissing these seemingly excessive standards of domestic labour as compulsive or as synonymous with pathological behaviour, Oakley instead describes how women regularly expressed calls for their housework to be *seen*, recognised and valued, and that they did this by adopting a range of creative expressions of domestic labour tasks. She writes: 'Housework generates *higher* levels of monotony, fragmentation and excessive pace than assembly line factory work, and is therefore liable to call for more *creative effort* on the part of the worker to find job satisfaction.'[17]

Work that is historically seen as lacking economic value, and labour that does not produce tangible results, is routinely rendered invisible, undervalued, unacknowledged and of course unpaid. Yet it is as equally exhausting, time-consuming, necessary and monotonous as paid work. As Oakley remarks in her study, paradoxically 'housework' itself was often described as the worst part of being a housewife. It is not surprising then that over time women have looked for ways to adopt new creative expressions for domestic labour, locate and create an aesthetic appeal, and even seek some sort of joy and pleasure from housework; expressions that at once insist on its value, make it visible and perhaps even provide new ways of seeking financial reward for their labour. Cleanfluencers frequently nod to the fleeting, transitory and even ephemeral nature of housework – 'I know it won't be tidy like this for long' – although of course we almost *never* see the messy version.

The almost total erasure of the word 'housewife' within cleanfluencing culture is of course intentional. Few today would willingly describe themselves as a housewife. Why would they? Housewifery carries none of the value or worth associated with neoliberal citizenship. Instead, its popular association with drudgery, complaining and judgement – the archetypal middle-aged, working-class, aproned woman, with saggy tights and curlers permanently left in her hair, standing, broom in hand, gossiping to her neighbours – is often parodied by cleanfluencers including Mrs Hinch, who uses an ugly Snapchat 'housewife' filter when she wants to 'have a moan'. Similarly parodied is the *Stepford Wives* style of impossibly perfect, fixed, robotic, idiotic and submissive housewife echoed in the infamous 1950s advertisements. In short, housework has variously been associated with dependence and submissiveness, lacking in 'real' glamour or femininity. Again, who would willingly describe themselves as a housewife?

Late modern capitalist societies, so heavily reliant as they are on the unpaid labour of women, have been tasked with finding a solution to this dilemma. If housework no longer carries value and is merely a stigmatised identity, how can women be persuaded to willingly comply? As Betty Friedan asked in relation to the supposed 'honour of being a woman', how is the occupation of 'housewife' periodically reinvented to ensure women's continued compliance? We know that women continue to perform the vast majority of unpaid and unseen domestic labour,[18] and, as Kylie Jarret has argued, this includes the majority of unpaid *digital* labour.[19] Consider the time taken to conceive, film, curate and manage the comments on a social media post. Housework today isn't simply about the visual representation of the home to visiting friends, family and neighbours; it must have a social media *public* visual presence too.

We can see how this relates to today's contemporary cleanfluencer who adopts a range of complex, often highly creative and sometimes sophisticated methods to record and curate not only the processes of housework but also the *display* of the fruits of their domestic labour. In the 2020s, cleanfluencers make use of digital platforms to find a creative expression for their domestic labour, and in doing so – paradoxically perhaps – reinforce standards, routines and ideals of efficiency, pace and often extreme standards of cleanliness and tidiness. Much cleanfluencing content features immaculately dressed and made-up women wiping down already perfectly clear and clean surfaces, vacuuming already lint-free carpets, mopping already gleaming floors and polishing taps and windows that were never dirty to begin with. Oakley proposes that rather than dismissing the rigid routines, standards and expectations of the housewife as a pathology, a disorder or an illness, we should instead examine the 'origins of the felt need to do housework',[20] and in doing so make sense of the 'compulsion' to uphold particular standards. Uncovering the feelings, emotions and even pleasures associated with housework is therefore key to making sense of the ties that continue to bind femininity to domesticity so tightly.

Of course, as Oakley makes clear in her work, mainstream academic scholarship has rarely taken the study of housework, and especially women's own accounts of their experiences and perceptions of housework, seriously. This is despite the fact that, as described in the Introduction, the stubborn persistence of inequalities of domestic labour remains a key barrier to meaningful gender equality. The central aim of Oakley's classic study is thus to conceptualise housework as *a form of work* rather than simply as a 'natural' feature of feminine roles. By recording the feelings around housework – as monotonous, lonely, dissatisfying, lacking in prestige, consisting of long working hours and adhering to a particularly rigid set of standards and routines – Oakley notes the close connection between housework and the construction of a feminine *identity*. Thus, women often reported that while they disliked the assembly line-type practices associated with housework, they reportedly enjoyed *being* a housewife. She asks, 'what are the origins of the felt need to do housework' and the 'compulsion to do it in accordance with particular standards'?[21] These questions remain pertinent today as women seek new meanings and creative expressions of self that transcend the processes and practices that are intrinsic to the performance of housework.

The deskilling of women's domestic and especially arts and crafts skills is noteworthy. During the industrial revolution, many traditional skills shifted towards mass production, factories and male labour. Ultimately, this preceded a shift towards women's domestic and homemaking skills being harnessed to execute male designs and concepts. A contemporary example of this is the 'minimalist' movement, which makes bold promises of freedom, self-expression, wellbeing and inner peace: 'Minimalism is a tool that can assist you in finding freedom. Freedom from fear. Freedom from worry. Freedom from overwhelm. Freedom from guilt. Freedom from depression. Freedom from the trappings of the consumer culture we've built our lives around. Real freedom.'[22]

Within the minimalism movement, clutter is vilified, pathologised and often ridiculed,[23] but in tandem, minimalism has become an aspirational aesthetic with women via their domestic labour and they are tasked with recreating it. Like the British arts and crafts movement pioneered by William Morris, the term 'beautiful and useful' used to set boundaries around what it was acceptable to have on display in the home. This coincided with Victorian feminine ideals of women as self-sacrificing, pious, pure and passive 'angels of the home', sweeping in and utilising their domestic skills to recreate the beautiful and useful homely aesthetic. Ironically, as Chapter 3 explores, rather than easing anxiety, concepts of aesthetic minimalism might actually intensify anxious thoughts around presentation, cleaning and tidying. The minimalist aesthetic finds its popular expression on cleanfluencing social media, which is visible in the multitude of posts featuring hyper-minimalist interiors: spotless, clear surfaces; neutral palettes of grey and beige; clutter-free rooms with only the bare minimum of selected objects on display.

One recurring feature of scholarship into housework is the finding that women continue to bear a feeling of 'responsibility' for it and the standard to which it is performed. This is the case even when women aren't doing the housework themselves and it is outsourced to others. The assumption of women bearing ultimate responsibility for domestic labour is almost never questioned in cleanfluencing culture and the tie between femininity and housework is hardly ever challenged. The fact that cleanfluencers, their followers and those who engage with digital housework forums are almost always women is also never brought into question. Narratives of choice, individuality and freedom of expression mean that there is very little in the way of a vocabulary to express these underlying inequalities or even to see this as problematic. In the shiny, bright, aspirational world of digital cleanfluencing, any woman would be happy to be involved.

How, then, do women find and demand that the labour they perform is imbued with value? How can value be reproduced within an activity where the labour invested in it is rendered invisible and where the activity itself is historically perceived as mundane, meaningless and apolitical?[24] We have seen so far in this chapter that the meanings of housework extend beyond the *practices* of housework themselves. Housework, then, *acquires* value when it is represented by cleanfluencers via social media.

From superwomen to tradwives

In order to further understand how housework became part of a personal project of the self, it is helpful to revisit earlier studies that situate popular, gendered representations of housework within the emergence of wider cultures. In 1987, Janice Winship identified what she described as the development of the 'superwoman' syndrome; a way of seeking highly personal and individualised solutions to the complex, deep-rooted structural problems of gendered inequalities at home and work. Superwoman syndrome, Winship argues, benefits only the most privileged of women, creating a type of competitive 'one-upmanship' of personal and individual successes and freedoms and little reflection on the mass scale of female exploitation: 'Superwoman is only the elitist and individual success story – "I'm all right sisters" – which leaves untouched the deep problems for most women of how to satisfactorily combine "home" and "work" without being made to suffer for it.'[25]

Some thirty-five years later, the solution to the ongoing inequalities of unpaid domestic labour and the balancing act between home and work in many ways remains similar. We are inundated with colourful, happy images of the few who have 'made it work'; who are at once beautiful, wealthy, happy *and* have actively embraced the domestic burden. In fact, it is more than this; the domestic burden has actually *enhanced* their beauty, wealth and happiness. I will pick up this idea again in Chapters 3 and 4 and show that today housework is no longer about simply *balancing* work and home but, in addition, welcoming domestic labour into the home as an act of self-care and love. This offers an interesting counterbalance to Winship's superwoman, whereby today women are often actively encouraged *not* to try to do everything; to accept the limitations on their lives but always without giving up on the housework. Instead of being encouraged, like our 1980s sisters were, to try and have it all, today we are told to accept that we can't. Which is worse? And why does the common denominator – the plodding, repeated demands of unpaid labour – remain steadfastly unchallenged?

As Winship noted, it has long been impossible to ignore the advances of feminism. The 1970s Women's Liberation Movement offered a fresh vocabulary for women to self-express their intersectional experiences of domestic drudgery and a solid recognition of the demands of unpaid labour. In the 1980s, the solution to inequality was a sort of 'aim high', *Cosmo*-style aspirational feminism of the individual; one which often meant that women who made it pulled the ladder back up behind them. Today, digital cleanfluencers in the UK and their sisters in the US – the middle-class, conservative, Christian 'tradwives' – have reframed housework and domesticity as freedom, liberty, choice and wellbeing; as '[l]iving truly free as our ancestors did', an expression of a sort of 'postcolonial melancholia'.[26] In the US, a recent example of this is the popular influencer

Hannah Needham, co-owner of 'Ballerina Farm', a vast ranch in the Utah mountains that also has its own highly successful meat, dairy, baked goods and homeware business. Needham's Instagram account, @ballerinafarm, offers regular updates on ranch living with her husband and eight home-schooled young children. The account depicts the perfect familial embodiment of the American Dream via regular posts and reels of domestic life on the farm. The family are God-fearing, church-going and patriotic; an American flag flies proudly from the front porch. Gender roles are usually segregated, with the boys heading to rodeo competitions while the girls help their mother to make food, always using fresh, home-grown ingredients. Everything seems natural, wholesome, organic and homespun. Family life is described as 'wild', and yet its depiction on Instagram is anything but. Hannah herself is picture perfect – slim, young and beautiful (she holds the Mrs American 2023 crown) – and is filmed effortlessly balancing her large family with managing domestic life on the ranch. She smiles as she serenely makes her own mozzarella, proves her own sourdough, bakes croissants, makes jam and cuts fresh flowers, all while her small children move around her, often one balanced on her hip or the baby strapped to her in a sling. Contrary to the claim to be 'wild', all is calm, languid and effortless. Comments from followers are a combination of admiration – how does she do it? – to praise for her 'simple' back-to-the-land family life. The Ballerina Farm aesthetic of linen aprons, bare feet and overalls is juxtaposed with trips to Las Vegas where Hannah competes in the Mrs American beauty pageant only days after giving birth to her eighth child. We see her sitting in a Las Vegas casino, breast-feeding her newborn baby while being heavily made up, hair blow-dried and sprayed, then strutting the stage in a range of swimsuits and ballgowns, and finally with her winner's bouquet and wearing her Mrs American '23 sash.

Despite their clear similarities – often tradwives and cleanfluencers are discussed interchangeably – there are notable differences, especially the tradwife steer towards Christian conservatism. In contrast, in the UK cleanfluencers tend to adopt a type of relatable resilience embedded in mass consumerism while the tradwives are more likely to centre their accounts on the farmyard, country living and a 'back to basics' lifestyle.

Yet Ballerina Farm helps to illuminate the contradiction at the heart of both cleanfluencing and tradwife culture. Namely, the deep, inescapable irony in the endless emphasis on seeking and gaining joy from simple domestic pleasures that are so often jarringly juxtaposed against images of ultra-consumerist agendas, such as trips to Las Vegas (the ultimate symbol of US hyper-consumerism), adverts for make-up and multiple opportunities to purchase Ballerina Farm-branded merchandise. For both the cleanfluencer and the tradwife, housework is reglamourised and framed as a lifestyle *choice* with a firm emphasis on personal liberation. There is never any acknowledgement of the impossibility of such a lifestyle for most, nor of the substantial privileges that benefit many of the most successful British and American influencers.

Cleanfluencing and the tradwife phenomenon can easily be seen as a sign of women's retreat to domesticity; a return to the 1950s stereotype of a passive, happy housewife, only this time with better clothes and domestic interiors. There is some critique of the anti-feminist message underpinning the tradwife, such as Hadley Freeman in the *Guardian*,[27] who described the fresh trend in 'submissive women' as having a 'dark heart and history' with associations with the alt-right in the US. However, the broadly uncritical celebration of the tradwife is also notable. An article in the *Daily Mail*, for example, featured four self-proclaimed British tradwives complete with glamorous photoshoot, dressed in 1950s-style clothes and make-up, including full skirts, high heels, aprons, coiffed hair and bright make-up, brandishing mops, brooms, dusters and mixing bowls.[28] Accompanying the smiling photos are four intimate stories describing the women's journeys to tradwifery. These are presented as accounts of personal redemption – escaping the false promise of the happiness of paid work that brought only stress, misery and the impossible double shift, rejecting the feminist critique of housework as exploitative unpaid labour as judgemental, and finding calm, order and personal and familial wellbeing and redemption in the process. The ethos of the efficient and savvy 1950s housewife, equipped in the art of household management, collides with twenty-first-century ideals of choice, personal betterment and diversity. Tradwifery resolves this contradiction by reframing housework as a choice, a type of freedom and a new-found personal liberty.

Of course, the *Daily Mail* article is also intended to verge on the humorous; there is an irony in the witty presentation of women dressed as 1950s housewives in an era when women supposedly have the same choices and career opportunities as men. Readers are even invited to consider how 'critics have denounced the tradwife trend as the ultimate betrayal of feminism'. Yet the article repeats many familiar tropes: 'The children were always in after-school clubs, the house was a mess, we'd eat takeaways because we were too tired to cook, and my husband and I bickered and rarely had time for each other.' The solution is a self-sacrificial turning inwards. Rather than looking outwards towards structural problems such as a lack of affordable childcare or meaningful flexible working practices, the solution to the complex juggle of family life and paid work lies with women taking control of the domestic sphere and relinquishing their participation in the paid labour market. Ultimately this also often means a loss of financial independence: 'It's only right that he gets the casting vote on our big expenditures; as the wage earner, he pays for it all.' Housework is ubiquitously presented as a personal decision: 'it's a *choice* and although I don't advocate that every woman's place is in the home, it's time we celebrate the importance of the role for those that feel it is'. The lack of monetary reward or recognition doesn't matter when pitched against the self-affirming notions of career sacrifice, keeping the home clean, tidy and well-ordered and the approval of one's husband who 'tells me the job I do at home is more important than any other'.[29] These anecdotes are offered up as a type of compensation for the perceived loss of status that comes from relinquishing paid work.

This repositioning of housework, and particularly of 'being a full-time housewife', as empowering and a way of 'taking back control of my life' offers a contemporary spin on old ideals of the white woman housewife and a set of aspirational codes that are certainly nothing new. In doing so, it reproduces other traditional positionings of femininity: the assumption of the financially stable household that can survive on a single salary; the presumption of a heterosexual family unit; and the unchallenged assumption of the importance of endlessly high levels of cleanliness, tidiness and 'order' that requires committed, continuous monitoring, crafting and labour.

It is a 'neoliberal' repositioning of housework underpinned by the same social inequalities and sexist assumptions around women's 'natural' competence in the home, but this time repositioned as offering the best deal scenario for *you*. Interrogating these contradictions helps to reveal what Shani Orgad terms the 'fault lines' in advanced capitalism that were laid bare in the narratives of a group of economically privileged middle-class women who had left behind careers in order to be stay-at-home mothers.[30] On the one hand, the women, such as the tradwives in the *Daily Mail* article, had benefited from the meritocratic choice and opportunities of the 1980s and 1990s and of the empowerment cultures of contemporary society. Yet Orgad notes how their lives were palpably constrained and subjected to 'gender retrenchment, the containment of desire and masculine domination'.[31] Importantly, Orgad points to the total absence of any easily discernible vocabulary to articulate any sense of disappointment, unrealised desire or protest. As with tradwives, popular narratives around choice, empowerment and personal satisfaction abound, while simultaneously the lack of any alternative vocabulary to express disappointment, unrealised desire, protest or even anger is palpable. In a world where it is assumed women have unlimited choice and freedoms, simply asking the question articulated by Betty Friedan in the 1960s – 'Is this all?' – feels ungrateful and remains subjected to widespread popular judgement, particularly given the assumption that, like motherhood, housework is still part of women's 'natural' role. Orgad continues:

> The women I spoke to colluded, often unwittingly, in enabling an almost complete separation between their husband's role in the public sphere of work and their roles in the family sphere – a gendered division which ... is ... rooted historically in institutional forms of capitalism and patriarchy.[32]

Thus, a dominant 'new feminine mystique' ensues, whereby cleanfluencers and tradwives similarly collude in cultural fantasies of women, ensuring the continuation of the gendered division of labour via narratives of personal choice and empowerment.

Chuck out that chintz! Enterprising selves

Keeping the house spick and span should be continuous: calm, effortless and almost unnoticeable.[33]

The invisibility of housework was further enforced via popular advice offered to women such as that cited above from *Good Housekeeping* in 1971, which recommended that women should keep a clean and tidy home while hiding the labour that went into creating it. In many ways, the hyper-visual presence of the digital housewife who offers regular, intricate and detailed retellings of her housework offers a rebuke to this type of earlier articulation of housework as valueless and invisible. It says: *Look! My labour exists! I exist!*

By the mid-twentieth century, popular representations of house-wifery had begun to focus on a middle-class 'ideal' of domesticity, and increasingly offered up commercial solutions to helping women achieve this. The post-war period also saw the beginnings of a type of 'dramatisation' of housework, especially within the burgeoning new advertisements of the post-war era. Advertisements for household products, and especially labour-saving devices, during this period often featured scripted and staged depictions of the housewife in direct dialogue with her viewers/consumers. The 1950s Christmas advert for the Hoover vacuum cleaner is a good example of this.[34] Featuring an immaculately dressed woman 'Hoover Home Consultant' made up to perfection – rather than looking like someone who has indeed been dragging a heavy Hoover vacuum cleaner around the house – she addresses the camera and viewer directly. 'I must just finish this', she smiles, as she carefully adjusts decorations on the Christmas tree then plumps the cushions on the sofa. Looking wistfully into the distance, then back to the camera, she sits down, resting her arm on the back of the sofa in an apparently casual pose. Like today's cleanfluencers, she enters into a personal and friendly conversation with the imagined viewer. Yet the talk is not 'confessional' – she is posed and perfect and there is no attempt to hide the fact that the advert is scripted rather than intimate, personal and 'fly-on-the-wall'. Moreover, the product itself – in this case the Hoover vacuum cleaner – is presented as almost superfluous to the story being told in the advert. Housework is present via the mention of Hoover but is alluded to rather than performed for the camera. In fact, the commercial contains no images of the Hoover vacuum, let alone it being used. Instead, the practice of housework is dramatised and retold as part of the story of familial happiness, festive joy and a presentation of relaxed self-satisfaction, but, in keeping with the *Good Housekeeping* advice cited above, the practice of housework is kept invisible. Crucially, the advert also emphasises the central role of the market and consumer durables in facilitating the perfect, happy home. The Hoover Home Consultant smiles as she addresses her audience of families across the country preparing their homes for Christmas. She says: 'In every home, Christmas trees will be decorated with gifts of happiness. Many of these gifts will be our own Hoover products. And we are very proud to think of the important part these gifts will play in helping to bring happiness to so many homes.' The advert ends with the popular, memorable jingle: 'Today and every day, it's Hoover for happier homes!'

Throughout the twentieth century, a uniform voice that articulated the role and purpose of the housewife as one who takes pride in her domestic practices gave way to a new form of 'domestic dreaming' whereby housewives began to realise the potential of new consumer cultures. Over time, the market opened up and advanced, promising new opportunities for women to hone their skills. Housework periodicals such as *Good Housekeeping* magazine, in addition to offering housework advice, increasingly offered tips on the consumption of cleaning products and practices. This was achieved through a combination of fostering new desires, alongside the promise of aspiration and has often involved the commercial construction of the home as a site of danger and infinite potential harms that must be cleansed.[35] Thus a 'culture of cleanliness' that underpinned the mass commercial expansion of housework.[36] This reached a nadir during the COVID-19 pandemic, when a renewed and heightened fear of germs and fresh concern around order and cleanliness became embedded in the marketing of household cleaning products.

Much earlier scholarship and activism around housework hails from a historical period when societal measurements of personal 'value' were bound up in old notions of production and labour. Today in consumer economies, value is increasingly tied to objects that we consume and the ways in which we display them. The mass fusion of selfhood and consumption – consolidated in the late twentieth century[37] – is key to making sense of the popular rise of housewives as consumer citizens whose value and 'worth' was increasingly centred around their consumer choices. Increasingly, the home became a place for self-expression, where changing its aesthetics can not only make you and your family happier, as with the Hoover advert, but can also change *you*.

Central to this process was a drift as consumer societies advanced towards seeking and sharing stories of personal gratification in housework, often simultaneously imbuing housework practices such as vacuuming, polishing and mopping with mystical, magical powers. The *fetishistic* qualities of mundane housework tasks also extend to the objects required to complete them. Thus, the Shark vacuum cleaner, the Minky duster and the Flash floor mop become more than simply objects to get the job done or to display a new type of aspirational consumerism as with the labour-saving devices of the 1960s. Rather, they are presented as *transformative* and as a route to self-enhancement, with predominantly women cleanfluencers demonstrating the products. Women are supposedly put in control of the narrative, emphasising what the product can do *for them*.

In 1996, the Swedish home-furnishing store Ikea, famous for bringing the flat-pack, affordable and 'minimalist' home aesthetics to the UK, launched an era-defining commercial that represented a shift away from the old ways of furniture advertising, which had previously focused on offering basic information about price and store location. The advert featured a montage of visual images borrowing heavily from the aesthetics of the Women's Liberation Movement: women striding forwards en masse, chanting and waving 'chuck out that chintz' placards, and feminist zine-style cartoon drawings of a woman carrying a 'liberation' sign. The women are strident; they throw open windows, march through the streets, throwing their 'chintz' – floral curtains, patterned lampshades, embroidered doilies – into giant skips as they go. Decluttering homes in the Ikea advert is presented as an act of protest and resistance – a grab at freedom from the suffocating old world of pattern and clutter which, in the Ikea commercial, is seen to symbolise domestic bondage. The solution is, of course, a commercialised one – buying mass-produced flat-pack furniture from Ikea, which was quickly establishing itself in the UK as a leading home-furnishing brand. The Ikea advert, now almost thirty years old, is an early example of the commercialised notion that political resistance and even equality and emancipation are, for women (there are no men featured in the commercial at all), tied to the presentation of their homes. Home is positioned as a way of setting yourself free, offering up opportunities to liberate yourself via self-expression:

Chuck out that chintz, come on do it today,
We're battling hard and we've come a long way,
In choices, in status, in jobs and in pay,
So don't let that doily go and spoil everything,
Chuck out that chintz!
Yes, chuck out that chintz today.[38]

The Ikea advert is symptomatic of the message popularised in the early 2000s that our 'true', liberated, free and happy self is always there, perhaps as Simone de Beauvoir argued, buried away under the crippling demands of domestic respectability. You just need to find it and set it free, then wonderful things will come to you.

As Chapter 1 showed, a minority of successful influencers have harnessed their cleaning to create a lucrative venture of high economic value. However, for the majority of women sharing cleaning and housework content on social media, there is little to no monetary value in their work. Rather, a different type of value is at play, whereby old notions of housework as the preserve of the tired, downtrodden housewife have been reinvented so that she emerges victorious with an enhanced sense of personal value in her labour.

You do you! Developing a 'respectable' domestic self

In 2022 the cleanfluencer @missgreedyshome published her book *You Do You!*[39] The book, launched to great fanfare including an event in a Chelsea restaurant attended by other celebrity cleanfluencers, featured a pink cover and the subtitle *Living the Life You Want*. *You Do You!* promises a 'motivational guide to celebrating your true authentic self'. Each page features a different set of motivational quotes and paragraphs, all interspersed with anecdotes of Charlotte's journey from feeling 'lost', 'stuck' and unhappy – describing poverty, bullying and low self-esteem – to turning her life around and 'learning to love herself' again, all through a story of self-improvement and inner transformation inspired by the ways in which she thinks about and experiences her home and family. In posts with the hashtag 'YouDoYou', shared across Instagram, the book is displayed alongside cups of tea and on coffee tables and bedside tables, accessorised with spotless surfaces.

Charlotte Greedy's story of a personal journey to happiness and life satisfaction is narrated against a backdrop of meritocratic aspiration: from tearfully leaving her council house behind and getting the keys to her own home; to home improvement on a shoestring, such as making a football goal post for her son from an old curtain pole salvaged from a skip; to endless reels of cleaning, tidying and organising the home. Home improvement 'before and after' shots stand as markers of success, not only of self-improvement or taking control of her own life but also of a renewed sense of order – an expression of a valued and respectable self. For working-class women in particular, respectable selfhoods are displayed through homes and bodies, and this is particularly the case with the digital domestic cleaning influencers. As Bev Skeggs and others have argued,[40] working-class women have long been subject to heightened surveillance from hostile social and political commentators, who combine centuries-old ideas of the 'undeserving' poor with intense judgement on the presentation of working-class homes and bodies.

Cleanfluencers not only represent one of the first sites for the unbridled, highly visual representation of working-class women's domestic routines, they also portray a hyper-visible and unique version of class and gender. Cleanfluencers are often women of working-class origin, narrating their journeys towards cleanfluencing stardom in terms of meritocratic ideals of making it against the odds. Stacey Solomon, for example, uses the afterword of her book as a way of challenging the snobbery and judgement that she faced as a 17-year-old working-class single mother from Dagenham, and uses these humble roots as further evidence of her success – as part of the rags-to-riches, 'working-class hero' fable increasingly embedded within popular culture: 'Where you came from, grew up, the level of education you got, the choices you made good or bad, your accent, how you look, just everything about you is what makes YOU and that is so special. Go out and GET IT yourself.'[41]

Within cleanfluencing culture, we see a highly visible articulation of anger at snobbery, elitism and class judgement that is probably quite new. However, in line with meritocratic norms, the solution is always found within and expressed through personal redemption stories; people make it through sheer strength of character, resilience and hard work. Luck or privilege are never mentioned. Rather, success, we are assured, can be found *within. Never give up! Just be you! You do you! Be the best version of yourself!* Importantly, the ongoing, grinding impact of inequalities on swathes of women, particularly during the cost-of-living crisis in the UK, are overlooked and social media platforms are rarely used to draw attention to the gritty reality of poverty and class. Instead, inequalities are played down; although classed *judgement* is challenged, the core message behind cleanfluencing culture is one that ultimately supports ongoing structures of inequality – namely that any need for wider change can be replaced with a more 'efficient' attitude to self-improvement.

Thus, the cleanfluencers today promise something more than simply advice on managing the home. They also offer a type of *self*-improvement alongside an often highly intimate description of their domestic lives. They present themselves as autonomous and aware of and able to articulate the dilemmas and difficulties of housework as working-class women did before them, and also how to navigate the process so that there is something in it for themselves. What we see is a range of personal affirmations such as 'You Are Enough' and 'Just be You' that not only offer space for articulating the struggles of housework but also sidestep rather than challenge the inequalities underpinning it. Protest at the never-ending domestic labour exists, but it is often a personal and individual search for the 'best version of myself' rather than political or radical. The cleanfluencer's response to her situation, then, is rational and highly instrumental, firmly positioning herself as a respectable mother, wife and homemaker. The most successful cleanfluencers are rarely single and never 'hyper-sexual'.[42] Rather, they tend to be presented within the confines of economically and emotionally secure relationships, striving towards the perfect display of what Bev Skeggs calls a 'caring self'.[43]

Within contemporary digital cleanfluencing cultures, the working-class caring self is displayed in glorious Technicolor. Returning to the example of @missgreedyshome and her journey of upward mobility, from struggling single mum to successful digital cleanfluencer and bestselling author, we see her story narrated alongside all of the markers of feminine respectability. Today, she is presented as having 'made it' against all the odds: she is happily engaged to her partner, she owns her own home, her house shines and we see her merrily cleaning and polishing; she is happy and smiling and strives for personal betterment. The icing on the cake, the final marker of her success, is of course a highly sought-after and lucrative book contract with Penguin publishers and a paid partnership with Procter & Gamble. Crucially, she is humble about her success as she offers her own version of the now familiar tale of meritocratic upward mobility.

And of course, the real secret to her success, in common with other cleanfluencers, is that she cleans, tidies and maintains her home as an act of care but also of *personal* betterment. Her work of carrying on regardless and against the odds by maintaining an impossibly ordered and happy home is rewarded by a society that above all else values responding to stresses and strains with a smile, by displaying superhuman resilience and striving for personal, commercialised success. Cleanfluencers do this very effectively, not only displaying the fruits of their labour via regular social media posts but also, crucially, promising to teach their legions of followers how to achieve this too.

Thus, the sort of life narratives we see throughout cleanfluencing culture represent a type of palatable response to class inequality; an acknowledgement of the struggle and pain that not only accompanies working-class life but is also a possible solution that avoids destabilising the meritocratic ideals embedded in neoliberal consumer societies.

Housework: The missing revolution?

The feminist movement that once held the unpaid labour of women as central to its struggle for the liberation and emancipation of women has in recent years tended to sidestep the topic of housework. Over time, the feminist focus on the body and fashion has intensified and the focus on the home and women's lived experiences of housework within it has diminished. In part, this growing absence can be explained by the mainstream dismissal of housework as frivolous, unimportant and apolitical. However, it also reflects a more general lack of visibility around housework and particularly working-class women's experiences.

Historically, the voices of working-class women and women of colour, and their experiences of housework, have tended to be ignored and overlooked in favour of an authoritative voice notable for its received pronunciation, such as that of the Hoover Home Consultant described earlier. The middle-class housewife is personable, approachable and understanding, with an aspirational but also *instructive* and *educating* presence. Working-class women were present during this time primarily as viewers and customers, who were presumably expected to aspire towards the advice of the middle-class woman educator.

Away from the gleam of popular cultures of advertising, there are other examples to be found of working-class women's descriptions of their domestic labour. In particular their difficulties in achieving the ideal home and keeping on top of the housework while working within a tight financial budget, alongside the often gruelling demands of paid work. The toil, burden, exhaustion and sheer intensity of domestic labour, particularly for working-class women in the early to mid-twentieth century, who frequently combined a demanding schedule of never-ending domestic labour chores with exhausting manual labour, such as factory work, have tended to be hidden from history and representations of housework in popular culture. The gritty realities of housework are regularly removed from the prim and neat depictions of the housewife, who is often presented as *separate* from the actual chores associated with housework.

Laura Schwartz cites a rare account from a working-class woman, Ada Nield Chew (1870–1945), a bricklayer's daughter and oldest of twelve siblings who combined factory work, women's Trade Union League work, housework and childcare.[44] Offering a detailed overview of the mundane minutiae of her daily unpaid domestic work helps to not only 'convey the incessant and all-absorbing nature of the daily round' but also 'force into public view a form of work that was usually hidden in the private sphere'.[45] Chew described the 'systematic, never-ceasing effort necessary to the keeping of an ordinary home clean by one pair of hands, *even when* bathroom and hot and cold water are all ready to hand',[46] and thus articulates the common burden of housework as it cuts across social classes.

Nevertheless, as Joanna Bourke has also argued, early feminist accounts of housework tended to position it as an unwilling and coerced type of 'slavery', thereby overlooking the ways in which women during the turn of the century were sometimes enthusiastic in their pursuit of the 'pleasures of housewifery'.[47] Rather, the decision to stay at home was sometimes driven by a rational choice that might have included part of embracing a new housewifely *identity* or of seeking some sort of status as wife and mother that may well have often been 'preferable to the difficulties of combining childcare, domestic duties and waged labour'.[48] But, as Schwartz argues:

> This should not mean we lose sight of the fact that housewifery was not just an identity, but also a form of labour that was invariably exhausting and frequently debilitating for the women who performed it. It was against this that not only middle- but also working-class feminists spoke out.[49]

The social and economic backdrop against which housework has always been situated is of great importance. The *labour* of housework brought to the fore so vociferously by working-class women is today compounded by the intensification of what Kylie Jarrett has termed 'digital labour', describing the digital display and curating of the home that is predominantly performed by women. But housework as an *aspirational identity* practice is also a feminist concern and absolutely core to the popularity of the cleanfluencer, a new type of highly mainstreamed culture that is both commercial and highly normative.

Today, housework has become synonymous with a type of post-feminist 'selfhood' that chimes with earlier popular forms of idealised 'respectable' feminine identities. The heroic, efficient housewife who stoically battled against the odds to create a sanctuary – a barrier – from the chaos is as strong as ever. Yet housework has been reinvented, repacked and reglamourised into a new set of representations of the housewife; one where her labour is seen in the most neoliberal and postfeminist reincarnations of 'doing it for herself'. Within cleanfluencing cultures, housework is not only celebrated but repositioned as being part of *who I am*. In 'just being me', I am being an efficient housewife, and we see new, never-seen-before entanglements between the self and housework.

Over time, the structural inequalities inherent in global capitalism and reflected in housework have remained fairly static. As discussed in the Introduction, globally women continue to carry the bulk of low-paid and unpaid labour, most of which is invisible. Increasingly, there is also a wider public awareness of the features of society that mean that it is historically harder for women than men to return to the workplace, particularly – although not exclusively – after having children. At the time of writing, in the UK the campaign groups Pregnant then Screwed and March of the Mummies have collectively organised the biggest and most high-profile protest around access to childcare and flexible working for decades. The campaigns succeeded in giving a voice to women's experiences of the huge financial and emotional cost of childcare, shedding light on the everyday gendered realities that have underpinned the structural inequalities of the workforce. Yet even for wealthy women, for whom childcare costs are less of a burden, a decision is frequently made to stay at home after having children. In *Heading Home*, Shani Orgad argues that the reasons for this are partly a lack of flexibility around childcare and partly a gendered sense of responsibility towards caring for both children and the home.

The continued gendered responsibility for housework is reflected and reproduced throughout cleanfluencing cultures and is rarely called out or questioned. Yet it is expressed alongside constantly changing presentations of self-identity. As we have seen, housework is routinely presented as synonymous with the enactment of consumer, caring, entrepreneurial and aspirational selfhood. As Rowbotham's socialist feminist critique of housework testifies, during the 1970s the emergence of the 'craft' of housework was valued primarily because of the ways in which a respected and valued self-identity was associated with performing domestic duties for the benefit of others. In contrast, in today's popular media discourses, women are increasingly encouraged to *centre themselves* in their actions and to seek a valued self-identity that puts oneself first – that has at its centre one's own needs, desires and 'self-care'. Cleanfluencing culture promises that rather than being self-sacrificial à la de Beauvoir, housework offers a route to finding yourself in the domestic sphere, enhancing yourself, being you.

Today, rather than housework itself – who does what within the home – the question has been reframed as to whether or not women do housework at all and the wider politics of who does the 'dirty work'. Unpicking the relationship between housework and feminism, Schwartz argues that:

> Housework was conceived of not only as an objective problem but also as a subjective form of political practice. How one performed housework, how one felt about it and whether or not one did it at all became important in debates about the formation of feminists as political subjects.[50]

Schwartz draws on evidence taken from the British suffrage movement to show how, in the early twentieth century, politics, housework and culture began to overlap in new and novel ways. For example, a range of suffragette-branded everyday household objects, such as teapots, plates and cups, helped to enhance everyday collective awareness of the cause, and feminist periodicals were increasingly used to advertise household cleaning products, offering a new manifestation of the overlap between politics and housework. Harnessing housework to the campaign for women's suffrage helped to advance the feminist cause by, first, making domestic labour *visible*, and second, presenting a range of labour-saving devices, presumably freeing up more time for political activism.

Discussions of housework from the political left have often focused on a thinly veiled critique of women who outsource their domestic labour. There is a tacit expectation that women should not only take responsibility for the housework but also that where working-class, low-paid women are paid to do cleaning work, it is other women who are exploiting them. The idea that men might also benefit from a clean and ordered home and might also be responsible for outsourcing their dirty work to less privileged people is rarely acknowledged. Nor is the almost entirely invisible labour of women during the night and very early hours of the morning in offices, hospitals, hotels, supermarkets and tech companies.[51]

During the COVID-19 pandemic, a Twitter debate (#cleanergate) surfaced around the politics of employing domestic cleaners during lockdown. In an apparent disregard for the safety of some of the lowest-paid people in society, the government's instruction to work from home did not extend to 'nannies, cleaners and tradespeople'.[52]

The opportunity to discuss how the pandemic might offer a moment to break down the gendered norms of housework was lost, with the debate stopping short of proposing radical domestic alternatives that might include men seizing the opportunity to shoulder their fair share of the housework. Women, and especially migrant women and women of colour, are disproportionately employed to do the dirtiest and least well-paid jobs globally, precisely because housework and care has long been seen as low-value 'women's work'; work that women are expected to do for free, in private and willingly.

The 'stalled domestic revolution'[53] that followed the Women's Liberation Movement of the 1970s occurred on the back of the *Cosmo*-era 'superwomen' of hyper-individualistic post-feminism, whereby earlier feminist interventions promoting a fairer balance of domestic life were displaced by a new 'race to the top' feminism. This inevitably meant that men were more off the hook than ever and that the age-old assumption of women's 'natural' responsibility for housework remained unchallenged. The deeply entrenched inequalities of the domestic sphere, which sees the continuation of mass exploitation of working-class women, migrant women and women of colour, were left untouched.[54] Sally Howard describes this as a deeply exploitative and unfeminist process of privileged women offloading their 'shitwork' onto other, less privileged women: 'British women had offloaded their shitwork down a racialised and working class labour line and, in doing so – here the inescapable feminist irony – reinscribed this work as "women's work".'[55]

A notable exception to the absence of left-wing feminist interventions into the subject of housework is Sheila Rowbotham's socialist feminist account of domestic selfhoods discussed earlier. By linking the emergence of a domestic 'self' to the everyday performance of housework, Rowbotham noted the ensuing willingness of women to partake in the unpaid labour on which capitalist economic systems of production are so reliant. Socialist feminists also often noted the ironic repercussions of domestic labour, as it simultaneously helps to support the continuing functioning of capitalist market economies while hindering women's ability to actively participate in radical politics. In *Sally on Saturday*, a bittersweet poem written in the early 1980s, Rowbotham describes the endless interruptions from her young children and exhaustion as waves of domesticity disrupt her ability to discuss politics with her friend:

You go out shopping
and return,
We search for tea -
and when you leave
anxious
because Daniel's cold
is making it hard for him to breathe,
I feel a loving sadness.
A Saturday spent
at the crossroads
without time
to journey between outlines.[56]

The 'loving sadness' – of conversations unfinished, ideas undeveloped, stuck 'at the crossroads' and running out of time – reminds us of the distracting qualities of domestic labour, its repetitive and endless nature leaving neither time nor energy to pursue alternatives.

Conclusion

Against the backdrop of increasing economic precarity and insecurity, and burgeoning living costs, it is difficult for households to manage on a single income. We are left, as Arlie Hochschild argues,[57] with generations of burned-out women attempting to balance the double shift of paid and unpaid labour. The structure of consumer capitalism makes it increasingly difficult to find time to think, resist and challenge. As I have shown in this chapter, the *willing* participation of women in cleanfluencing is made possible by making cleaning fun, sociable, glamorous and self-aspirational. As has long been the case, capitalism is endlessly repackaged in order to present ever new ways of ensuring its palatability.

In this chapter I showed that feminists have often described housework as a flight from self; a debilitating, thankless and endless set of tasks that sap the soul and leave little time or energy for any meaningful expansion of self. And yet, within contemporary digital cultures of housework, the tasks associated with domestic labour are reglamourised and repackaged as offering a type of freedom, liberation, choice and, as Chapter 3 shows, happiness. Today, cleanfluencers have devoted digital content to making housework hyper-visible. Yet the real work – the real labour of housework – remains broadly hidden, as the unpaid or low-paid labour power behind curating an outward-facing image of the idyllic, happy home remains disguised and distorted as much as it was in the 1970s.

In 2019, the British celebrity cleanfluencer Mrs Hinch launched her first range of Procter & Gamble cleaning products, sold exclusively at Asda and featuring 1950s-style, hand-drawn illustrations of her cleaning, tidying and relaxing, hair piled high, dressed in jeans and a T-shirt rather than apron and dress, with a beaming smile on her face as she is depicted navigating the laundry. As one Twitter user at the time asked, 'have I just woken up in 1972?' Her bestselling children's book, *Welcome to Hinch Farm*, reinforces the tale of a personal journey of selfhood, from cleaning to happy family, large home and immaculate children, with everything clean, fresh, unsoiled and blissfully content. The image is not vastly dissimilar to the advertising of the smiling, white, middle-class nuclear families in adverts for the new suburban housing estates in 1950s North America. Mrs Hinch herself often reflects on her own shock at her success; for everyone else it is a daydream, but one which we are told, if we believe in enough, we can achieve for ourselves too. Follow the rules of capitalism, conform merrily to gender norms, and you will reap the rewards – *just be you* and great things will happen.

Today, the growing scale of critique of the exploitative, exhausting and thankless nature of unpaid domestic labour has become too widespread and obvious to ignore. Both Oakley's and Hochschild's books became bestsellers that are still regularly reviewed and discussed in the mainstream media. In Chapter 3, I show how housework has been reframed in a way that simultaneously acknowledges the inequalities of domestic labour, and also proposes new ways of seeing housework as joyful and good for the soul. It has become at once a witty riposte to the feminist refusal of inequalities within the domestic sphere and a rebuttal of the idea that housework is the enemy of the fully formed self. As the mass popular use of digital media was consolidated and the cleanfluencer firmly established as a core component of contemporary popular culture, housework was about to be rearticulated as a route to happiness, wellbeing; a way of self-soothing and seeking to enhance selfhoods.

3

'I'm broken and it's beautiful': Digital housework and the promise of happiness

> When you've finished putting your house in order, your life will change dramatically. Once you have experienced what it's like to have a truly ordered house, you'll feel your whole world brighten.[1]

In Chapter 2, I traced the history of housework and the emergence of new, highly individualised consumer selfhoods. I argued that creating the ideal home and performing housewifely duties in high-consuming ways became integral to the late modern project of selfhood. I described feminist discourses around the emergence of the housewife as an identity and the dangers of the self-limitations of this. In this chapter, I develop this argument further by exploring how the latest stage of housework – cultivated via a new curation of digital domestic labour – promises a digitised and highly commercialised solution to low mood and anxiety. To do this, I explore in more detail the relationship between housework and the positive-thinking and self-help movement, showing how cleanfluencing connects with the burgeoning 'confidence culture' movement.

'Sparking joy'

In 2011, the Japanese 'organising consultant' Marie Kondo published *The Life-Changing Magic of Tidying Up*. The book became a global success, published in more than thirty counties, and was a bestseller in Japan, Europe and the United States. The book was later accompanied by two hugely popular Netflix television series, the first in 2019,

Tidying Up with Marie Kondo, and the second in 2021, *Sparking Joy with Marie Kondo*. Kondo also offers an expensive formal training programme for the KonMari 'method' that promises to 'bring the joy, weightlessness, and upward pointing trajectory of a clutter-free life to others'.[2] The global reach and commercial success of Kondo is further evidenced by a range of celebrity endorsements, culminating in her being added to the *Times* list of '100 most influential people' in 2015 and some even arguing that 'KonMari' has become a verb.

Kondo herself is dressed simply and immaculately in neutral colours, reflecting the decluttered lifestyle that she advocates. Her demeanour is always calm, gentle and smiling. Her petite physical appearance is often remarked upon; she is variously described as like 'a little doll' and 'like a tiny perfect 29-year-old Japanese woman',[3] but with a positive and powerful message making her *the* 'decluttering diva'.

Kondo's books and her Instagram account, which has over four million followers, offers the opportunity to learn Kondo's decluttering and tidying method. We see tidying occurring in intricate detail, almost in slow motion, as a set of purposeful, meaningful and precise actions. Kondo advocates a decluttering practice that begins with carefully holding each individual item, close to the heart, closing the eyes, breathing slowly and allowing 'the cells in your body' to determine whether or not the object 'sparks joy'. The method also advocates tidying by category of object rather than location in the home. Objects that don't make the cut can be discarded or donated to charity, while those that do are allowed to progress to the next stage: the organising, filing and storing process. In Kondo's videos on Instagram and YouTube, such as 'Folding for Perfect Appearance', we see her folding clothes calmly, gently, neatly and with extreme care in her own KonMari way and placing them into perfect order in boxes and drawer dividers. It is soothing and almost meditative to watch; nothing is out of place and the objects slot into the boxes perfectly. They are not crammed in too tightly or rattling around in too much space. Boxes are always the perfect size and the objects inside them fit in easily, calmly and without effort. This aesthetic, sensory order and calm underpins Kondo's successful brand where nothing is out of place.

Purging and organising the clutter that defines domestic space is repeatedly framed by Kondo as 'life-changing'. As she carefully curates her belongings, she promises that tidying and decluttering will not only bring joy, order and calm but also create life-changing possibilities. The practice of intimate, repetitive processes and purposeful activities enhance the likelihood of feeling 'joyful' and attaining personal happiness and wellbeing. As Kondo remarks, '[t]aking good care of things leads to taking good care of yourself' and this will 'increase your sensitivity to joy'.[4] In other words, we see in 2011 the beginnings of the idea that cleaning and tidying have a type of magical potential to turn lives around and are central to discourses of personal self-improvement and emotional growth.

The KonMari method promoted by Kondo is represented as a lifestyle choice that will positively impact our lives in other ways too. This method of tidying, we are assured, will help inform positive decision making around finances and at work, and will even facilitate the ability to make more meaningful, careful decisions around grocery shopping. As Kondo reminds us, '[t]he perspective we gain through this process represents the driving force that can make not only our lifestyle, but our very lives, shine',[5] creating for ourselves a 'bright and joyful future', all attainable through decluttering and tidying our homes.

The altruistic message underpinning Kondo's work – of sharing the domestic secrets and tips that will bring joy and happiness – threatens to mask the ways in which the heavily marketed and extreme popular success of the KonMari brand in many ways reproduces highly traditional, heavily gendered, cultural expectations of keeping a spotless, hyper-organised and efficient home. At times, Kondo's tone becomes patronising and bossy, reminiscent of the home economics educationalists that came before her, as she reminds her readers that first, clutter and mess are *the* barrier to happiness and personal fulfilment, and second that achieving the perfectly organised and decluttered home is possible for anyone possessing the right sort of 'mindset'. This reflects wider cultural ideals which tend to deny the existence of external barriers to reaching the broadly held markers of accomplishment – the perfect body, the perfect home – and instead advocating that the real secret to change and success comes from within. The mantra that 'I alone am responsible for my own successes and failures' is rife within contemporary popular culture and is especially prevalent in the discourses curated by the cleanfluencers. The antithesis of KonMari – the disorganised, cluttered, messy, chaotic home – comes not from a lack of time, energy, space or money but from not having the right 'mindset'. Kondo writes:

> The act of tidying is a series of simple actions in which objects are moved from one place to another. It involves putting things away where they belong. This seems so simple that even a six-year-old should be able to do it. Yet most people can't. A short time after tidying, their space is a disorganised mess. The cause is not a lack of skills but rather lack of awareness and the ability to tidy effectively. *In other words, the root of the problem lies in the mind.* Success is 90 per cent dependent on our mindset.[6]

Kondo is an early, high-profile and phenomenally successful example of the reconfiguration of domestic labour as an autonomous, personal choice, and moreover as an act which serves to aid personal development, happiness and wellbeing. The idea that infinite popular representations of the 'perfect home' and the idealised, impossible to recreate images of immaculate, picture-perfect drawers, cupboards and shelves might be culturally determined is never considered or mentioned. Instead, Kondo offers up a new representation of domestic labour – specifically cleaning and tidying – where women are not only expected to bear the brunt of the responsibility to create the perfect neat, tidy, decluttered-to-the-extreme home but also to work on their own emotional health, strength and resilience while they are at it. This all chimes with the contemporary popular individualistic mantra of doing it for yourself;[7] the implication is that rather than doing housework for the benefit of others, here housework is positioned as something I like to *do for myself*. The very idea that in contemporary life, such a seemingly intense and sometimes desperate search for joy is necessary at all acts as a tacit acknowledgement that all is *not* well. Kondo rose to fame with her books and Netflix shows making an appearance in tandem with multiple political shifts, unpredictability, nervousness and uncertainty. For example, the controversial election of Donald Trump in the US, the Brexit vote in the UK, the COVID-19 pandemic and subsequent lockdowns,[8] and in the UK the sense of precarity around the cost-of-living crisis and austerity policies, combined with moments of broad political activism such as the global climate change movements, Black Lives Matter and MeToo. During moments of political flux and change, anxieties are often played out and manifested at the site of the domestic. The scale of recent social and political uncertainty, precarity and chaos that might often feel unmanageable and unwieldy means that turning away from the public and towards the domestic to transform and manage what it is possible to control is understandable. The trauma of the outside world is perhaps more palatable when one can turn one's focus instead to exerting extreme control over intimate domestic spaces and practices; folding, filing, storing, decanting, decluttering. It is an act of what Casey and Littler describe as 'scouring away the crisis'.[9] In this regard, the popularity of the KonMari method might be understood in terms of its proximity to crisis; a hyper-controlled domestic sphere standing in stark contrast to the chaotic and dangerous outside world that might quite reasonably seem impossible to change. This is reminiscent of the recent self-help mantra: 'Don't try and change what you can't control.' Instead, we are promised that happiness, joy and an easing of stress and anxieties is a journey, a *project* of self – a route towards personal redemption.

These journeys of redemption, self-fulfilment and personal satisfaction are narrated most clearly in Kondo's Netflix shows. In her 2019 series *Tidying Up with Marie Kondo*, each episode is framed around a personal dilemma or crisis, with decluttering and tidying proposed as a solution to finding and creating peace, calm and order in amongst the chaos. Often the stories are highly personal, intimate and painful, such as relationship breakdown and bereavement. They share a common theme of a family going through some sort of personal struggle that is juxtaposed against the families' parallel battle with clutter, which is regularly described in strong negative and visceral terms such as 'heavy' and 'overwhelming'. Kondo's strategy is to show how these problems are connected, and how together they constitute a 'problem' that can be solved simply by following the KonMari decluttering method. Each episode then follows a similar formula: participants learn the unique 'magic' of decluttering that ultimately culminates in feeling happier and more joyful and enjoying a more harmonious family life.

As discussed in Chapter 2, the idea that, over time, the home and housework came to be associated with practices of the self is further echoed here, whereby the connection between the home and a supremely resilient and steadfast self that is 'strong enough to change me' is strengthened. The idea that cleaning and tidying has the potential to change me as a person is powerful and one that is pioneered by Marie Kondo. As one of the participants in her Netflix show remarks: 'We are on board; I want it to change, I just want it to be strong enough to change me.' Similarly, the notion of the powerful life-changing potential of tidying and decluttering is emphasised in the accolades regarding the KonMari method that are included in her books. One KonMari convert describes the positive impact that decluttering has had on her marriage, remarking that, 'My husband and I are getting along much better'. Another describes how following the KonMari tidying method enabled her to lose weight, 'I finally succeeded in losing three kilos', while another sums up the seeming personal transformative potential of KonMari, 'I'm amazed to find that just throwing things away has changed me so much'. A tidy home, we are promised, means a tidy mind, better relationships, personal growth and better physical health. Choosing to follow the KonMari method is presented as part of a life-changing decision to follow the personal path to joy. It is an extension of an advancing discourse of what Elizabeth Nathanson has described as 'domestic aesthetics promis[ing] to be therapeutic'.[10]

Underpinning all of Kondo's work is the idea that by cleaning out clutter we *choose joy*. The use of the word 'choose' is important here because it implies that joy and happiness are feelings that we alone have control over and that being joyful is a choice. This of course implies that feeling sad, anxious, depressed or unhappy is also a choice rather than something that might be the result of myriad factors completely beyond our control. Yet the relentless focus on finding and seeking out joy and happiness, which is fore-grounded not only in Kondo's books and videos but also in self-help popular culture more generally, speaks to the clear implication that all is not well. And, as pioneered by Kondo, there are a plethora of easily accessible self-help gurus, inspirational guides and Instagram therapists, all of whom promise to teach us how to seek and find happiness within ourselves.

In 2019, the KonMari brand took a new turn as it launched an official online store selling Kondo-style homeware. In tandem with the decluttering KonMari mantra, the shop promised to maintain the goal of purging clutter, but this time with a fresh twist: the space that decluttering has created now enabled KonMari recruits to 'make room for meaningful objects, people and experiences'. In other words, *some* objects, namely those approved by the KonMari brand, are acceptable. Thus, in the opening blurb for the online shop, Kondo reminds us that not all objects are problematic, but also that – perhaps slightly confusingly – some household objects can actually spark joy. She writes: 'I can think of no greater happiness in life than being surrounded only by the things I love.'[11]

The online shop itself features a vast selection of strikingly ordinary household objects, the majority of which would be available cheaply on the high street. In particular, the plethora of everyday, rather unremarkable storage objects is stark. The main section is labelled under 'Tidying and Organisation' – Kondo's speciality. There are stacking storage boxes, under-bed storage boxes, handbag organisers, storage canisters, decanting jars, 'neat and tidy' Japanese label makers, document storage boxes, a box for letters, drawer organisers, woven storage baskets, metal storage baskets, kitchen utensil organisers, desk mats, jewellery boxes, kitchen and pantry food labels, newspaper and magazine trays, shoe racks, maple wood book-ends and glass jars with lids. Of particular note are the special boxes for 'sentimental' occasions such as weddings and the birth of a baby. These feature multiple tiny drawers, compartments and pull-out folders in which you can put keepsakes and photographs that might otherwise look 'messy' and cluttered. Once filled, the whole box of memories folds in on itself into another neat, single box which can be carefully filed away.

Kondo's everyday tidying and decluttering aids are all displayed and photographed against the familiar KonMari minimalist style and neutral backdrop, and Kondo herself regularly integrates the products into her YouTube videos and Instagram posts. Out of context, the objects would feel profane and mundane, but placed within the scene of the KonMari method, with its beautiful aesthetic appeal and the promise of joy that seemingly exudes from Kondo-styled homes, the objects acquire a fresh appeal that is also reflected in the relatively high price tags. The US online shop includes, for example, a 'let go with gratitude' paper bag for charity donations at $15, a 'rotating glass organiser' for $39.99 and a small glass storage jar for $14.99. All are available to purchase using Klarna – the 'buy now pay later' credit company.

Yet not all of the objects on the online shop are useful household objects. There is also a section of 'Decorative Objects' that don't appear to serve any function other than to exist as objects in their own right – in other words, 'clutter'. There is a 'tuning fork' and quartz crystal set, a set of hand-carved Japanese wooden animals, a matte black candle wick 'trimmer', a desktop Zen garden and a lava stone diffuser. This selection of quirky, disjointed and clearly unnecessary objects appears particularly dislocated from the KonMari method of purging our lives and souls of unnecessary, overbearing clutter. The irony of the KonMari online shop was not lost on many social commentators. A satirical column in the *Guardian* focused on the Mari Kondo 'therapeutic tuning fork', asking, 'Why is Marie Kondo selling the world's most unnecessary item?'[12] The KonMari shop serves as a reminder that despite the altruistic and wellbeing platitudes, cleanfluencing can be an immensely lucrative business model. The decluttered and extreme tidied homes that are represented in Kondo's books and social media, which are reproduced multiple times across different social media platforms via the KonMari and SparkJoy hashtags, offer an endless reproduction of a type of visual, aesthetic ideal that never deviates from the logics of consumer capitalism. This lays bare the contradiction inherent in the 'Spark Joy' mantra – that despite the endless insistence that happiness and joy can be found within, through actively choosing it and via a careful decluttering of homes and thoughts, consumerism, and particularly the appeal of mass-produced products, is offered up as a way of helping people to achieve this. As the *Guardian* article continues: 'A woman who built an army of fans by espousing the notion of living in an empty house is now asking the same fans to fill their houses up again, specifically with her stuff.' The KonMari method, then, is a reincarnation of the long-standing commodification of domestic life that was described in Chapter 1. Happiness can be located within and through the active purging of clutter in our lives, but if and when that doesn't work, there are plenty of consumer goods available to buy that can help.

Kondo's immense popular success and the widespread appropriation of the KonMari decluttering method reveals much about the roots of the relationship between cleaning, tidying and the self-help movement. What we see embedded within Kondo's pitch is a heavily aestheticised visual ideal of the home that is inextricably linked to personal wellbeing and happiness. The long-standing pressure and responsibility to create an ordered, tidy and managed home is in evidence throughout, but this time round it is compounded by a simultaneous pressure to seek and find personal happiness and joy within that work. Within KonMari, we see a combination of domestic labour entwined with a new type of labour of the self; a method of *turning inwards* to find the solution to anxiety, stress and disorder. As the next section shows, this new, popular, digital self-help movement pioneered by Kondo among others frequently goes hand in hand with traditional norms of femininity, particularly around housework and the home. As we shall see, it is often accompanied by a strong aesthetic appeal and slick marketing, never deviating too far from the usual conventions of consumer capitalism.

'Redirecting your mindset': The rise of digital self-help culture

As the external social world we inhabit has become ever more precarious, chaotic and unequal, women have increasingly turned to popularised notions of 'self-help' and 'self-care' in order to find ways of coping with accompanying feelings of stress and anxiety. I began to explore this idea in the previous section, where I examined how Marie Kondo's tidying and decluttering method helps to exemplify the emergence of the now widely held belief that happiness and wellbeing can be pursued and attained via the performance of everyday domestic labour practices. In this section, I want to push these ideas further by considering how the increasingly intensified turn towards the self has cemented the belief that women are personally responsible for their own wellbeing, emotions, successes and failures, and moreover are entrenched to the point that challenging these discourses and narratives becomes virtually impossible. Here, I do not mean a narcissistic turning towards the self but rather the adopting of increasingly individual and digital ways of utilising the myriad 'self-help' strategies to navigate and cope with the ravages and demands of highly unequal and exploitative late capitalist consumer societies. I show how the huge popularity of the recent cleanfluencing movement owes much to its harnessing of contemporary self-help and self-care mantras.

Of course, the self-help and wellbeing movement is nothing new. The late 1980s onwards were awash with books and instruction manuals offering a plethora of take-home advice promising easily accessible and implementable techniques that made bold promises to improve relationships, stay calm, overcome fear and generally cope with whatever traumas or difficulties might come your way. Every bookshop worth its salt had a 'Mind, Body and Spirit' section aimed at promoting emotional and physical wellbeing and calm. *The Little Book of Calm* published in 1996 and offering simple tips around 'harnessing serenity in your life', such as taking a moment to pause and eat an orange or taking a bath with lavender oil, sold over two million copies; while *Feel the Fear and Do It Anyway*, first published in 1987 and still a bestseller today, promised to teach the reader 'how to handle what life throws at you, allowing you to take control, move forwards and live the life you want'. The books emphasised and popularised the notion of taking personal responsibility for emotions and feelings, whether positive or negative and whatever the cause. These self-help narratives echoed the cultural shifts occurring throughout the 1980s and 1990s, when neoliberal and highly individualistic notions of reaching inwards, looking within for care and help, alongside burgeoning ideals of personal betterment and aspiration were popularised, replacing old ideas of community and 'society' and ultimately protecting a widespread belief in the logics of the market and consumer capitalism. The new mantra that happiness is a personal project of the self, detached from social and economic forces, has proven to be a highly lucrative one. As William Davies describes in his book *The Happiness Industry*, the ever-advancing, highly lucrative business of happiness pivots on the promise that being happy is a commodity that can be bought and sold.

The idea that individuals can be taught the skills necessary to guide them in successfully navigating the search for happiness, and conversely the strategies needed to combat unhappiness, has gained further prominence in recent years. During the COVID-19 pandemic and 'lockdown', many of the accepted methods for combatting anxiety and depression, such as seeing friends or family, taking an exercise class or talking to a therapist, were unavailable. In addition, research shows that the pandemic itself intensified feelings of stress and anxiety, disproportionately so for women.[13] The combination of a deterioration in mental health alongside financial strains meant that, for many, the search was on for affordable and easily available self-help solutions. What we see from 2020 onwards is a particularly intensified use of digital media to access mental health support, particularly for women. In tandem with this was the rise of the so-called therapist bloggers – digital self-help therapists and gurus who curate digital content designed to offer quick, accessible and motivational tips to navigate some of the harshest health, financial and interpersonal crises in a generation.

In 2022, *You* magazine ran a feature on Dr Julie Smith ('Dr Julie') under the headline: 'The TikTok Doctor with Four Million Patients'. A qualified clinical psychologist, 'educator and vlogger', Dr Julie uses her social media accounts to post regular short videos of herself offering visual 'snippets' of her self-help strategies. For example, in one video she uses wooden Jenga blocks to illustrate the importance of maintaining boundaries and balancing your own needs with those of others; in another, she uses an origami bird to illustrate how each fold represents a small action that accumulates over time to create 'big results'; in yet another, she pushes an inflated balloon into a tank of water that works to demonstrate the ways that numbing emotions with alcohol, drugs and social media leads to an eventual surfacing and 'overflowing' of negative thoughts. Dr Julie has become a global popular success, with millions of followers on TikTok, Instagram and YouTube combined. This social media success is accompanied with her bestselling book, *Why Has Nobody Told Me This Before?*, published in 2022, which has been translated into over thirty languages. Dr Julie also regularly appears on daytime television shows such as ITV's *This Morning*, where she replicates her videos in the studio.

Dr Julie's digital profile presents a relatable, friendly and respectable femininity (she is 'Dr Julie', not 'Dr Smith') and the sort of normatively attractive appearance that is favoured on social media. She is white, young, slim, beautiful, middle class and femme. Her Instagram, TikTok and YouTube videos are carefully shot and curated so that she always appears with immaculate hair and make-up, usually with a filtered camera effect and colourful, tidy and aesthetically appealing, homely backdrops. Like Marie Kondo before her, Dr Julie describes her digital therapy in altruistic tones. For example, in a *Guardian* interview she declares that she would like everyone to be able to access her advice for free. Chiming with the current, austere economic backdrop in the UK, the cost-of-living crisis and the intensification of poor mental health and social isolation during the pandemic, Dr Julie offers a free, accessible and quick form of self-help. 'It is my mission to help as many people as I can to thrive', she writes, 'I want to make top quality mental health education accessible online. This means that even those who cannot access therapy can get off to the best start in their recovery journey.'

Therapy is offered on Dr Julie's website via a range of snappy three-minute videos on topics such as 'Signs of a Highly Sensitive Person', 'Beat a Low Mood and Depression: 7 Top Tips' and 'Anxiety Thought Bias that Makes You Feel Worse: 7 Top Tips'. It is easy to see the appeal of the videos for time-pressed, cash-strapped people experiencing unprecedented levels of low mood, anxiety and depression. Although the videos rely on the viewer essentially self-diagnosing as well as making sense of and applying the strategies by themselves, we are promised that the free advice offered draws on evidence-based research. The advice given is necessarily generic and broad, rather than targeted to individual experiences and personal biographies. Much is made of shifting your mindset, for example 'setting intentions' by clarifying why something is important to you, defining what the changes are that you want to see, and finally working out how you can make those changes happen. Another video advocates 'practising gratitude'. Expressing sentiments around thankfulness and appreciation for the 'positive' things in your life has become one of the most potent and widely reproduced mantras of recent years; as we shall see, this is habitually used throughout cleanfluencing cultures via the hashtags #Blessed, #Grateful and #Thankful, for example. Accompanying the videos on the website is a range of blog articles, including a section on the power of 'motivational quotes' that have become almost synonymous with contemporary social media. Dr Julie tells us that 'returning to a powerful quote can be a great way to redirect your mindset when you find yourself slipping off course' and advocates a daily 'gratitude' practice focusing on things to feel grateful and thankful for. This can be something as small as a comforting sip of tea, a chat with a neighbour or a breath of fresh air in the garden. The intention is that by shifting one's focus towards positive thoughts, an improvement in your mood will naturally follow.

Within the digital self-help world, the acquisition of happiness is presented as a 'battle', with personal *action*, self-compassion and a positive mindset viewed as a type of magic dust or 'superpower' that holds the power to transform lives. As Dr Julie reminds us, 'In the fight against fear, action is your superpower', and 'what you do changes how you feel', with 'inaction' and 'avoidance', or committing the ultimate sin of not taking personal responsibility for your feelings and emotions, potentially making anxiety worse. This idea of actively self-soothing yourself through pain via widely and freely available tips that anyone with a smartphone can access is the ultimate in *leaning in* philosophy where happiness, wellbeing and joy can be found through self-compassion, self-help and self-care. Conversely, failing to achieve success in any form, whether personal, interpersonal or career, is held up as a consequence of not believing in yourself hard enough, or as Dr Julie says, having a 'fear of failure, a fear of success, feeling undeserving, feelings of guilt and shame for obtaining something good.' 'Self-sabotage' and its popular sister concept, 'imposter-syndrome', both pathologise and personalise what are often the effects of social and structural problems and inequalities. Indeed, there is very little reflection within popular digital self-help media about the *causes* of mental health problems or of the existence of wider social forces that might underpin them. Thus, the transformative power of feelings and the potential that can be harnessed simply through self-belief is integral to the new social media and influencer cultures.

What we see expressed throughout Dr Julie's videos, then, is the repeated mantra that the solution to low mood and depression can be found within yourself, without the need to acknowledge, reflect on or challenge the status quo. This parallels multiple other scenarios within popular culture where the solution to entrenched social problems is a set of skills that can be acquired by anyone willing to 'work on themselves'. For example, a popular response to food poverty is often to advocate for greater education around cookery, shopping and recipes; in other words, the idea that a set of taught personal skills should be enough to combat even the gravest of social problems. None of this is to deny the comfort and relief that the advice provided by Dr Julie might provide, but in common with the majority of popular digital self-help cultures, depression, anxiety and low mood are *always* decontextualised from social forces and inequalities – indeed, the precise factors that are known to have a detrimental impact on mental health. Of course, the riposte to this is the mantra that 'trying to change what you can't control' can exacerbate feelings of helplessness and stress. However, there is a wider risk in denying the existence of external forces in triggering low mood. While self-help strategies might offer a temporary solution, it probably isn't the case that truly life-changing moments can be achieved simply by restructuring our thoughts and 'choosing' happiness and joy.

The contemporary self-help movement bolsters the current situation in which women are not only more likely to experience inequality but also are tasked with finding ways of coping with the effects of it. The language around mental health and self-help therapy popularised by digital therapists such as Dr Julie is important because, as we shall see, it has been so firmly incorporated into the discourses of digital cleanfluencing.

Performing vulnerability and the rise of confessional culture

In this chapter so far, I have examined the ways in which self-help discourses today are an entrenched feature of everyday digital cultures. Multiple social media influencers centre their content around a type of altruistic offering of self-help and self-care tips and advice to their followers. In the two examples discussed above, I describe how first, Marie Kondo's tidying and decluttering method has become a global brand promising to bring calm, joy and happiness to those who subscribe to it; and second, how the popular digital self-help guru Dr Julie offers her followers snappy tips for vanquishing the storms of everyday stress and anxiety. The type of advice proffered here is framed as 'expert'. Dr Julie is a qualified clinical psychologist while Marie Kondo has decades of experience as a professional 'organiser and consultant'. What I want to turn to now are the social media influencers who are still offering their followers a range of self-help tools, advice and knowledge, but this time *centring their own vulnerability* as they do so.

Increasingly, being open and honest about and sharing one's own vulnerabilities has become an essential part of becoming a successful influencer. Whether it is sharing intimate experiences of anxiety and depression, feeling 'low', lacking self-esteem, suffering from a sense of unworthiness, having low body confidence, suffering the judgement of others or experiencing feelings of failure as a parent, partner or friend, the most popular social media accounts are those that don't 'talk down' to their followers; rather, followers are positioned as 'equals' with whom they are happy to share details of and confess their own vulnerabilities. This shift from 'confidence' towards vulnerability is central to the idea of relatability discussed in Chapter 1 and works to compound the all-important 'authenticity': the holy grail of influencer culture. Orgad and Gill describe this as 'obligatory vulnerability',[14] which, as we shall see, is also core to the popular appeal of the cleanfluencers. The public disclosure of often painful and traumatic experiences is framed as at once empowering and inspirational, and crucially it works to help validate the core message of influencers.

In order to help illustrate this shift in digital self-help cultures from the instructive to the vulnerable and confessional, I want to draw on the example of another social media happiness celebrity. Fearne Cotton is the author of multiple bestselling self-help books and guides about wellbeing and happiness, the presenter of a hugely successful, prizewinning podcast, *Happy Place*, and of course the owner of a very popular Instagram account with 3.8 million followers. Fearne is young, rich, successful and beautiful. Her father-in-law is a member of The Rolling Stones and her husband is in the rock band Reef. She lives with her family, including her young children and teenage step-children, in Richmond, a wealthy suburb in south-west London. And yet, despite her significant privilege, Fearne manages to use her Instagram account to present a very appealing and friendly relatability. In particular, she shares personal, intimate and often brutal details of her emotional state and intense feelings of vulnerability, shame and a lack of self-belief. Fearne's account juxtaposes pictures of herself in glamorous, fashionable outfits, often with glimpses of her tidy, chic home in the background, with pictures of her make-up free, hair matted, in an oversized towelling dressing gown looking exhausted, fed up and resigned. The latter are usually accompanied with an explanation, often related to a lack of sleep, exhaustion with looking after young children, a dip in energy or low mood. This juxtaposition adds to Fearne's relatability. Her 'no judgement' ethos and her honesty surrounding her anxiety concerning criticisms from her internet trolls combined with her warmth and humour adds to her approachability; Fearne feels like a friend you'd go to with your problems.

Fearne's hugely successful podcast, *Happy Place*, was launched in 2018 and by July 2023 it boasted 100 million downloads.[15] Links to the show and its themes are regularly shared on her popular Instagram account. Each week on *Happy Place*, Fearne interviews a celebrity guest about their mental health journey. The podcast gives an unusual prominence to the profiling of highly personal discussions of, for example, bereavement, sexual abuse, childhood trauma, domestic violence, single parenthood, depression, suicide, alcohol and drug dependency, anxiety and post-natal depression, many of which have been previously glossed over in mainstream media. The centring of mental health and emotional wellbeing alongside interviews with some of the most famous people on the planet makes for fascinating listening and fits seamlessly into the self-help and confessional zeitgeist. In 1995, when Princess Diana gave her now infamous interview detailing her personal trauma, sadness and anxiety to the journalist Martin Bashir, the widespread shock and even disgust at her openness and perceived indiscretion was palpable. Today, we almost expect intimate disclosures. On the *Happy Place* podcast, Hollywood stars, television actors, MPs, pop singers, rock-and-roll icons and authors queue up to discuss in public the innermost details of their personal stories of mental health with Fearne.

The *Happy Place* podcast is illustrative of a wider process of breaking the stigmas and taboos around mental health and personal struggles. It also represents a new mainstreaming of men, in particular, talking publicly about their anxieties and experiences of trauma and stress. Although these are clearly positive shifts, *Happy Place* is firmly situated as part of a broader social media culture which reproduces rigid self-help narratives, especially around personal growth and transforming mindsets. Ultimately, as with a plethora of other popular self-help celebrities, Fearne's followers are encouraged to take personal responsibility for resolving their own internal struggles, while mental health remains firmly dislocated from wider social forces and inequalities.

The idea that happiness lies within us all, sometimes dormant but always with the potential to re-emerge, is central to the digital self-help movement; we just need the skills to uncover and rediscover it. We are constantly reminded that underneath the layers of mess, busyness, clutter, anxiety and self-doubt there is a 'real' and 'authentic' self waiting to be uncovered. As Fearne writes in her 2017 book *Happy: Finding Joy in Every Day and Letting Go of Perfect*: 'Calm is a place that exists in us all, we just have to find our way back to it.' In the same book, Fearne also reiterates the idea that happiness is buried away deep within us, available to everyone who accepts personal responsibility for finding it and not just to a privileged few: 'I think we often assume [happiness is] just around the corner, in the hands of others, or only for a chosen category of people. The beautiful thing is, it's actually there for the taking, inside us all the time, bubbling away waiting to be embraced.'[16] The notion that we have a happy and 'true' self that is hidden away beneath a weight of emotional chaos and mess is reproduced repeatedly across contemporary digital media. By 'speaking our truth' and seeking and articulating our 'true selves', we are able to uncover and celebrate *who we really are*. The idea is that the resulting 'authentic state' will bring about happiness.

Within self-help culture, being vulnerable and sharing our vulnerabilities with others is seen as the first step in uncovering our 'true', 'authentic' selves. Alongside being vulnerable, and truly focusing on ourselves, we are also reminded of the importance of 'living in the moment', 'rediscovering everyday joy' and crucially not trying to change things that are beyond the sphere of one's control. This centring of the individual and the self is a hallmark of contemporary neoliberalism; it is a seductive narrative that helps to persuade women in particular to internalise and personally soak up the residue messes, strains and traumas of late capitalist society. This message is repeated in Fearne Cotton's 2021 book *Speak Your Truth: Connecting with Your Inner Truth and Learning to Find Your Voice*. Writing about the chaos and stress during the COVID-19 pandemic, Fearne urges her readers to enjoy the moment, to take the opportunity to find pleasure in the 'everyday' and the domestic and to avoid thinking too far ahead, which would only 'spike fear'. Instead, 'we must *be in the moment* and deal with the daily washing of hands, scrubbing of clothes, cooking every leftover, planning our shopping trips thoroughly and Facetiming family'. The inescapable pandemic that no one could control is presented as a life lesson, 'this is how we should always live – in the present moment'. Although injustice is briefly mentioned, with 'insecurity, inequality and struggle' described as the 'new normal', in common with other popular self-help discourses, it is reframed as an opportunity for growth.[17]

The idea of finding joy and pleasure in taking control over one's immediate domestic surroundings reminds us of the tidying and decluttering tips described by Marie Kondo in the opening section. When these tips are fused with a heavily entrenched, often confessional popular narrative of self-help and self-care, we get a new type of discourse which emphasises the transformative power that taking control of minute aspects of domestic life has in helping to reveal your true self, and simultaneously releasing the happiness held within. Chaos, mess and clutter thus come to represent a possibility for personal growth, and inequalities are not just tolerated but also often either ignored or glossed over completely.

These narratives are central to the popular appeal of influencer culture and they are carefully framed so that they never threaten the assumptions of consumer capitalism. In common with most successful influencers – as discussed in Chapter 1 – Fearne's self-help account is peppered with opportunities to buy into her enviable lifestyle. She has a paid partnership deal with Nobody's Child, a fast fashion clothing company whose products are responsibly made, and another with the cookery brand Hello Fresh. As such, the self-help mantra is heavily commodified. The tacit acknowledgement running through Fearne's account is that although life is difficult for many, it is solvable via reframing thoughts and perhaps also by buying a new dress or subscribing to a cookery box.

Cleanfluencers and the confessional

In this section, I further examine the dichotomy underpinning digital media culture between, on the one hand, chaos, mess, public life, the future and uncertainty and, on the other hand, stability, home, order, the 'here and now', calm, 'truth' and peace. I do this by drawing on the ways in which cleaning and housework are framed as first, self-help, second, a route to happiness and joy and third, a means of 'control'. To do this, I focus on the example of another Instagram celebrity who has used her account to develop the type of narrative around home, cleaning and housework that fits very much within the ideal neoliberal context of the consumer citizen adept in self-help strategies described above.

Like Fearne Cotton, who had a successful career as a television presenter and popular radio DJ before she built her podcast and Instagram career, Stacey Solomon's celebrity status began in 2009 when she became an *X Factor* finalist. In common with the rags-to-riches fable underpinning the reality television genre, much was made of Stacey being a teenage, working-class, single mother of one from Dagenham. As she remarked in a 2022 interview on her upward mobility journey: 'You have no idea what it's like to be a teenage mum from Dagenham, carrying her kid up the station stairs every day in a pram, then being in a room with Whitney Houston and singing to her. It was just insane! Incredible.'[18] Following the *X Factor*, Stacey has carved out a successful career as a television presenter, including as a panellist on ITV's *Loose Women*; she also won the reality television show *I'm a Celebrity Get Me Out of Here*. Since then, Stacey has become a highly successful influencer with 5.9 million followers on her Instagram account where she shares content centred around her home, family, domestic life and tidying tips. Stacey effortlessly breezes through parenting her five children with her husband, the television actor and presenter Joe Swash. Her popular Instagram account is almost always centred on her home, 'Pickle Cottage'. Indeed, we rarely see her in any other space; the emphasis is firmly on the home and the pleasures that both being in it and looking after it bring. We see her lovingly decorating, tidying, organising and renovating the house – including the outdoor swimming pool – all the while playing with and caring for her children. Everything looks effortless, bright, clean and sparkly tidy.

Crucially, Stacey is candid about her vulnerabilities and experiences of anxiety and post-natal depression, regularly sharing details of this with her followers in her interviews, books and Instagram page. Alongside this, Stacey pioneered the 'Tap to Tidy' Instagram trend where users post an image of a messy room, dirty sink or pile of laundry, for example, then invite followers to 'tap' to see the clean and tidy version. Beginning with sharing a photo of 'mess' and disorder, Stacey then clicks her fingers and the room is instantly and seemingly magically cleaned and tidied. Tap to Tidy has become widespread across cleanfluencing accounts. From the perspective of the cleanfluencer, it serves two purposes. First, by sharing images of messy and 'real' content, it reminds followers that despite their celebrity status, the cleanfluencers are in fact *just like you*, thus enhancing their relatability. Second, Tap to Tidy acts as a contemporary and digital manifestation of the idea that housework need not be exhausting, difficult, time-consuming and monotonous; on the contrary, with the right skills and attitude, it can be achieved quickly, effortlessly and as magically as a fairy tale. Some cleanfluencers actually use songs from Disney princess movies as background music for their Tap to Tidy stories. The seemingly never-ending Tap to Tidy stories on Instagram and TikTok are appealing and seductive (you could potentially scroll through similar stories for hours) because in Tap to Tidy fashion, it makes the impossible (an endlessly bright, clean and tidy home) seem achievable. Stacey Solomon's bestselling book of the same name, *Tap to Tidy:*

Organising, Crafting and Creating Happiness in a Messy World, was published in 2021. In true relatable style, Stacey announced the launch of her book personally to her Instagram followers in a quasi-glamorous, filtered photoshoot wearing loungewear and fluffy slippers, but with perfect make-up and hair and beaming smile, holding the book towards the camera: "Honestly, I've never been so nervous!", she laughs. The shoot represents a strange sort of heavily stylised and carefully curated relatability that has come to define the cleanfluencers, which is at once aspirational *and* relatable.

In Chapter 1, I explored the friendly intimacy curated by influencers and demonstrated how this often works to couch the aggressive marketing, advertising and multiple consumption opportunities bolstering it. Here I want to focus more on the idea of decluttering as 'wellness'. In between tips for household organisation, tidying and crafting, *Tap to Tidy*, as the title suggests, reiterates the stress and anxiety that is central to the experience of living in increasingly 'messy' and 'uncontrollable' worlds. Repeated use of the words 'mess', 'messy', 'anxiety', 'lack of control' and 'worry' are endlessly juxtaposed against ideals such as 'achievement', 'gratification' and 'satisfaction', with decluttering, tidying and organising at home presented as helping to navigate a path through the chaos towards a happier life. Describing tidying and organising as like a 'form of meditation', Stacey uses the opening section of her book to extoll the mental health benefits of housework:

> When the tidying's done, there's the satisfaction of looking at some-where that was once a tip and knowing I've just sorted that all out! There's a real sense of achievement. The gratification is just so good. I love that feeling: It makes me feel like I've accomplished something and, on top of that, like I'm in control. A lot of my anxiety comes from feeling very out of control – which might be the case for you too. I think for a lot of us those worried feelings are about not being able to change certain things or make certain things happen. But you *can* make little things happen in your own world.[19]

Throughout Stacey's social media and books, the idea that happiness and wellbeing starts at home in cupboards, drawers and shelves is palpable. The notion that personal joy is something that can be created and curated by individuals so long as they are equipped with the right skills is central and echoes the digital self-help ethos described above. In this way, there are some parallels with Marie Kondo's KonMari method described earlier, but Stacey's openness about her vulnerabilities sets her apart from the cleanfluencing celebrities that came before her. As we see in the quote above, vulnerability is celebrated and stripped of stigma, but only insofar as it doesn't disturb the self-care, personal growth mindset and its reinforcement of individualistic consumer culture. The huge popularity of the narrative of creating your own opportunities for self-care, happiness and wellbeing was further galvanised in 2021 with *Sort Your Life Out*, a BAFTA-nominated BBC reality television show presented by Stacey where 'ordinary' families are invited to transform their homes and therefore their lives via a dramatic decluttering process where the individual contents of each home are laid out in a huge warehouse and participants – guided by Stacey – must make decisions about what to keep, what to donate and what to recycle. Stacey is always warm, relatable and caring, taking time to listen to problems and offering solutions, often sharing personal stories, feelings and challenging life experiences of her own. Much of the clutter consists of what Sophie Woodward has termed 'dormant objects', which participants share their emotional and personal connection to.[20] In what often ends up being quite an emotional and sometimes distressing process, Stacey encourages participants to shift the way that they relate to the objects in front of them. She advises participants to see happiness not in the 'out of place' object but in the disposal, tidying or organising of the object, which is reframed as a barrier to happiness that is dragging its owner further away from wellbeing.

The show almost always follows a set format, with, in common with the reality television genre more broadly, life-changing narratives underpinning the show. Contestants regularly express awe: 'I can't believe this is happening to us!' Tidying up is reframed as a 'life-changing declutter' and culminates in the 'big reveal'; almost always an emotional scene where often complex and chaotic lives are transformed via the decluttering process. The show is the latest in the long tradition of the home makeover genre and offers viewers a *Tap to Tidy* experience par excellence – a fantasy scenario achievable only because of the skilled, professional team (including a carpenter, cleaner and professional declutterer) working round the clock, presumably with a substantial budget, to make it happen. The idea that decluttering and tidying might transform lives is a worthy one, but it is difficult to see how this would be achievable in the real world, with just one woman adopting *Tap to Tidy* decluttering methods alone at home.

Conclusion

In this chapter, I have explored the contemporary discourses of decluttering and tidying the home and mind that have become a hallmark of influencer culture. I have illustrated this with some of the most well-known figures from the online self-help cleaning, tidying and wellbeing communities. Within these hugely popular social media accounts that promise to empower followers to seize the day and to find ways of making their inner happiness blossom, women in particular are held personally accountable for their own successes and failures. As Laurie Oulette and James Hay have also argued,[21] 'self-responsibilization' discourses proliferate throughout media cultures, with the 'techniques of everyday self-management' bonded into popular cultural narratives and beyond. I now move on to a discussion of the ways in which the popular digital self-help movement has, in recent years, been adopted by the cleanfluencers to great effect.

4

'Laughter can get you through the hard days': The cultural politics of housework

You are braver than you believe; stronger than you seem; smarter than you think; and loved more than you'll ever know.[1]

The irony behind the idyllic happy family as a place for repose is the consumption of female labour power.[2]

Within cleanfluencing cultures, self-help discourses abound. In this chapter, I explore the prevalence of these powerful discourses in more detail and consider how cleaning, tidying and housework more generally have become repositioned as pivotal to personal satisfaction and contentment. One of the core findings of recent research examining the power of popular cultural discourses around post-feminism is that structures of injustice, inequality, exploitation, insecurity and struggle, and the harsh realities of late modernity (particularly for women), are made visible. Moreover, anxiety, stress, struggle and a sense of failing to meet the exacting standards of normative femininity are reframed as first, a 'new normal', and second, as an opportunity for growth.[3]

The steep increase of recorded mental health 'disorders', now estimated to be prevalent in 50 per cent of the world's population,[4] is well documented, with the relationship between mental health and income inequalities especially clearly established. And yet, research from the 1960s onwards has sidestepped the social and cultural context of mental health, with solutions to a range of symptoms including stress, anxiety, depression and trauma increasingly personalised and individualised with a seemingly never-ending range of commercial solutions on offer. Today, a quick scroll through social media channels reveals a plethora of discourses directly and candidly articulating a variety of highly confessional 'lived experiences' of mental health issues and even pathologies which are, it is promised, solvable and manageable via personal 'growth' and taking individual responsibility.[5] In tandem with this, welfare and the role of community and the state have increasingly been exorcised from debates around mental health, in place of individualised, self-help, often aspirational and commercialised solutions such as those described in Chapter 3.

Although scholarly literature has long pointed to a link between poverty and mental health, this is routinely ignored in popular discourses. Instead, mantras around 'thinking yourself happy', 'setting your happiness free' and 'changing your mindset' prevail. The raft of personalised, individualised solutions to low mood, and the seemingly infinite range of commercially available products to help facilitate these, are paralleled by rapid austerity and welfare cuts. After all, the logic goes, if mental health discourses are all in the brain and mind, without any external social reality, then there is no need for any economic or political solution.

In this chapter, I unpick some of the entanglements around cleanfluencing, popular social media cultures and mental health discourses. Cleanfluencers offer a novel and highly seductive invitation to voice self-expressed ideas around mental health centred around a freshly glamorised version of housework. This plays a significant role in reproducing the separation between mental health and social, political or cultural contexts. I argue that within cleanfluencing accounts we see a *normalisation* of psychological suffering.

You and your home deserve to shine: Normalising anxiety

Recent years have seen a plethora of social media accounts and hashtags that extoll the mental health benefits of cleaning and tidying. Online cleanfluencers have been particularly vociferous in describing their experiences of anxiety and stress in candid detail. Sometimes this extends to interspersing cleaning stories with film reels and posts showing boxes of antidepressants, personal accounts of journeys through depression and heart-to-heart confessional conversations with followers about mental health struggles. From the perspective of the cleanfluencer, the intention is to destigmatise mental health problems by normalising not being OK. The #ShineNotShame hashtag that is popular on social media, particularly within cleanfluencing communities, illustrates this. Coined by the Clean & Tidy Home Show in 2021, it purports to take the stigma out of talking openly about mental health issues, and of course seamlessly presenting cleaning and tidying ('shining') as the solution: 'The Clean & Tidy Home Show believes there is no shame in asking for help or sharing a problem. We are committed to supporting our community no matter their experience or approach to homemaking.'[6]

The post feels inclusive: the Clean & Tidy Home Show is 'open to all' without shame or judgement. The 'Shine Not Shame' page on the website promises a feeling of community 'for all homemakers, no matter their budget, time or other constraints'. Importantly, the message that is most vociferously reinforced is that the show exists for those who 'need it to ask for help'. 'Help' is provided via a raft of corporate organisations – The Pink Stuff, Cillit Bang, Harpic, Surf, Vanish and Persil all have stalls – but notably also by Clean & Tidy Home Show 'Shine Not Shame' ambassadors, who promise to offer tips and advice to those who are struggling without judgement or stigma. The sort of 'help' that people might need within this context is never fully explained. It is unclear whether it means help for mental health struggles or help with the burden of housework. The underlying assumption – embedded in the fusing of 'shine' and 'shame' – is that this exciting new concept in cleaning and tidying can offer both. As part of the advance promotion of the 2023 event, the Clean & Tidy Home Show introduced Instagram followers to their 'Shine Squad'. The Shine Squad consists of 'ordinary' cleanfluencers from around the UK, overwhelmingly white, working-class women, who are introduced as 'ambassadors' responsible for 'promoting the show and the wonderful brands exhibiting'. Months before the show, held in October at the Excel Centre in London, the ambassadors are introduced and then create their own Instagram posts – which are paid partnerships with the Clean & Tidy Home Show and include a link to ticket sales for the event on their Instagram pages. The announcement posts are a mixture of excitement and pride that directly address their followers: 'I've been keeping a secret … I'm part of the Shine Squad this year and I'm so excited!' Members of the Shine Squad tend to be 'ordinary' women, often with paid jobs, who have some sort of uplifting story to tell about how cleaning and tidying has helped them to cope with the stresses and strains of their everyday lives. This correlates with the discussion in Chapter 1 around the importance of relatability. Although the Clean & Tidy Home Show features prominent and high-profile cleanfluencers, the proffered focus on destigmatising mental health is promoted with stories from 'real' women who are smaller-scale cleanfluencers.

The 2023 Shine Squad team member @mrscleans, for example, is candid about the stressful reality of her life as a full-time employee in a care home, but she says she enjoys spending her spare time cleaning and organising. The closest she gets to revealing the stress and exhaustion of the double shift is to remark that 'with the dog and the husband … sometimes life gets in the way', but also that ultimately 'cleaning is very much my therapy and helps me to escape and helps me cope with my mental health'. In one post, @mrscleans stands at the top of a tight stairwell pointing to a huge pile of shoes, coats and bags and other generic hallway clutter. Still in her work uniform, she is bent over, clearing up an enormous pile of shoes, sorting and piling until they all fit into two storage baskets. Filmed against a Whitney Houston remix, we then see a speeded-up vacuum of the stairs followed by a bottle of air freshener being sprayed. Done! Without the extreme speeded-up video that makes the job seem fast and effortless, it is *almost* a realistic portrayal of housework – acknowledging the scope of 'mess' to be cleared and a reminder of paid work too. Yet the volume of mess to be sorted, the cleaning and tidying that is performed after the paid shift ends, is reconfigured as resilience, the 'imperfect' standing as a reminder to followers of the relatability and, importantly, of her resilience in the face of adversity.

In a separate post, @mrscleans shares a video reel of her immaculate but small first-floor flat which she and her partner moved to after their previous landlord gave them notice to leave. 'It's a perfect cosy little flat for us while we work hard to pay off some of our debts.' The post offers a fascinatingly extreme positive spin on what are by any standard enormously difficult circumstances ('it was a stressful time') alongside a ruthless commitment to old gender norms around uncomplainingly submitting to the exhausting demands of unpaid labour. In one post, @mrscleans opens up the popular self-help book *How to Find Joy in Five Minutes a Day* that offers tips and advice on squeezing some of joy into lives where every moment is accounted for. Where time and money are scarce resources, the book promises to provide tips and ideas to 'transform your outlook' and 'find a small oasis of calm'. The idea that 'all you need is five minutes' speaks to the extreme scarcity of time and space, especially for women in late modern societies. For working-class women in particular, like the junior cleanfluencers described here, a full-time, low-paid, demanding job, combined with cleaning, tidying and organising a home and of course also an Instagram account, means an absolute paucity of spare time to access that elusive time for 'self-care'.[7] The solution is to *maximise efficiency*: @mrscleans turns the pages of *How to Find Joy in Five Minutes a Day*, landing on a tip called 'Move while the kettle boils'. In an accelerated reel presented against upbeat, speeded-up pop music, we see the switch on the kettle flicked, at which point @mrscleans springs into action; we see her putting away the dishes, cleaning the sink, 'refreshing' the plug and cleaning a mirror. The kettle finishes boiling and the reel ends with @mrscleans pouring her tea. The story is tagged with the hashtag #cleaningismytherapy that is absolutely celebrated and championed throughout cleanfluencing culture.

Cleanfluencing culture is packed with endless attempts to resist judgement, shame and stigma around mental health and the normalisation of anxiety. The message is often one of resisting self-monitoring and campaigning against 'unkindness', but ironically this is often via a fetishisation of housework and an almost ruthless reproduction of impossible normative ideals of the home. This has the effect of: first (as already discussed), seeking solutions to the pain of anxiety by turning inwards; second, seeking solutions and distraction via housework; and third, gaining support from online cleanfluencing communities. The account @lifewiththetomkins,[8] run by the cleanfluencer Shannon Tomkins and cited in the opening quote to this chapter, has 79,000 followers on Instagram and offers a combination of family life and cleaning motivation. In an act reminiscent of the type of online 'community' that cleanfluencing promotes, it also invites followers to 'share our special moments with us'. Almost all of the very colourful posts are to do with cleaning and tidying an immaculate semi-detached home, peppered with images of a wide variety of cleaning products. In common with other cleanfluencers, the account includes a 'mental health' stories tab featuring a video diary of Tomkins' mental health journey and inspirational quotes. Antidepressant medication frequently features prominently, such as in one 'Happy Sunday' post from 2022, a bright, carefully arranged kitchen bench display against a clean wooden bench, white tiles, fresh Minky sponge, cup of tea, lit white candle, vase of flowers and opened box of antidepressants. The way in which medication is displayed first serves to normalise mental health support, but second it positions the home and house-work as the *real* spaces of sanctuary, where recovery is most likely to happen, never giving up on the idea that happiness lies at home closely associated with housework routines and practices.

After an absence on Instagram following a bout of depression, Shannon returns with a 'reset' reel. Filmed against the Kelly Clarkson song *Stronger (What Doesn't Kill You)*, her return is accompanied by a message of thanks to her followers for their online support. The reel is accelerated, intending to be motivational, peppered with multiple branded cleaning products: 'Nothing gets me motivated more than NEW cleaning products.' In a short, thirty-second reel, we see a bed being made, laundry being done, kitchen surfaces being cleared and wiped and a floor being mopped. There are multiple product placements squeezed into the reel, including Flash, Zoflora, Mrs Hinch's Tesco home range, Fairy Liquid and Lenor. By the end of the reel the rooms that we see are shining and immaculate. In the final scene we see Shannon pouring the dirty water from the bucket down the toilet. The sight of the slightly grey water might be seen to symbolise the type of relatable-resilient content that has become so popular and lucrative across cleanfluencing cultures. As Shannon assures her followers, 'My house is an absolute state if I'm honest. Check out the water at the end [sick emoji].' This chimes with Angela McRobbie's description of the entanglements of the 'perfect', 'imperfect' and 'resilience' within contemporary neoliberal culture;[9] not only the omnipresent but never articulated contradiction between the relentless circulation of images of normatively perfect homes and families but also the so-called celebration and embracing of imperfections and vulnerabilities.

Thus, within cleanfluencing cultures, the endlessly reproduced yet impossible demands of perfection – home, family, job, physique, etc. – are tempered by an acknowledgement of the *imperfect*, most often of struggles around anxiety and depression but also by sharing glimpses of the imperfections of home: of 'mess', clutter and, as with the above, the 'dirty' residue of housework. This is particularly important when one considers that feminist scholars and activists are increasingly vocal in articulating the heavy demands that contemporary life places on women. As Catherine Rottenberg notes in her review of Angela McRobbie's book *Feminism and the Politics of Resilience*: 'The imperfect, in other words, helps to dilute the relentless demands of neoliberal feminism, particularly in the wake of renewed mass and more radical feminist mobilisations.'[10]

As the Kelly Clarkson lyrics so frequently used across cleanfluencing social media accounts remind us: 'What doesn't kill you makes a fighter.' Followers are given glimpses of the mess and dirt, but only to provide a contrast to the transformed, finished product and to help illuminate the resilience and relatability of the cleanfluencer.

Popular messaging around resilience in the face of often extreme adversity has become one of the hallmarks of cleanfluencing culture. The almost total normalisation of mental health problems, particularly stress and anxiety, is framed first as a process of destigmatising and removing shame and judgement, and second as fixable and manageable through the right types of cleaning and tidying processes and routines. Central to this messaging is a reframing of often very severe problems and demands (including debt, homelessness, single parenthood, abuse, exhaustion, stress and anxiety) as an opportunity for personal growth via a mindset of vulnerability-to-resilience; and of course to a sparkling clean home too. This message is also widely and enthusiastically endorsed by 'celebrity' cleanfluencers. Lynsey Crombie, the resident cleaning expert on the popular British ITV daytime talk show *This Morning*, also known as 'Lynsey Queen of Clean', has a popular Instagram cleanfluencing account (309,000 followers) of the same name where she shares housework tips and hacks in colourful posts. The posts are interspersed with accounts of her mental health struggles, her journey to recovery aided by cleaning and tidying. In a 2021 interview live on *This Morning*, Crombie describes a set of what must have been hugely stressful personal circumstances: the discovery that her partner was a sex offender, and the judgement and shame that came from being a single mother whose children were on the Child Protection Register owing to their father's crimes. In what has now become a familiar tale of adversity–vulnerability–resilience–recovery, Crombie describes how cleaning helped her to navigate a path through her torment. It is a story of personal redemption, of 'scrubbing away the pain', where cleaning becomes a coping mechanism or, as is often postu-lated, a type of therapy. In a post created by @LynseyQueenOfClean in recognition of 2023 Mental Health Awareness Week, Crombie directly addresses her mental health struggles and the role that cleaning has played in easing them:

> I have used cleaning as a form of therapy and a coping mechanism to deal with daily stresses and anxiety for many years ... Whenever I am angry, dealing with a stressful situation or tired, I clean. It awakens my body and it gives me a different perspective on the day ahead. A clean house is definitely a happier house.

In the post, @LynseyQueenOfClean stands facing the camera in her impossibly gleaming, shining, and bright kitchen. The white, shining surfaces are completely clear save for a vase of brightly coloured flowers. Crombie is equally immaculate, her bright clothing and make-up, including trademark red lipstick, pink nails and bright waved hair illuminated against the minimal white background. She holds a sponge in one hand and a bottle of surface spray in the other, seemingly mid-housework task. Her stylish, bright patterned maxi dress is linked in her post – available to buy for £100.

The depiction of cleaning alongside mental health struggles, peppered with stories of personal struggle and resilience, echoes the contemporary politics of resilience as fundamental to new postfeminist cultures, as postulated by Angela McRobbie. It's fine to feel that you are failing so long as failure is harnessed towards personal redemption of self and home. As the Clean & Tidy Home Show reminds us, 'You and your home deserve to shine!'; and also, of course, you deserve that dress!

Of course, the carefully curated everyday glamour that accompanies the depiction of housework is not new. In 1964, Betty Friedan noted the ways in which the glamourising of housework by cleaning companies was a lynchpin in ensuring the continued willingness of women to partake in unpaid labour:

> Consider, as a symptom, the increasing emphasis on glamour in the women's magazines: the housewife wearing eye make-up as she vacuums the floor – 'The honour of being a Woman'. Why does 'Occupation: Housewife' require such insistent glamorizing year after year?[11]

The difference today is the accompanying promise of good mental health. Whereas Betty Friedan noted the catastrophic impact on mental health of the binds of housework and unpaid domestic servitude, today, perhaps as a way of sidestepping those debates, cleaning and tidying is routinely presented as a salve to rather than a cause of stress and anxiety. In a live interview streamed on Instagram with the Tower Hamlets branch of Mind, which is a project partner of the Clean & Tidy Home Show, the show's founder interviews a Mind social media coordinator. The interview is smiley, light-hearted and fun. We are reminded that in these 'tea break' interviews children, dogs and interruptions are welcome. The interview coincides with Mental Health Awareness Week, and the emphasis is on 'reaching out' via online cleaning communities and in person at the Clean & Tidy Home Show, and on breaking down the stigma around mental health. The tone is friendly and warm and viewers are invited to join a slow fashion decluttering event. We are reminded again of the links between a tidy wardrobe and good mental health and that all events are inclusive – everyone is welcome. The interview ends with a question for Mind: 'what's your secret to keeping a clean and tidy home?' The response is a combination of tips – dealing with one room at a time and having an efficient housework routine, for example. The assumption that there is a positive correlation between housework and good mental health is never questioned or unpicked.

Does it matter and are these discourses harmful? What do we really know about the impact of unpaid domestic labour on mental health? In the absence of peer-reviewed research, we do not know enough to claim so uncritically that it eases stress and anxiety however, we do know that women, and working-class women in particular, feel judgement, shaming and stigma acutely. What we see echoed in the examples above are the ways that cleanfluencers tap into the unease around the pain and stress of judgement. But, in a twisted contradiction, the repeated pleads not to judge and to 'be kind' are juxtaposed against endless images of the perfect home. It is a strange irony that many long, carefully written posts about the very real emotional harms of judgement are so regularly illustrated with images of domestic and often bodily perfection.

It is fascinating how, in the early decades of the twenty-first century, the relationship between emotional harm and the unremitting demands of housework have been rewritten. Once, harm was associated with a lack of societal and cultural recognition of housework as valuable and with the persistence of an unequal system of work that relied on the unpaid labour of women. In 1966, Hannah Gavron, known colloquially as one of the first women sociologists, wrote her celebrated and only book, *The Captive Wife*. Shortly after its publication, Gavron killed herself in the kitchen of her home leaving behind two young children. It is hard not to see the parallels between Gavron and the American poet Sylvia Plath, who died by suicide a couple of years earlier only a few streets away. Both women left behind prolific personal accounts of the emotional captivity of home and motherhood and the often suffocating trappings of domestic life. Gavron's study identifies the conflicts of housebound mothers bound by the utter incompatibility of motherhood and paid work, and notes the reduction in status of housewives who 'do not feel themselves to be at work' no matter how arduous the work is. Gavron describes a vast commonality of experience of stay-at-home mothers, and yet, '[a]t the same time there is no community of experience of women whose lives have so many factors in common, and who share a common interest in the activities of the home'.[12]

This sense of 'commonality but no community' stands as a precursor to the sort of extreme individualism that I have already described and which plagues neoliberal societies. It manifests itself in a situation whereby women might share the same or a similar set of circumstances but without the means of sharing their experiences.

To a certain degree, cleanfluencers acknowledge the sense of captivity, burnout and loneliness, and place huge importance on bringing people together either online via the cleanfluencing community, or by coming along to the Clean & Tidy Home Show and 'making friends'. In promotional posts for the 2023 event, the Clean & Tidy Home Show lists 'making new friends' as its top reason for attending. In a nod to the loneliness and fear of judgement that has long plagued women's experiences of housework, the Clean & Tidy Home Show introduced an alternative to the usual industry awards, by renaming the judging panel members 'Not a Judge': 'We don't like the idea of a "judging panel". Instead, we have a series of super-passionate experts who can't wait to get excited about everything your brand has been doing for the cleaning and tidying and homemaking community.'[13]

In addition, the suffocating demands of domestic labour are acknowledged and addressed in a light-hearted way by the daily Clean & Tidy Home Show 'tea-breaks': live-streamed chats with guests, often other cleanfluencers. A typical tea break chat begins with one of the show's founders directly addressing the camera – smiling, friendly and approachable – and asking, 'How are you all getting on today?' In pre-digital media times, women's magazines often centred around this idea of offering a quick break from the housework. The popular magazine *Take a Break*, for example, was cheap and offered a combination of quick boredom-busting tonics for the time- and money-pressed housewife, such as crossword puzzles, celebrity gossip, jokes and tips to ease the domestic load. Thus, we see that the boredom and monotony of housework has long been reflected in various popular culture offerings. The magazines offered something else too – a comforting recognition of not being alone. Housework might feel lonely and isolating but mirrored in magazines such as *Take a Break* was the comforting realisation that others are there too. Millions of other women with the same routines, anxieties and sense of isolation existed everywhere. As Hannah Gavron noted in the 1960s, the commonality of experience did not translate to *communities*. This separation of common experience from community intensifies isolation. Digital culture attempts to recreate some of that community via descriptions of 'my Insta-family', for example, and the promise of making new friends, but there is no evidence of how effective this digital 'community building' has been. The comfort of being a member of the online cleanfluencing community is often tempered with an expression of fear at meeting other cleanfluencers 'in real life' at the Clean & Tidy Home Show and nervousness around getting on a train to arrive at the show. It is a stark reminder of the *virtual* nature of most cleanfluencing communities and maybe of the temporal comfort that these communities might offer. Like the magazines that came before, readers were promised an illusion of community, shared experience and comfort in being part of something.[14] In our attempts to explain why feelings of shame, stigma, fear, loneliness and anxiety aren't going away, we turn to individualised explanations; 'blame' lies with the unkindness and individual judgement of others and solutions are positioned as commercial and individual.

Returning to the Clean & Tidy Home Show 'tea break' interview, we can see echoes of the familiar attempt to cajole women into a soothing, temporary space where some of the repetition,

monotony and routinisation of housework is temporarily inter-
rupted. The underlying message, like the women's magazines that
came before, is 'we hear you!' but this time it is infused with the
promise of helping to restore mental wellbeing. Before the live
video, followers are gently cajoled into coming along: 'Go on ...
have a cuppa with us.' The top tips offered during the discussion
with the cleanfluencers are very familiar, from cleaning 'little and
often' to 'putting things back where you found them'. During the
tea break the invited cleanfluencer sits with her baby son bouncing
on her lap – a reminder that cleanfluencing might be one of the
few career options where the visibility of children is accepted and
even celebrated as part of the job. The interview quickly shifts to a
focus on how cleaning can 'help you'. Alongside affirmations around
being authentic, showing 'real life and all that', we are reminded
that of course, no one's home is perfect – that no one lives in a
show home. Because of course, the juggling and the descriptions of
'mess' and 'chaos' are only accepted within the context of subsequent
achievement. Failure and mess are acceptable so long as they are
just prefixes to redemption, success, happiness and ultimately 'a
clean house and a clean mind'. Alongside this is a familiar and
stubborn refusal to challenge inequalities of domestic labour: top
tip, 'Don't have kids or a husband!' – *laughter*. Men's assumed lack
of involvement in housework is fleetingly mentioned but framed
as women's responsibility to find ways of involving men. 'How
can we make men feel welcome?' asks the interviewer following a
discussion about favourite cleaning products. The question comes
at the end of the interview, almost as an afterthought; tagged on
to long discussions about products, tips and advice to make the
relentless juggling more bearable. It's an interesting choice of words
too – combatting inequalities in domestic labour is reframed as
making sure men don't feel 'pushed out' of the housework; that
communicating and addressing issues around discrepancies of housework remains firmly the responsibility of women and an additional
part of the domestic burden. The discussions propose new ways of
delicately trying to address the domestic burden more fairly in a
light-hearted, non-confrontational way. The key is *communication*

and mutual understanding, with women gently guiding men towards 'helping out'.

It is interesting looking at the contemporary cleanfluencers' occasional takes on the active participation of men in the housework (or lack of it) to see that this is still presented in broadly the same terms. Men are described as 'helping me out'; as 'needing a bit of encouragement' perhaps by providing a list of tasks to allocate to men who, it is assumed, simply don't see the jobs that need to be done. Implicit in the Clean & Tidy Home Show interview, and the nod towards gender inequality, is the idea that women have somehow locked men out of housework, that they must therefore take personal responsibility for inequalities and that it is up to women to draw men in and to show them how it is done. In a set of comments that would not look out of place in a 1950s women's weekly, the unequal share of cleaning and tidying is reduced to a type of in-built, fixed 'difference' between men and women. Continuing with the jocular tone to the interview, the cleanfluencers share their thoughts on how 'women think differently' to men. Cleanfluencers are habitually presented as independent and empowered; they advise followers to 'be yourself' to not follow trends, follow the crowd or be a sheep. In doing so, independence and personal empowerment are proposed, while simultaneously and ironically reproducing the assumption of 'natural' differences in men and women's attitudes towards and ability to perform housework. Of course, here women are asked questions about their husband's participation in the housework that men themselves are never expected to answer. Here we see that resolving the problem of inequalities falls to women who are also expected to provide justifications for their roles as housewives; roles that are habitually denigrated, unpaid and lacking in value. Women are thus tasked, first, with justifying their participation in these unequal systems and, second, with reglamourising and finding value in their labour. They do this by describing how, although their husbands are completely at the mercy of their careers and therefore have very little time (they would do more if they could), they nevertheless 'help out' and 'muck in' where they can. Often cleanfluencers describe how their husbands take charge of the garden and the DIY; how 'he does the bins' or 'every so often he helps with something I can't manage, like the high parts'. In this way they are also part of a collusion in normative gender expectations. They help to silence the disquiet that might emerge from deep thinking around these inequalities, which instead are articulated as natural and fair – we like it this way.

Twentieth-century media cultures have long been flooded with celebratory representations of motherhood and women as paid workers, yet despite its ubiquitousness, women as housewives have long been devalued to the point of invisibility. Not only is 'housework' lacking in value and status, it is often invisible too. Cleanfluencing helps to bridge that contradiction as predominantly women use social media in an attempt to imbue their labour with value and personal purpose. They do this by rejecting the idea of housework being a trap or a disavowal of self and instead fall back on popular vocabularies of self-care and familial harmony to quieten any sounds of ambivalence around being a housewife. Rather than being a 'selfless' act, it is, in the lexicon of confidence culture, reframed as 'doing something for myself', as a form of self-care and as a way of expressing one's individuality and purpose. The endless insistence that housework is joyful and fun and brings with it personal satisfaction; the fresh expression of this across social media further aids this collusion and silencing.

It is also, of course, an example of the further individualisation of collective problems. This is further exemplified by the inclusion of a 'relationship expert' at the Clean & Tidy Home Show alongside the kitchen expert, upcycling expert and cleaning science expert. Clarissa is a 'psychotherapist ... who shares effective tools and strategies we can all adopt to develop healthy, stable, and authentic bonds with the people around us'. The domestic load thus becomes about *personal* family and relationship dynamics. There is no mention of gendered norms, expectations or stigmatising women who complain or don't assume responsibility for the domestic role. Instead, we see the familiar repertoire of 'survival skills and daydreams',[15] and the perfect fantasy lifestyle is displayed in vivid detail by the cleanfluencers. It is a new way of personalising a political problem that has its roots in the logics of post-industrial capitalism, which still rests on the assumption of someone at home taking control of the housework and childcare.

In 2021, a cleanfluencing account inspired by the cleanfluencer Mrs Hinch, originally named @LetsHinchandBeHappy and later renamed @TheBelfastGirl, featured a daily video of a cleanfluencer taking antidepressants. Each day, played alongside uplifting music, such as Kelly Clarkson's 'I'm Broken and It's Beautiful', she shares another video story of herself opening a plastic pill organiser and taking out three blue and white pills, which she holds up to the camera in the palm of her hand and swallows with a swig of cola. The videos are accompanied with positive affirmations around breaking stigmas and confronting the shame, taboo and silence that has historically surrounded mental health. The Belfast Girl is candid about her emotional trauma, especially her everyday anxiety and stress around being a stay-at-home, often solo, parent and army wife and being displaced from her family and friends in Belfast.

In a world long characterised by silence around mental health, Instagram is used here as a space to normalise the articulation of stress and depression and creating online communities around mental health: 'It's time to know it's OK not to be OK!' she writes, along with the now familiar mantra, 'You've got this!' As a video diary, the antidepressants serve to remind followers of the ubiquity of anxiety and depression. It alludes to ideas around the supposed power of online communities to engender openness, positive thinking and self-help to win the battle against emotional pain. Crucially, beyond the discussions about anxiety and depression, The Belfast Girl extols the mental health benefits of cleaning and tidying. In a 2020 interview with the *Belfast Live* newspaper, illustrated with a picture of an immaculately well-organised cupboard packed full of cleaning products, she explains the influence of Mrs Hinch and cleanfluencing more broadly on her decision to launch her own cleanfluencing account: 'I just felt that there was something about this page that I could relate to and that was loving cleaning products and just loving my home.'[16]

As The Belfast Girl's account helps to illustrate, cleanfluencing culture has been part of a contemporary trend towards easing the taboo and stigma associated with talking about mental health. In many ways, particularly to the extent that women are increasingly producing their own narratives of their experiences of mental health, this is revolutionary. Cleanfluencers habitually devote a significant amount of their content to discussing their emotional and mental health. Interestingly, more medicalised terminology such as 'stress', 'anxiety' or 'depression' are avoided in lieu of more euphemistic descriptors such as 'overthinking', 'having a day off' and 'it's OK not to be OK'. Being confessional and sharing intimate feelings and thoughts around mental health adds to the relatability of the cleanfluencers described in Chapter 1, reminding followers of the similarities between them and of the invisible threat connecting their experiences of anxiety. But being confessional serves another purpose. By couching complex, painful emotions and accounts of fragile wellbeing in accessible terms, mental health issues appear ubiquitous but also temporary and solvable: 'I know I'll be better tomorrow.'

The relatable – solvable – highly personalised axis underpinning the articulation of anxiety that has become such a familiar feature of cleanfluencing accounts is nicely exemplified in a recent 2023 video blog posted by Mrs Hinch, who appears on Instagram after an absence of a few days to offer an explanation to her followers for her absence. It turns out that her anxiety – which is well documented in her media interviews and books as well as on her social media – accounts has 'flared up', leading to her almost complete incapacitation. In her self-filmed video, Mrs Hinch lies on her bed, heavily made up, trademark bow in her hair, wide eyed, anxiously touching her face and fiddling with her necklace. The video is filmed in the semi-darkness and Mrs Hinch whispers her thoughts to the camera, almost as if she is confiding a deeply personal secret with a friend. She appears overwhelmed, scared, fearful, like a heroine in a horror movie anticipating imminent danger. In the video, Mrs

Hinch offers a lengthy, detailed and highly personal description of the physiological effects of her current mental state on her mind and body. She says:

> It's like, I can't explain it. Um, when you get like a moment of like tense vibration in your tummy and then it stops. You know then it'll be alright for a minute and then it'll go again and then it'll stop. It's like a bloody little electric shock that goes in your stomach ... I call them the tummy shivers ... Maybe it's something in the air today. Sending lots of love.

Straight after posting, Mrs Hinch is inundated with messages from followers describing their own 'stomach shivers'. I think it would be accurate to say that the feeling Mrs Hinch describes that appears to strike a chord with so many of her followers is an experience of anxiety, which is a notoriously difficult physical sensation to describe.[17] It is interesting, though, that the word 'anxiety' is avoided by cleanfluencers, and yet the symptoms redolent of the epidemic of anxiety that is increasingly reflected in official data are articulated and addressed in a most omnipresent way within cleanfluencing cultures.

It is imperative that we listen to and pay attention to these fresh articulations of anxiety. First, because they help to illuminate some of the lived experiences of anxiety and domestic life, and second, because the corresponding message that is so rarely challenged – that it is individuals themselves who must take sole responsibility for addressing and finding solutions to their mental health – is deeply harmful. Moreover, what we see reflected in cleanfluencing is a deeply problematic normalising of psychological suffering, where a constant nagging, gnawing stress and anxiety is perpetuated by the increasingly unrealistic demands of consumer capitalism and perfected normative femininity. In the absence of, first, any meaningful vocabulary to address suffering and, second, a juggernaut of heavily corporate messaging around the absolute normalisation of self-help, it is of course not surprising that women seek ways of coping and strategies of resilience within the boundaries of options available to them.

As Orgad and Gill note, in contemporary confidence culture, 'not being OK' or even 'failing' completely is tolerated and deemed acceptable so long as it is preceded with success; in this case, joy, happiness and personal and familial wellbeing.[18] Being happy has become a project of the self, with infinite self-help books dedicated to teaching women the tips and hacks that will enable them to shed their unhappiness, revealing a 'true', shining, serene, happy and satisfied self. In recent years, the digital self-help movement has focused on exercise, diet, yoga and even gardening, all centred around aspirational images of a perfect normative body shape and reproduced endlessly on social media. What we see is a fascinating contradiction between the thing that is supposed to improve mental wellbeing (in this case cleaning and tidying) and the phenomenon that is often described as provoking anxiety – namely the obsessive, competitive disorder of late capitalism.

In a Lacanian sense, we might see anxiety as broadly stemming from the perceived desire of others and, within late modern or neoliberal societies, individuals locked within endless cycles of crisis management. Within such structures, the 'real' – inequalities, injustice, exploitation, etc. – is purged and replaced with a sort of normalised, ubiquitous suffering which we are all compelled to resolve in our own personal ways. For women in particular, life is defined by endless cycles of responding to the multiple demands, desires and expectations of others.

Of course, many might dispute this, and increasingly there are calls for the further recognition and celebration of women as wives, mothers and domestic labourers. But the increasingly rigid conformity and reproduction of unrealistic expectations, alongside a lack of support for those who would like to move beyond low pay and restrictive domestic roles, helps to explain the central role of narratives around anxiety within cleanfluencing culture.

The extent to which anxiety, fear and resilience are ruthlessly repackaged by neoliberal consumer culture is abundantly evident throughout contemporary popular discourses of domestic labour. In a move that seems to erase the history of the Women's Liberation

Movement that has long posited housework as repetitive, dirty, tedious, demanding, undervalued and imprisoning, housework within the corporate imagination is increasingly advocated as having a unique power to *alleviate* stress and anxiety. Not only that, individuals can make use of this self-help strategy themselves without outside support, and for free, in their own homes. The only financial cost relates to the burgeoning market in cheap, mass-produced, colourful, celebrity-endorsed cleaning products, but other than that there is no cost, no need for expensive therapist sessions and crucially no need to turn to others or the state for help. In short, this is the latest repackaging of the idea that happiness is attainable to those who most enthusiastically adopt and make the most of their unpaid labour and the self-affirming messages alluding to a stress-free lifestyle. The notion of cleaning as good for your mental health has, unsurprisingly, been enthusiastically adopted by a whole range of global cleaning brands and companies, increasing profits while simultaneously persuading women of the mental health benefits of a particularly regressive form of domestic conformity.

One of the cornerstones of cleanfluencing culture is the relentless association between cleaning, organising and decluttering, on the one hand, and 'positivity', good mental health and a feeling of calm and overall life satisfaction, on the other. Increasingly, these associations are interwoven into popular media cultures and narratives of housework. There are numerous examples of this, including an article published in 2019 in *Good Housekeeping* magazine extolling the relaxing and stress-reducing qualities of cleaning and tidying. Illustrated with images of women cleaning and tidying their homes, the article posits that 'putting in a little elbow grease can do wonders for your mental health' and that 'the act of cleaning makes me feel good'.[19] Similarly, the British newspaper the *Daily Mail* has published multiple articles attempting to celebrate the mental health benefits of cleaning. An article published in 2018 cites a woman blogger who found that after intensifying her cleaning schedule, '[n]ot only is my house now spotless but I am happier in myself. I haven't felt that lack of motivation I'd feel every day, and my mood has sky rocketed. And that's the power of one women ... cleaning.'[20]

Multiple other newspaper and magazine articles describe how cleaning might help ward off panic attacks and regain a sense of control during moments of anxiety. The articles are almost always illustrated with pictures of well-groomed, femme white women with lipsticked smiles, often wearing aprons, posed against the backdrop of immaculately sparkling clean and tidy kitchens and homes. It is hard to look at these images and not see stark similarities to the ubiquitous post-war images of the happy, smiling, 1950s housewife. The message today remains strikingly unchanged: housework is women's work and the happiest and most content women are those who seek and gain personal satisfaction from performing their domestic duties to a high standard. Rather than wasting time complaining or 'overthinking', they have the last laugh by simultaneously reaching coveted levels of happiness and contentment.

These powerful narratives around happiness and housework are also increasingly echoed in official health service documentation. For example, in 2021 the Oxford Cognitive Behaviour Therapy (CBT) site published an online article describing the mental health benefits of decluttering and cleaning, suggesting that 'keeping clutter and mess at a minimum will have a positive effect on your focus, stress and mental health'. Even more impressive is the promise of the mood-lifting capabilities of housework. We are promised by the psychologists at Oxford CBT that since 'clutter and mess can be linked to negative emotions like confusion and tension', the clear solution is to engage in more mood-lifting labour. Again the message couldn't be clearer: first, cleaning has a magical power to transform and uplift mood; and second, in keeping with the value of a neoliberal cultural economy, cleaning gives individuals the power of 'self-actualisation' and the ability to reach one's own personal potential. The article comes with a warning that the ordinary trappings of everyday life, the 'dirty plates from breakfast, an overflowing bin, piles of laundry or the children's toys everywhere... can all raise your stress levels'.[21]

The joy of clean: Cleaning your way to a positive mindset

The link between happiness and housework has long been reflected in popular culture in its various guises, as mentioned above, and is completely at odds with the seemingly forgotten feminist history of housework. The suffocating and often unrealistic domestic demands placed on women was once central to the Women's Liberation Movement, yet the feminist gains of the 1970s did not extend to dismantling the inequalities around housework. As capitalist society has advanced, along with the supposed opening up of women's freedoms and rights, the structure of the working day has remained largely unchanged, still resting on the assumption of someone at home carrying the domestic burden. As Betty Friedan noted long ago, the 'feminine mystique' or the 'problem that has no name' that blighted middle-class American suburban housewives is characterised by an absence of a vocabulary available to explain emotional afflictions. Today, we still see the same sort of blurry and vague accounts of mental health that Friedan described, which are often experienced by women who, unlike the wealthy women of Friedan's study, do not have the economic privilege of being stay-at-home housewives. The Belfast Girl's feeling that cleanfluencing offers 'something that I could relate to' taps into fresh attempts at relatability.

'Keeping your clothes clean and you happy!'

The much-loved online cleanfluencing expert Laura Mountford knows how overwhelming and confusing putting a load on can feel. But, with the right tips and tricks, she's turned her washing into a straight-forward, stress-free task. And now it's an essential part of her self-care routine.

Many of the most successful cleanfluencing accounts are centred around offering tips and advice on cleaning and managing the domestic load. Yet, looking at these, I am struck by how many of the activities depicted in the videos are fundamentally no different to ancient processes and practices – generally a variation of mopping, sweeping and wiping. The detail of the tips – for example, how to wash wool, leather, curtains and rugs; how to remove baby milk stains from upholstery and lint from clothing – are almost identical to those offered to women for centuries, albeit with new products and devices to make the job more manageable. At the time of writing, for example, the steam cleaner has become ubiquitous on social media but the tasks that it is used for are unchanged – cleaning around taps, shining windows, cleaning sofas and curtains. Women have long been lured with the promise of ever-evolving 'labour-saving' gadgets, devices and cleaning products and with the promise that this time the hunt for a solution to the burden of housework is over. What is different this time round is, first, the entertaining, expertly filmed and edited video montages that operate as a sort of video diary, and second, the promise of *self-care* – the fun and joyful experiences of housework.

One recent popular cleanfluencer who exemplifies this is Laura Mountford, whose Instagram account with 560,000 followers, depicts her immaculate and perfectly ordered home and offers a sort of daily video diary of her domestic life. Mountford herself is young, white and femme with a down-to-earth, accessible glamour. She often cleans in leggings and T-shirts but with a perfect manicure, make-up and hair. The video blogs invite us to join her as she cleans the floor, or shops in Home Bargains, a gleaming smile never leaving her face. She is filmed outside the shop beckoning us inside to 'spend the day with me at one of my favourite shops, Home Bargains! One of my favourite brands!' After introducing followers to her 'favourite' Flash products, she is filmed happily behind the tills serving customers; 'I had such fun with the team!' she says as she waves to the camera alongside the uniformed Home Bargains team. Everything is happy, airy and fun. Everyone looks joyful, excited and exhilarated by the opportunity to buy and sell the brightly coloured, jolly cleaning products on offer.

This breezy delight in cleaning is echoed in Mountford's other Instagram posts. There is, of course, no visible clutter; no books, mess, dirty dishes, fingerprints on windows, wires, cables, footprints on the floor, rubbish, piles of magazines and unopened mail or empty jars waiting to be recycled. In short, there is no evidence of a home that is lived in; no marks of other people at all. An exception to this is the occasional appearance of Mountford's husband – 'Clean with us!' – but this is rare. I discuss this in more detail in Chapter 5, but in the main it is just Laura, her home and her cleaning products – and of course her Instagram followers, who are invited to watch and join in her journey.

Self-care narratives are central to Laura's cleanfluencing account and occupy a prominent position in the accompanying bestselling 2023 book, *Live Laugh Laundry: A Calming Guide to Keeping Your Clothes Clean – and You Happy*.[22] Promising that 'caring for laundry can truly be caring for you' her Instagram 'reset days' featuring fast-edited, effortless deep cleans of her house are reframed as a way of 'resetting my mind'. The reset days, 'clean with me' and 'shop with me' video reels are never described as work, labour or housework. Instead, they are depicted as 'self-care for me and my home'. Yet lurking within Mountford's account and accompanying book is a tacit reminder of the unrewarding, hard, monotonous nature of housework that can often feel, as Mountford herself describes, 'overwhelming', 'confusing' and 'stressful'. Yet, time and again, we are reminded that the solution comes from *within*. The mantra that 'I alone am responsible for my own successes and failures' is rife within contemporary culture and especially prevalent, as we have seen, in the discourses curated by the cleanfluencers.

Commodifying self-help

The coalescence of self-help and cleaning has been ruthlessly commodified in recent years. For example, the Procter & Gamble Instagram account recently renamed itself 'The Joy of Clean', with an associated website 'Making Cleaning Fun' offering cleaning tips and advice. Similarly, in 2021, the cleaning brand Minky launched a campaign alongside the Samaritans, a UK-based charity providing support for people who are struggling to cope with emotional distress or are at risk of suicide, to design their own 'positive' Minky antibacterial cleaning brand to promote 'positivity, kindness and mental wellbeing'. The Minky brand has become a central feature of the cleanfluencing trend with multiple hashtags, shares and video montages devoted to promoting it. In 2023 the Clean & Tidy Home Show also sought to capitalise on the expanding narratives around cleaning and self-help. Part of their promotional campaign for the 2023 event featured a post of the '10 mental health benefits of a clean home', including relieving stress, boosting positivity, improving your mood, building social confidence and sparking creativity.

There is often a tacit acknowledgement that cleaning and housework is monotonous, unrewarding, difficult and overwhelming. Yet we are endlessly promised that the solution lies not with challenging inequalities or proposing radical change but rather that the solution comes from within; by changing your personal attitude, mindset and reframing housework less as an invisible, valueless and thankless set of cyclical, never-ending tasks, performed selflessly for the benefit of the family, and rather as a route towards personal happiness, success and fulfilment. As Chapter 5 shows, it is a particularly regressive and harmful mantra that fixes women in positions of dependency and exploitation, making entrenched inequalities ever more difficult to challenge.

Conclusion

This chapter has identified some of the ways in which the sort of Instagrammable self-care aesthetics described in Chapter 3 are firmly entrenched in cleanfluencing cultures. The solution to low mood and anxiety is one that further fixes women into regressive categories as arbiters of the domestic sphere and the housework; one where she can find joy and worth.

As the example of The Belfast Girl demonstrates, the rapid increase in popular discourses of mental health has been broadly accompanied by a heavily commodified self-help movement. The pursuit of happiness is thus not only something that can be bought and sold, it is also to be found *within*. Alongside this, cleaning products are positioned as offering a joyful experience that can facilitate an almost meditative state acting as a distraction from the stresses and strains of late modern societies. 'Mess' and 'messy' become metaphors for the wider world while deflecting our attention towards organising and purging the mess from our homes. Thus, while digital media abounds with personal and intimate accounts of mental health, there is rarely any discussion of the causes of anxiety and depression, particularly not of the detrimental impact of striving towards impossible to achieve ideals of homes, families and bodies that are endlessly and relentlessly reproduced on social media.

Instead, the solution is a combination of cleaning, tidying and buying an endlessly available range of cheap, mass-produced products. In other words, what is created and reproduced is an individualised and neoliberal solution to a *social* problem.

5

The return of the housewife: Housework in the aftermath of crisis

The cleanfluencers occupy a key moment in the history of the white woman housewife. Their popular appeal is rooted in wider social trends and change, particularly postfeminist responses to gender norms, and the increasing commodification of domestic life. In this penultimate chapter, I explore in more detail how cleanfluencing both replicates gendered inequalities of domestic labour and might also at times offer the potential to challenge or at least present a response to these inequalities. In many ways, cleanfluencing, like North American tradwifery, can easily be seen as representative of a regressive, even anti-feminist technique which reproduces ubiquitous images of young, perfectly groomed heterosexual women as the natural arbiters of the perfect home. I do not want to dismiss the problematic nature of these representations and in particular the risk of a return to rigid representations of a feminine identity that locates women within the home, performing housework with a smile. There is a real and growing risk that the intensification and increased ubiquitousness of these representations will limit choice and freedom and potentially, as Laura Bates has noted, see a return to 1950s levels of gender inequality at work and at home.[1] Certainly, I think we are witnessing a dramatic resurgence of conformist notions of women as willing, savvy and worthy arbiters of the domestic sphere, with a renewed sense of worth and value being tied up in the ability to perform housewifely roles and to reproduce not only the division of labour but also to defend the boundaries of the nuclear family. An additional pressure in neoliberal and postfeminist societies is how to perform this labour while simultaneously hiding and even denying the effort and work that goes into producing it. This is an important change because identifying as a 'housewife' today does not hold the same value as it once did. The final product (an immaculate home, cheerful, rosy children) remains steadfast, while the effort that goes into creating it is rendered invisible.

This has been clearly epitomised in recent years, for example on British World Book Day,[2] when primary school aged children are invited to come into school dressed as their favourite character from a book. Since the Instagram success of Mrs Hinch described in previous chapters, and the publication of her books (a household tips book, autobiography and children's picture book depicting life at 'Hinch Farm'), there has been an upsurge in children – the vast majority of whom are very young girls – dressing as Mrs Hinch for World Book Day, with images of the girls in their costumes often shared widely across social media and beyond. In March 2020, the Scottish newspaper the *Daily Record* ran a story of a Glaswegian three-year-old girl in her World Book Day Mrs Hinch costume featuring a tulle skirt adorned with Zoflora boxes, holding a duster in one hand and a box of Mrs Hinch-branded Lenor laundry tabs in another. Nicknamed 'Little Hinchers', the children quickly become social media sensations with Mrs Hinch herself regularly sharing photos of girls dressed up as her on World Book Day and accompanying the images with tearfully happy emojis; a mix of expressions of 'cuteness', 'beauty' and 'little darlings'. Costumes include buckets of cleaning products, 'Eat, Sleep, Hinch, Repeat' T-shirts, hair in scrunchies and rubber gloves, and often they are accessorised with a copy of one of Mrs Hinch's books. Pictures are often shared by Mrs Hinch fans, such as the 'We Love Mrs Hinch' Facebook account, who are often adamant that their daughters have chosen their own outfits and that 'she loves Mrs Hinch as much as I do!' I argue that this fresh, heavily popularised and increasingly mainstream representation of young women and, as we have seen, even very young girls as willing participants in cleanfluencing culture should be of significant concern. It represents a vicious combination of narrow versions of aesthetic femme beauty, happy housewifery and buying into the norms of an increasingly harmful commodified influencer culture. In short, the representation of housework as glamorous and the reproduction of sexist roles that draw on women and girls as willing domestic workers is potentially harmful, particularly where one considers the volume of young women who are increasingly watching cleanfluencing tips and videos on social media.[3]

In written evidence submitted to the UK Parliament in 2020, drawing on the report *Changing the Perfect Picture*, Ros Gill noted the significant and growing pressures and anxieties particularly experienced by women as a consequence of their increasing social media use. Gill found that 80 per cent of women felt pressure to look a particular way. She argues that '[y]oung women growing up today live in a world with an unprecedented number of visual images, and feel under intense pressure to look perfect and to present a perfect life'.[4] Concerningly, a pull towards 'compulsory perfection' on social media was felt by the vast majority (95 per cent) of young women. The impact of COVID-19 is notable here and echoes what I said earlier about the importance of the global health pandemic in precluding the ideal context within which cleanfluencing is able to thrive. A new, hyper-intense focus on and fear of germs, hygiene and health, and the harnessing of this by corporate giants, combined with renewed discourses of the home and the reconfiguring of domestic space, dovetailed perfectly with the increased use of social media in disseminating these narratives. In the immediate aftermath of the pandemic, Gill found a disproportionate impact of social media pressures on young women: 80 per cent of her sample said that they now spent more time on social media, while 95 per cent of women reported an intensification of pressure about body image, 70 per cent reported a pressure to create a 'perfect life' and a vast majority (90 per cent) said that they felt increased pressure to look attractive.[5] Cleanfluencing contributes an additional heavy burden on young women – the pressure to both create and digitally *curate* the perfect home.

Regarding this latter point, it is well documented that standards of cleanliness – what counts as a 'clean' and 'tidy' home – have intensified over time. Today, social media cleaning cultures, where the already spotlessly clean home is endlessly recleaned, polished, dusted and scented, reminds us that in the contemporary digital age, nothing is ever clean enough. The ever-evolving technological solutions to the domestic burden, which have long promised to lighten the load of housework, have conversely intensified domestic labour as standards have been pushed further and further towards impossible to achieve perfection. The promise of relief from drudgery that was made by profit-hungry home appliance manufacturers was clearly a false one. The intensification of the allure and striving towards impossible standards has opened up a contradiction at the heart of late modern societies. Namely that, in tandem with the promise made to contemporary individuals, especially women, that the capacity for free time, for 'me time', has been improved through new technologies, strategies and tips to lighten the domestic load, we have witnessed a simultaneous evolution of norms, standards and expectations of social reproduction in all its guises – including housework – that in reality renders this capacity more curtailed than ever.

This contradiction does not go unnoticed, with cleanfluencers increasingly using their platforms to poke fun at the recommendation to squeeze 'self-care' into an already packed and unmanageable schedule. However, this is also often offset by the message that cleaning can be fun, pleasurable and good for the soul. Rather than dismissing the pleasurable possibilities of housework, feminists have often noted the fleeting, tactile, even sometimes sensual pleasures afforded by the acts of cleaning and tidying. 'Satisfying' has become a key part of the cleanfluencing lexicon and the temporary gratification of housework is in part what makes cleanfluencing so compelling – and what makes 'power' and unequal gender roles hold good. Women are more likely to be willing participants in activities that provide at least occasional pleasures. Of course, it would be untrue to say that housework is never pleasurable, particularly when it is self-directed. It is easy to imagine the rhythmic, soothing pleasure of ironing a T-shirt in a large, fresh and well-organised laundry room, without myriad other distractions: a pile of washing in the sink, the phone ringing, a mound of dirty laundry by your feet, hungry children arriving home from school. In other words, as Hester and Srnicek argue, the pleasures of housework generally emerge when it is self-directed rather than *coerced.*[6]

Notions of housework as coercive rather than self-directed and pleasurable stand against recent popular framings of housework as joyful and exhilarating. Cleanfluencing reinforces a set of restrictive and heavily gendered norms of reproductive labour while also sidestepping the unacknowledged post-work, labour-intensive imagining of the 'perfect home'. In the post-Covid period, social reproduction is more firmly located in the home than ever, and fears of being judged by others, of getting it wrong, of the family suffering when jobs are left incomplete abound. The increasingly ubiquitous spectacle of the immaculate home that incorporates a refusal to acknowledge the labour-intensive practices involved in producing it, alongside the fear of judgement emerging from restrictive norms, creates a perfect storm for the proliferation of gender inequalities. Discourses surrounding women's 'natural' ability to sweep up mess are everywhere; whether it is picking up the bulk of time- and energy-intensive but often under-rewarded administrative tasks and emotional labour at work, or shouldering the burden of housework and caring labour, in 2023 that assumption remains not only dramatically unchallenged but also devoid of a language to resist. When the comedian Russell Brand decided to 'settle down' after a long period of public promiscuity, it was with a woman who, he boasted in a 2019 interview in the *Times*, was imbued with an almost saintly, pure and *natural* domestic and caring disposition:

> I don't have much experience of how to organise domesticity. I do whatever I'm told ... I'm still of a romantic and reflective and, possibly, to give it its proper name, a religious disposition. That's my worldview. That's not necessarily what you want, organising pragmatic, bureaucratic, managerial stuff ... Laura does all of it. It turns out that she is extremely well versed in the nuances and complexities of child-rearing.[7]

Generations old sexist attitudes, here shrouded under words such as 'romantic' and 'reflective', reinforce ideas of the natural abilities of women as 'well versed' to shoulder the bulk of domestic labour. As the quote above reminds us, we need to guard against the slow drip of sexist cultures. At the time of writing, debates around the hyper-sexualisation of young women and girls are being revisited, but it is important to resist narrow representations of women as willing housewives too and to challenge the same sexist cultures that box women as 'naturally' caring and nurturing. The popularity of cleanfluencing is a timely reminder of the need to guard against the proliferation of sexist attitudes and rigid categories of femininity. Often we have these conversations too late. A 2023 Fawcett Society study looking into housework and social attitudes found that, '[w]hen those who lived in mixed-sex households were questioned on what actually happens behind closed doors, 63% of women said they did more than their fair share of the housework'.[8]

Housework and the 'natural order' of femininity

The unequal, gendered division of unpaid domestic labour is built into the bedrock of capitalism. Without it, the logics of capitalism fall apart. A division underpinning capitalist economic thought that values reason, freedom, independence and conquering over emotion, dependency, caring and thoughtfulness can only exist because the two spheres are kept physically and ideologically separate. It is a reactionary division that is celebrated and routinely venerated within cleanfluencing cultures that offer a new narrative of an old dichotomy that divides home and work into separate entities.

Since Adam Smith, economists have long calculated and concluded that women's subordination is rational. The task, as ever, is to persuade women of this in new, ever-evolving and more convincing ways, ideally while stamping out signs of dissent in the process. Historically, economists ignored women's unpaid domestic labour; the childcare, cooking, cleaning, washing and home administration that they conducted was rarely or never acknowledged at all. Since those activities didn't produce tangible, exchangeable goods, they were deemed to be unimportant because they didn't contribute towards prosperity. As a set of cyclical, never-ending tasks that don't

142

appear to 'create' anything that can be seen or measured, housework stands in direct opposition to traditional definitions of 'economic activity'. As a consequence, these beliefs were accompanied by an insistence that the chief impetus for housework was not economic; rather, it occupied a different logic which was a key part of the 'natural' order of femininity. Thus, Marcel writes:

> What she did was just a logical extension of her fair, loving nature. She would always need to carry out this work, and so it wasn't anything that one needed to spend time quantifying. It came from a logic other than the economic. Out of the feminine. And Other.[9]

This explains why, as an activity that does not produce tangible economic goods, domestic labour is so badly paid or not paid at all – because it is seen as a set of skill-free tasks that should be done by women for free, out of pride, love and duty. As we saw in the previous chapters, cleanfluencing offers the potential for turning the unpaid into paid, and represents one way in which women have found ways of making their labour visible. As the next section shows, this is not the first time that housewives have fought back.

Irish Housewife of the Year: Passive housewives or pushing back?

The hugely popular annual event Irish Housewife of the Year ran in Ireland from 1968 and was televised from 1982 to 1995. From 1978 the event was sponsored by Calor gas making the commercial interests of the show apparent. The event invited 'ordinary' Irish housewives to enter the competition for a chance to win a cash prize. Women were given the opportunity to demonstrate their cooking prowess and other domestic skills, all under the watchful eye of the popular Irish television presenter Gay Byrne who compered the televised event. Watching video footage of the 1993 show today makes for uneasy viewing. Byrne's tone is gentle but patronising, on the one hand appearing to show an interest in the domestic skills of the housewives, but on the other hand devoting much of his opening interviews with contestants to amusing stories about marriage and courtship. Throughout there is a celebratory focus on the family. The male presenter is omnipresent and the co-presence of a male judge, who also presents the winner with a sash and large cellophane-clad bouquet of flowers, is a stark reminder of how, although this is a competition about and ostensibly 'for' women, it is men who control the narratives. This is true not just in the screening and production of the show itself but also within the wider patriarchal political context of Ireland at the time. Irish Housewife of the Year, right up until its 1993 finale, took place against a broad cultural and social climate of particularly regressive policies around women and domestic life. The Irish Constitution, for example, still makes reference to the assumption of domestic roles as the core occupation of women, effectively limiting freedom of choice, making assumptions about the heteronormativity of the family and including no mention whatsoever of the duties of fathers. In December 2023, the Irish government approved a referendum on a proposal to amend the constitution to remove Article 41.2, first written in 1937, which promised that the state will 'endeavour to ensure that mothers shall not be obliged by economic necessity to engage in labour to the neglect of their duties in the home'.[10]

Until 1973, Irish women's freedom of choice was further curtailed by the 'marriage bar' that required women civil servants and wider public sector workers to leave their jobs upon marriage. The state had thus created a situation enshrined within the constitution where women were not only constrained by rigid gendered norms around their roles as unpaid domestic labourers but were also rendered economically dependent on their husbands. By officially classifying women as 'dependents', this often had the effect of leaving women with nothing if their husbands refused to hand any money over.[11] In *Women and Poverty*, Mary Daly notes that by the late 1980s, women's share of family welfare payments were usually only 60 per cent, but that this was never guaranteed since it was entirely dependent on the goodwill and discretion of husbands.[12]

This state-sanctioned curtailing of women's lives helps us to make sense of the huge popular appeal of Irish Housewife of the Year and other, more contemporary digital configurations of the housewife. Irish Housewife of the Year, with its seemingly one-dimensional focus on women as wives, mothers and domestic workers, is often dismissed as a retrograde and best-forgotten part of Ireland's popular cultural history. Yet such an account dismisses the experiences of many Irish women whose lives were of course curtailed by heavily gendered state policy but who were not victims or dupes without any say in how they portrayed their lives and labour. The contestants were always more than simply 'lovely girls'.[13] There was, for example, a commercial interest in taking part in the competition, not just for the television channel and producers but also for the contestants themselves. Winners – and also sometimes runners up – were often granted marketing, sponsorship and promotional work, in addition to a Calor cooker or a year's supply of Calor gas. Women crowned 'Irish Housewife of the Year' were also often invited onto the popular *Calor Housewives Cookery* television show featuring past winners, offering live demonstrations and showcasing their recipes.

It is easy to dismiss the competition as a relic of a sexist bygone age, fuelled by a particularly conservative, religious Irish patriarchy. However, at a time when women's lives were regularly unmarked, and their contribution to domestic life particularly underacknowledged, it is perhaps unsurprising that so many women wanted to take part in a competition that brought their private, domestic labour into the public and shone a light onto their hitherto overlooked skills. A deeper understanding of the motivations of the women themselves, who were so ready to take part in the annual, flamboyant and highly public spectacle of the Irish Housewife of the Year, might reframe participation as a way of pushing back against the endless devaluing of housework. Reliance on 'partial payments' given to married women by their husbands had understandably put a great number of women into vulnerable positions. Irish Housewife of the Year offered one means to combat the invisibility of domestic labour and the expectation that it is conducted with no moral or economic support.

'We get absolutely nothing'

Resistance to the long positioning of housework as 'non-work' came from women in other ways too. The Women in the Home (WITH) campaign, for example, was founded in 1982 to combat the lack of 'moral' or economic support that housewives received.[14] In a 1986 interview with the group's founder, Nora Gilligan, a self-described housewife from the Dublin suburbs, she expresses her frustration with the ways that the role of housewife has been 'downgraded' and positioned as 'non-working' women, gaining little to no legal, economic or moral acknowledgement of the contribution of those who stay at home. For groups such as WITH, this perceived injustice adds to the pressure on women to leave the home, devaluing the idea that for many, housework is a 'way of life'. Describing housework as playing a vital role to the family and society, and as 'a stabilising influence on the family and on the community as a whole', Gilligan advocates for increased legal rights and status for women in the home and discusses her plans to bring the group's influence all the way to the European Economic Community. She is palpably furious that her work and her decision to stay at home is increasingly devalued, and crucially that there is no financial reward for 'home-workers'. 'Our husbands', she says, 'are contributing to social welfare. We get absolutely nothing.' As with the Irish Housewife of the Year, with no legal right to an income and their work continuously devalued, women sought other ways to resist, and in the case of WITH to 'organise ourselves'. The emphasis throughout is placed firmly on 'the job' of the housewife. In the absence of adequate communal and community support and accessible, affordable childcare, it is understandable that women became frustrated that the work that they were doing for free in this regard – including providing emotional support to children, looking after the home, etc. – was so routinely devalued and ignored.

It is thus easy to see how the opportunity to make visible and to gain financial reward for domestic skills and labour, and the opportunity to advance their own narratives of hitherto invisible domestic labour, would have seemed appealing. Yet in the examples above, narratives, agency and political organising around housework are often lost beneath the commercial and patriarchal framing of housework. In the case of Irish Housewife of the Year, women are paraded in front of male television presenters and judges to both discuss and be assessed on their domestic prowess, with the main line of questioning regularly turning towards family life and marriage: 'Tell us about how you met your husband.' Meanwhile, the male journalist who interviewed Nora Gilligan from the WITH campaign endlessly attempts to focus Gilligan's palpable frustration towards 'radical feminists'. Gilligan's comments around legal frameworks and state support for housework are swiftly deflected so that, instead, the conversation turns to feminism, and in particular the popular distortion of feminism that suggests feminists have pressured women to go out to work and have ignored the contribution of women who stay at home. 'Are you saying to the radical feminists "get knotted"?', she is asked mischievously.

This patriarchal and anti-feminist framing of housework has a double-edged consequence. First, it positions inequalities of house-work as a *choice*, and second, it implies that the solution to painful feelings of exhaustion, financial hardship and invisibility often associated with housework is to resist calling for changes to unequal structures. In the 1980s, rapid social change increasingly came to be associated with supporting yourself and finding one's own solutions to external problems. Against this backdrop of early neoliberal framing it is easy to see why the popular representation of housewives as entrepreneurial, anti-feminist and ultimately *willing* participants in unequal domestic practices proved popular. Although she might include a witty rebuke of her husband, who doesn't do much around the house and gains some visibility and possibly financial gain from her usually unpaid labour, the popular housewife of the 1980s ultimately left inequalities safely unchallenged.

We see above some examples of housewife activism and organisa-tion. These stop short of constituting 'uprisings' given the lack of challenge they pose to established power structures or inequalities of domestic labour; however, they help to reveal the agency of housewives that is so often ignored in popular dismissals of brainless, oppressed housewives. It is clear from the activities of both WITH and Irish Housewife of the Year that housewives historically have organised and fought for the visibility of their domestic skills and reframed themselves as educators with discernible sets of skills. Of course, this isn't new – from Mrs Beeton onwards, the twentieth century is full of examples of women reframing their domestic labour as technical, even scientific skills. Martens and Scott argue that technological advances and the scientific skills of housework, for example the renaming of it as 'domestic science', not only helped to make housework appear to be a technical skill but was also a way of giving it the extra academic status and gravitas that might have appealed to middle-class parents and their daughters.[15]

This ideology was consolidated in the 1980s, with Margaret Thatcher explicitly courting housewives on her campaign trial, beginning in the late 1970s. This is an important historical moment because it helped to consolidate the idea of the savvy, consuming, knowing housewife, who is able to cultivate a happy home for her family while gaining personal value, status and happiness in the process. Previous popular accounts of housework had tended to focus on either presenting an impossibly ephemeral image of the housewife – unattainable in her perfection – or as downtrodden and exploited. The dramatic shift from production to consumer economies required popular support that Thatcher sought to achieve by speaking directly to housewives, simultaneously advocating for individual solutions to the everyday impacts of everyday problems.

In 1978 a *Daily Mail* women's supplement featured an interview with Margaret Thatcher, soon to be the British Prime Minister and the first woman leader of the Conservative Party.[16] From the outset, the interview sidesteps politics, a fact that is particularly ironic given the cataclysmic impact that Thatcherite policies would have on the everyday lives of women, the reverberations of which would be felt for generations. And yet 'politics', says Barbara Henderson, the journalist who conducts the interview, 'will be forbidden'; rather, 'it is Margaret Thatcher, woman, wife and mother I have come to talk to'. The interview is a fascinating précis into the state of gender relations in the late 1970s. Women, including the soon-to-be Prime

Minister, are reduced to their domestic labour and child-rearing abilities and importantly their ability to calmly and efficiently absorb and resolve the stresses and strains of everyday life. We see a very visible shift towards a new, highly personal and individual focus on savvy and worthy women who can absorb and handle any crisis that comes their way, or, as Thatcher describes it, using womanly domestic skills to patch things up when 'anything is going wrong': 'You know, dear, when anything is going wrong, I'm the one who is still calm and just getting on with it. It's characteristic of many a woman.'[17]

Thatcher's political campaigning spoke, often for the first time, directly to women's lives and experiences within the home. On the campaign trail in 1979, for example, she was famously photographed holding up two bags of groceries, one half-full and the other bulging at the seams; a visual illustration of the effects of inflation between 1974 and 1979 under the Labour government. Similarly, domestic photos of her doing the dishes in her apron in her Chelsea home or ironing her husband Denis's shirts became as commonplace as formal Downing Street or House of Commons shots. This repositioning of the willing housewife as acquiring value and status with women who 'get on with it' is lauded. For Thatcher, 'the enemy within' didn't just extend to trade unions but also arguably to 'women's libbers' intent on dismantling gender inequalities, especially around the domestic sphere. Borrowing from the strategies of relatability adopted by her closest ally, the ex-Hollywood film star US President Ronald Reagan, Thatcher introduced the importance of inviting voters to see the 'real' woman behind the politics. She offered an opportunity for women to hear and see themselves reflected in the stories of social mobility (from grocer's daughter to 10 Downing Street) and to take pride in domestic roles and responsibilities, in supporting personal and familial aspiration via domestic thrift, in household management and in curating homeliness against the chaos of the outside world.

In the 1978 interview, Thatcher adopts a relatable but authoritative tone, quite distinct from the politicians that came before here, but one that today has become commonplace among digital social media influencers. Describing a daydream of her perfect home, she says, 'I'd love a large kitchen. If I had money, if I really had a lot of money, I would like to build the sort of house that I want to suit my type of life.' Discourses around aspiration, consumerism, personal responsibility and women's roles became increasingly entrenched during this time, and maintaining a 'respectable' status manifested itself for many as the struggle to run a visibly respectable home. As Bev Skeggs has also noted, in late capitalist societies, 'homes and bodies are where class is lived out in the most omnipresent form'.[18] In the 1980s, the idea that home was central to the family's display of wellbeing, status, aspiration and respectability was galvanised. Having a clean, tidy, well-decorated and well-furnished home thus became one of the hallmarks of respectability, with women expected to shoulder the labour necessary to achieve this.

What we see during this time is the birth of a new type of 'magical femininity' and the beginnings of the popular narrative of women keeping things going, often in very depleted post-industrial economic conditions. The interview reminds us that keeping things going, sweeping up the mess and fallout of crisis, or what Sheila Rowbotham calls the 'rags and bones of capitalism', has long been perceived as a job for women. Moreover, what we see in the 1980s is a period where women are given a central space and new sense of visibility for their concerns, but without the prospect of any real change. Beatrix Campbell calls this the 'politics of paternalism'; a marking of responsibility and duty while removing any power to transform. Thatcher centred and made visible the domesticity that was already being performed by women but simultaneously reaffirmed housework as 'women's work'. Her interviews reveal a set of affirming and relatable ways of speaking about housework while ignoring its solitude, thanklessness and wageless, monotonous and mind-numbing facets, and remaining silent about the existence of poverty, exploitation and racism that accompany women's experiences of domestic labour. Thus, Campbell argues that the 'housewife is worked into Thatcher's representation of the "national interest": she is seen as an isolated, free-standing citizen, with no affiliations or responsibilities other than to her own family'.[19] She is heroic, willing, steadfast and individual – connected to other housewives only insofar as she shares the same characteristics. What we see in the 1980s, then, is a revival of the notion of housework as a *moral* conviction and a renewed focus on the heroic housewife who single-handedly shoulders the burden and mops up the messy residue of capitalism. Women were inserted into political dialogues but only in ways that were assumed to be acceptable. Housework itself was granted a new status as a precious womanly skill in time management and economic efficiency that Thatcher jokes in a knowing way the men in Westminster are often lacking: 'Perhaps it takes a housewife to see that Britain's national housekeeping is appalling.'[20]

'As every housewife knows'

The Organised Mum Method will give you a structure. You won't suddenly find yourself with a few spare minutes and panic about how you can use them to your best advantage. You now have a list and a system and you will tick everything off as you go along.[21]

No book about contemporary representations of housework would be complete without a discussion of Gemma Bray, otherwise known as 'The Organised Mum'.[22] Bray founded The Organised Mum Method or TOMM in 2017 and at the time of writing has a popular Instagram account with 260,000 followers, along with a bestselling book of the same name. Her approach to housework differs from the other cleanfluencers discussed in the book in two key ways. First, her regularly updated Instagram stories are structured like educational videos. We generally only see Bray's head and shoulders talking to the camera where she sits in front of a neon 'Just be yourself!' sign. She looks serious rather than light-hearted and fun, wearing glasses with straight, neatly blow-dried, bobbed hair. Her glamour is understated and she doesn't share the same sort of personal anecdotes or videos and pictures of her family that have become commonplace among other cleanfluencers. Although we occasionally see a snapshot into Bray's large, clean and tidy home and garden in the London suburbs, we never see her actually doing any housework. Instead, her role feels instructional – a sort of friendly bossiness as she

gives her advice on how to keep on top of the housework to her
followers.

Bray is relatable in a different way. Her live video streams and
stories address a different 'real life' housework dilemma each time,
all beginning with a tale intended to speak to the everyday demands
of housework placed on busy followers. Bray's guidelines for dealing
with housework dilemmas are always instructional, advocating a
rigid timetable, organisation and management of the housework
that is intended to present a rational solution for the complex
demands of domestic labour. TOMM offers a different approach to
cleaning to the cleanfluencers discussed previously. Although there
are still a few upbeat positive affirmations – such as the 'Just be
yourself!' sign – the idea perpetuated in other corners of cleanfluencing culture that housework is mindful or good for the soul or that
it enhances personal wellbeing is rejected. Instead TOMM begins
from the premise that housework is recognised as an annoying but
necessary set of tasks, with 'organised mums' – those who follow
Bray's method and are savvy enough to leave time for the 'fun stuff'
– best placed to navigate them. Alluding to the stresses and strains
of housework, its 'treadmill' nature and its 'drudgery', Bray encourages
her followers to get with the plan and banish housework before it
interferes with the ability to have fun and 'to live'. It is unclear
what is meant by 'getting out there and living' but the positioning
of housework as the opposite of freedom and pleasure is interesting
and different from other digital representations of housework. Instead,
housework is presented as a chore and a bore that needs to be swept
away as quickly and efficiently as possible. In her 'Monday morning
musings', Bray addresses her followers:

> I know it might seem like we are on a constant treadmill of domestic
> drudgery but there is so much more that you are capable of, so much
> more fun that you could be having and so much life out there for
> you to live. Let's get the housework done and dusted early and then
> let's get out there and live. Because there is more to life than house-
> work. Lots of love Gem x.

Bray's account epitomises a kind of post-Fordist housewifery with
an emphasis on maximising productive efficiency, clearing the way

for personal freedoms and pleasure. In this way, housework itself is not associated with self-fulfilment, as it is with Mrs Hinch; rather, self-fulfilment comes from an efficient eradication of the daily domestic load. There is no mention within TOMM of cleaning as fun, rewarding and good for mental health and wellbeing as with the other cleanfluencers discussed so far. Instead, Bray offers a space where she confides with her followers, sharing the often unspoken knowledge that housework is tedious and that no one really wants to do it. 'Reminder', she writes, 'you were *not* put on this earth to just *cook* and *clean.*' TOMM offers a type of Gina Ford style efficiency to housework; Gemma will teach you the tricks and skills necessary to get it out of the way as quickly and efficiently as possible, leaving time for the fun stuff and promising to leave the weekend free for those who follow the plan. Motivational language around 'blitzing those housework tasks', being a 'cleaning whizz' and offering to be a 'personal trainer for housework' alludes to feminist ideals of independence and freedom from domestic drudgery, while contradictorily instructing thousands of mainly women followers to adhere to a rigid plan of housework efficiency.

The front cover of Gemma Bray's book, *The Organised Mum Method*, features a pop art style cartoon image of Bray with glossy hair and shining red lips, winking through long eyelashes. The cover design offers a perhaps ironic nod and a knowing wink to the followers who are in on her secret. The pop art style cover design feels like a kitsch version of Lichtenstein's iconic images of disappointed 1960s housewives constrained by the walls of domestic suffering. The knowingness comes from Bray's constant rejection of the idea that housework can make you happy. TOMM, then, is not so much about dismissing the 1950s ideal of the perfectly organised home but about recasting the role of the housewife responsible for creating it as hyper-efficient and able to enjoy the fruits of her labour, freeing up time 'to get on with the fun stuff in life'.

In addition, TOMM does not include multiple product placements, commercial partnerships or discount codes, which is unusual in the world of cleanfluencing. In fact, cleaning products themselves rarely feature at all. Instead, it is the 'method' that is for sale. In addition to the successful books and Instagram account, TOMM offers 'guided housework' projects via printable worksheets, guided cleaning sessions and podcasts. Starting in September, there is also a weekly 'Organised Christmas' checklist, designed to avoid the stress of last minute preparations and planning. All tips, lists and plans are designed to maximise housework efficiency; a clean and tidy home in just thirty minutes a day. There are multiple reminders on TOMM that 'there is more to life than housework', and the uplifting 'Rock the Housework' podcasts and '20 minute company sessions for you to chip away at the ironing' promise to make domestic chores more bearable by adding music and 'company'.

TOMM promises to make housework easy, at least for those who are efficient enough and are doing it properly, leaving time for fun and freedom. Ultimately though, the message embedded in the title, that housework is women's ('mum's') work, sidesteps the politics of housework. An asterisk on the front cover of the TOMM book in small font – '*and organised dads!' – references the inequalities of housework as an afterthought that is left unchallenged.

Ultimately, TOMM, for all its promises of a fresh approach to housework, is a rearticulation of decades-old practices, long embedded in the focus on helping women to 'be better' at holding it all together rather than reducing the domestic burden. Within TOMM, grinning and bearing it through the hard work and multiple, often impossible to achieve and conflicting demands are venerated. This is evident in abundance throughout contemporary popular culture, such as in Paris Fury's autobiography *How Does She Do It?* The book promises to share the secrets of Fury's skills in creating order at home up against a particularly chaotic, complex domestic situation:

> Paris Fury can pack a week into everyone else's day. So how does she do it? Looking after six children, keeping house, while being there for her World Heavyweight husband Tyson, still looking amazing – and finding time for herself – is just a shortlist of what she manages. A lot can go wrong and often does, but Paris takes it all in her stride.[23]

'How does she do it?', 'superwoman', 'miracle worker', even 'faultless' have become common descriptors of women in contemporary society. Superhuman qualities are celebrated and used as compliments towards women who seemingly achieve the impossible while looking happy, glossy and uncomplaining throughout. That life is often difficult, rarely straightforward, imperfect and often imbued with failure is all the more important because this helps to narrate a more compelling tale of survival, tenacity, superhuman household management skills and hyper-efficiency. Women within popular cleanfluencing narratives such as TOMM are firmly located as chief arbiters of the domestic sphere; as endless takers and organisers of shit and mess who can solve anything and respond and protect no matter how great the crisis. The huge popular success of the digital cleanfluencer in the midst of a coalescence of multiple crises, including the cost-of-living economic crisis, the climate emergency and COVID-19 pandemic, is no coincidence. Rather, the regulatory frameworks of capitalism render cleanfluencing an entirely logical response to the crisis of capitalism; a response which of course carries little to no scope or space for the imagination or the advancement of alternatives. If anything, cleanfluencing proposes the opposite – an almost total avoidance of interrogation or challenge to the norms of domestic labour.

Women thus hold together the threads of crisis capitalism. Moreover, they must look great while they do so; don't complain, don't make it look hard, do it with a smile and always with humour and grace. These expectations are compounded by the habitually entrenched and familiar ethic 'work smart not hard' that is reinforced both at home and work.[24] In other words, the creation of perfection must also be effortless, its breezy aesthetic standing as proof of the curator's efficiency, drive and hard work. Cleanfluencing, as we have seen with the example of TOMM, offers multiple invitations to achieve this. '*Clean* smarter not harder' suggests Gemma Bray on the TOMM Instagram account in a neat variation of the 'work smart not hard' mantra. It serves as a reminder that any overwhelm or exhaustion must be down to personal inefficiency rather than societal expectations of overwork and perfection.

Gender inequalities in the home thus remain stubbornly naturalised and unchallenged. As with TOMM, the frustration and thankless drudgery of the domestic load is sometimes articulated but never directly challenged.

It's only me who notices

The majority of housework is still done by women. Where men make a contribution they tend to 'help'.[25]

Yet social media is also used at times to directly articulate the injustices at the heart of domestic labour. In 2023, the social media influencer Cat Sims (@notsosmugnow) wrote a deeply heartfelt article reflecting on the frustration of being solely responsible for the domestic burden and particularly the 'mental load'. Cleanfluencers often use social media as a way of relating to the frustration around the sheer invisibility of the mental load that accompanies housework. 'Mental load' is certainly part of the popular lexicon,[26] and it is increasingly reflected in cleanfluencing content. In her purchasable worksheets, 'The Mental Load List', Sims describes the mental load as feeling 'like you're the swan and I'm the f*cking legs'. It is, we are promised, 'the list you've all been waiting for', enabling followers to 'get the mental load out of your head and onto paper. Edit it to suit you. Delegate the shit out of it.' The list is intended to assist with 'difficult conversations' around the mental load by naming each domestic task and offering suggestions for having constructive conversations around the unequal distribution of the mental load while avoiding 'toxic habits':

It's also designed to show the people you love exactly what the mental load is and what it consists of so that you can have constructive conversations about how to manage it better. It should help you delegate some of this stuff and you need to be ok with things being done in a slightly different way if necessary. Accept the help.[27]

As with the quote above from *Feminist Mothers* by Tuula Gordon published over three decades ago, today cleanfluencers at times express similar frustration with the unequal division of domestic labour: 'He just doesn't see the dirt!' In 1990, the solution was often radical – at times even used as a precursor to separatism. In 2023, cleanfluencers often wittily, sometimes painfully, articulate the stress of the second shift and their frustration and anger with the misogyny and lack of equality in sharing domestic tasks. And yet the solution is personal, to be found within the confines of inter-personal relationships and always disconnected from the historical context of domestic inequalities. To overlook the historical context of the gendered inequalities of domestic labour is a mistake because it is key to making sense of the fact that for women, worth and value has long been bound up with one's ability to perform domestic labour. Historically seen as a valueless, non-economic and non-productive activity and therefore not the 'natural order' of masculinity, it is unsurprising that men don't appear to carry the same mental load and that recognising, struggling with and looking for ways to overcome the problem of injustice and inequalities within the home remains the role of women. Carefully dividing up the mental load while avoiding conflict is yet another job to add to the domestic 'to-do' list.

As the popular, glossy, social media activism centred on the celebrity of the influencer, whose content is often heavily curated and peppered with lucrative paid partnership deals, repeatedly remind us, failing at the housework – the juggling, the mental load, the double shift, etc. – is fine, even normal, but it is women's responsibility to fix it. Inequalities affect women the most but ironically it is women who are repeatedly tasked with finding solutions to them. In her discussion of the 'female complaint', Lauren Berlant argues that neoliberal feminist discourses tend to reject overt exclamations of female unhappiness; frustration and a sense of injustice are rarely welcomed and they 'broadly by and large repudiate[s] female suffering, disappointment and complaint. They render such negative effects abhorrent, uninhabitable and unimaginable.'[28] What we see in the contemporary popular digital depictions of housework is *some* articulation of suffering, and a frequent recounting of 'failures', such as @notsosmugnow describing her marriage almost breaking down because of the stress of the mental load, but always with a happy ending – as the magical femininity and hyper-efficiency that comes to the rescue. As Lyndsey Crombie (the Queen of Clean) asserts in a 2023 Instagram post – 'Delegate!': 'Running a home is all about teamwork. If you are feeling overwhelmed with your household chores, DELEGATE! Do NOT feel pressured to do everything at home yourself. Looking after the home is all about TEAMWORK.'

Thus, cleanfluencers sometimes offer a type of 'pushing back', not only by offering – possibly for the first time – an intimate and highly visual display of the nitty-gritty of housework but also by insisting, as TOMM does, that housework should not be your 'sole' purpose, that housework can be lonely and boring, that housework can be overwhelming and that the inequalities of the mental load are unjust. But the solution remains the same – to get better at it. Take hold of the reins and organise your relationship and your home, take control of the domestic load, make a list, become more efficient in your labour, get it done, delegate, ask for 'help', *just do it!*

Why does it matter?

The recent focus within cleanfluencing cultures centres on both articulating the stresses of the mental load and offering guidelines to lighten it by taking the time to delegate tasks to others. In one sense, this appears to offer up a means of disrupting the gendered norms of domestic labour by pushing hitherto invisible, unrecognised and unrewarded domestic labour practices to the fore. The recent popular appeal of these accounts is palpable, and yet these fresh articulations of housework are also notable for the ways in 'which they cannot fully move beyond [the] logics'[29] of the cult of the housewife that merges with confidence culture to form a dangerous, highly restrictive discourse whereby avenues to meaningful transformation are endlessly blocked. What we see in cleanfluencing cultures are a set of confidence, self-help narratives that are powerful, persuasive and seductive enough to render refusal nigh on unthinkable and impossible to imagine. Thus, while we see flashes of anger, frustration and resentment at the pressures of the domestic load and women's uneven role in taking responsibility for it, resistance is 'partial and uneven', with the challenge to inequalities being remade along neoliberal lines.[30]

As we saw in Chapter 2, earlier feminist responses to gendered inequalities of housework need to be understood within the context of pre-neoliberal cultures whereby the obsessive and impenetrable focus on the individual and personal responsibility for 'fixing' crises did not exist as it does today. As I discussed earlier in this chapter, this hyper-individual response to the heavy normative burden of domestic labour has its roots in the ideological shifts of the 1980s and in particular in Thatcher's courting of women housewives as worthy, savvy consumers. A new type of altruistic discourse speaks to the labour of housework – 'we see you' – but simultaneously venerates it, encouraging unfettered consumerism to help manage the domestic load, a steely determination to get the job done and, crucially, a reluctance to say no. As others have also argued,[31] this was central to Thatcher's battle for popular authority; a battle that was indisputably won and now rarely brought into question.

Today's new generation of social media influencers and cleanfluencers, who mostly have no recollection of pre-Thatcher or pre-neoliberalism, makes the task of finding the appropriate language to make sense of and to challenge domestic inequalities even more difficult. But we must try. Evidence suggests that younger people share a similar lack of ability to imagine or employ more flexible gender roles at home. Orgad notes a 2017 report by the non-profit, non-partisan American Council on Contemporary Families, where increasingly large numbers of Millennials *do not* support more egalitarian family arrangements.[32] The 'not good enough' social media message is embedded throughout the highly seductive but endlessly distracting TikTok reels perpetuating the enduring promise of the ultimate satisfaction that comes from a clean and tidy home. It is not just about the psychological effects of the not good enough message but also the impact of popular digital representations of housework as fundamentally women's work on gender inequalities more broadly, particularly in paid work. The expectation that women are the most adept at certain types of work – cleaning, caring, organising[33] – remains firmly entrenched and broadly unchallenged. As I have shown in this chapter, cleanfluencers often express frustration, pain and even anger with the misogyny and lack of equality in sharing domestic tasks. As we have seen, social media is awash with funny, witty, painful and ironic articulations of the stresses of the second shift which we are reminded remains stubbornly persistent. Yet there remains no discussion of alternatives, with the solution still firmly fixed within the heteronormative family and the unequal division of labour. In this sense, we see in the cleanfluencing accounts a type of muted and contained frustration and ironically a reproduction of the split between the home and domestic life versus public and economic productivity. Cleanfluencing, then, might also be seen as a way of making use of cultural narratives to disavow disappointment and fury and to mask, or at least restrain, the contradictions and frustrations inherent in the unfettered demands of domestic labour, such as the telling lockdown memes discussed in Chapter 1.

Addressing the stubborn persistence of inequalities around housework will only be possible if it is understood within the broad historical, cultural and economic contexts within which it exists. We need to take note of the ways in which economists since Adam Smith have long concluded that women's subordination is 'rational'. The task has been to persuade women of this in evolving, new and convincing ways, ideally stamping out dissent in the process. Thus, cleanliness for centuries has been consciously bound up with class-based respectability and seen as a key civilising practice. The tight association between a clean and tidy home and respectable femininity is further reflected in the fact that it is women who are most often blamed when things related to the home go wrong. Women are thus not only expected to *desire* to take control of the housework but are also scapegoated when the house is not deemed clean *enough*. As we have seen, this long-standing thread of surveillance and blame was exacerbated during the COVID-19 pandemic, with its renewed focus on germs, bacteria and the importance of cleanliness as literally central to survival.

In *For Her Own Good*, Ehrenreich and English argue that the mass marketisation of cleaning has long exploited the rigid cultural association between femininity, cleaning and 'worthiness', with the 'neglect of house cleaning ... tantamount to child abuse' and with advertisements 'play[ing] directly to maternal fears and guilt'.[34] Today, these standards are exacerbated within cleanfluencing culture via a new ultra-minimalist, extreme spotlessness and hyper-organised aesthetic.

The 'cruel optimism' of cleanfluencing

Historically, attempts to counteract inequalities around domestic labour and to debunk the cult of the housewife have been twofold: first, positioning housework *as work*, for example during the 1970s Wages for Housework campaign; and second, by making it visible, with a tangible *value* that fulfils clearly identifiable social needs, for example the Iceland women's strike. Recent interviews with Sheila Rowbotham and Hilary Wainwright describe a recent 'burying' of the radical histories of socialist feminism during the British Women's Liberation Movement.[35] This is compounded by the deep entrenchment of postfeminist ideals that coalesce with the principles of neoliberalism, particularly the ways in which today all human activity invites the naming of a *price* determined by a ruthless negotiation between the individual and the market.

The popularity of cleanfluencing cultures is a perfect example of the deep entrenchment of liberal feminist solutions to complex structural inequalities. Arruzza et al. discuss the impact of liberal feminism on culture, describing the corporate enthusiasm for 'diversity',[36] condemning 'discrimination' and enthusiastically advocating 'choice', all while it 'steadfastly refuses to address the socio-economic constraints that make freedom and empowerment impossible for the large majority of women' and, 'rather than seeking to abolish social hierarchy, it aims to "diversify" it, "empowering" "talented" women to rise to the top'.[37]

Cleanfluencing perfectly reflects the embedding of liberal feminism into popular culture. It is synonymous with an individualised approach to the domestic burden whereby individuals seek solutions to crisis capitalism by 'leaning inwards' – in the case of cleanfluencers, towards the home, building a cosy, soft and bacteria-free barrier between themselves, their families and the outside world. A type of corporate diversity is often embraced and promoted via unrelated cultural events, for example Pride-themed cleaning products during Pride Month or the inclusion of a post dedicated to cleanfluencers of colour during Black History Month on the Clean & Tidy Home Show Instagram account. Yet for all the promises of diversity, as we have seen, cleanfluencing culture focuses on the commercial success and 'empowerment' of a small number of chosen 'talented' women who are routinely celebrated, promoted and venerated. All the while, inequalities around domestic labour remain stubbornly unchanged globally, and the pressure on individual women to conform to increasingly rigid ideals of domestic femininity runs rampant.

And so within cleanfluencing cultures we witness an odd con-tradiction between a hyper-normative representation on the one hand, of women as 'happy housewives', and on the other a grinding reproduction of the mainstream liberal feminist language of empower-ment, diversity and choice. Sometimes, as with the 1990s Ikea advert discussed in Chapter 2, this also extends to co-opting feminist discourses, making feminist criticism of the cleanfluencing genre more complex.

A good example of this incongruous positioning of housework as both appealing and pleasurable, while at the same time unequal and unjust, is further illustrated at the 2023 Clean & Tidy Home Show. Alongside the usual stalls, 2023 saw the inclusion for the first time of a feminist 'craftivism' stall. The Domestic Dusters project curated by Vanessa Marr invites women to embroider a response to the question 'Women and Domesticity – What's Your Perspective?' onto a yellow duster. The duster collection was displayed at the show, where attendees were also invited to contribute a message of their own on a giant 'community sized' duster. Messages already in the collection vary from the heroic 'I am a member of a superhero group', to the invisible 'I care … do you?' and 'We are being swept under the carpet', to the importance of kindness as an impetus for sharing the domestic load: 'Kindness is important, share the chores.' Some of the messages displayed are undeniably feminist, offering a rallying call for a more equal division of domestic labour, raising the visibility of housework and taking the 'work' element of housework more seriously; others, I think, offer an ironic reference to tropes of 'kindness' and the 'superwoman' syndrome which I have discussed in previous chapters. The Domestic Dusters project taps into the feminist potential of subversive crafting.[38] For example, the medium for the display of the message – the ubiquitous yellow duster – which is pegged up for display on a washing line, and the red embroidery, references women's domestic skills: dusting, laundry and sewing. These activities, long associated with respectable, virtuous femininity, are then subverted into the embroidered statements of resistance.

The gallery of embroidered dusters offer a nod back to the second-wave British feminist campaigns which often included homemade banners featuring statements of resistance. To me, the recreation of the aesthetic style and also some of the sentiments of 1970s feminist campaign materials demonstrates an awareness of earlier debates around housework and the injustices of inequalities of the domestic load. One might look at the dusters and their embroidered messages and see seeds of resistance or at least an element of consciousness raising around who does what; a quiet protest against inequalities, a token gesture and an outlier within broader popular cleaning cultures, sure, but a gesture nonetheless. And yet, the incongruous setting of the Domestic Dusters gallery among the mass commerce, the heavily normative and gendered displays of cleaning and of course the mass celebration of cleanfluencing cultures blunts any meaningful disruption of entrenched structural inequalities.

Instead, we see a type of 'girl powering' of cleaning,[39] whereby multiple, highly individualised depictions of cleaning – in this case a space to embroider your thoughts on a duster – obscures the lived experiences and the unequal conditions and structures of the domestic load. Like the witty lockdown memes discussed in Chapter 1, Domestic Dusters, when placed within the context of a cleanfluencing event such as the Clean & Tidy Home Show, offers a type of temporary light-touch and feel-good conversation around inequalities without highlighting or addressing the structural fabric of these inequalities.

The interchangeable way in which cleaning is positioned as both personal fulfilment and agency and an unequal and unjust domestic practice works to fuel the authenticity and appeal of the cleanfluencers. Although we all know, see and feel the inequality, sometimes acutely, any protest is carefully curtailed and rendered palatable. Occasional references to the awareness of inequalities around housework also helps to embolden the claim, reinforced in cleanfluencing cultures, that women have authority over their choices and that their participation in the machinery of cleanfluencing simply reflects their autonomous decision making. In common with other forms of contemporary popular culture, cleanfluencing offers, as Lauren Berlant describes, a type of 'cruel optimism'; the cultivating of desires that ultimately stand in the way of a flourishing selfhood.[40] Within cleanfluencing cultures, we see a compartmentalising of frustration without any real resistance; a carefully restrained, polite, unthreatening and, as Rottenberg dubs it, 'defanged' feminism.[41]

Backlash? 'Team work makes the dream work!'

Where next? What happened to the critiques of housework that were such a cornerstone of feminist activism? At the beginning of this chapter, I sketched some of the early feminist campaigns around home and domestic labour. I showed how, as the decades have worn on and neoliberal consumer culture has tightened its grip, political responses to unequal domestic loads have tended to offer: first, individual solutions; second, blaming feminists for taking away choice and 'judging' others; third, an increase in leaning in and outsourcing domestic labour; and forth, transforming cleaning into a lifestyle choice and type of self-care. All of which offer a type of acknowledgement of inequality but a neat sidestepping of the socio-economic structures that give rise to it. We can contrast this with earlier feminist demands for *social* change that linked the unequal experiences of women in the domestic sphere with wider political and ideological structures. This is clearly epitomised in the 1970s women's liberation campaign posters which, in contrast to individual messages of frustration, directly linked the exploitation of women's domestic labour to the cogs of capitalist labour production. For example, a red screen-print poster made by the Red Women's Workshop in 1976 presents an image of the 'split woman', her work as an assembly line worker devalued in equal measure to her unpaid domestic labour. The images of women cooking, cleaning, ironing, looking after children and labouring on an assembly line under a ticking clock are presented alongside the slogan: 'A Woman's Work is Never Done'. Another poster, also made by the Red Women's Workshop in 1979, entitled 'My message to the women of our nation … ' includes an image of Margaret Thatcher rubbing her hands gleefully with a speech bubble that reads, 'Tough!' Around the image of Thatcher are various newspaper clippings depicting Conservative cuts that disproportionately affected women. The homemade zine quality of the posters is a direct contrast to the shiny commercialisation that was simultaneously emerging at the time.

The seduction of commercialisation, combined with rampant individualism, has gradually drowned out dissenting voices around the expectation of women and domestic labour. The grassroots consciousness-raising initiatives and collectives of the 1970s had helped to embed new discourses around the inequalities and injustices of housework into popular, collective forms of resistance and protest. Yet today, the incorporation of feminist discourses of equality into cleanfluencing discourses has led to an anti-feminist, highly conservative repackaging of notions of gendered injustice in the home. For example, the recently popularised hashtag 'team work makes the dream work!' in posts, depicting cleanfluencers involving their partners in the cleaning and tidying, supposedly advocates an equal share of the tasks. Yet the cleanfluencing 'star' is almost always a woman, posts depicting men doing the housework remain rare and, crucially, men are very rarely depicted cleaning alone – usually they are there to 'help out' their female partner. When men do appear, their images are generally accompanied by affirmations of love and gratitude – 'helping out' positioned as an extraordinary act of love and kindness rather than as part of the mundane daily reality of housework. The 'team work makes the dream work!'

posts are almost always accompanied with responses from female followers that reiterate the 'problem' (the unequal domestic load) while situating the solution at home within the confines of inter-personal relationships: 'So nice to see this, can he train mine!', 'He's a good helper. I don't think Mr C has changed a bed for the last 10 years!', 'I need my husband to watch this for motivation lol', 'Can I borrow him sometime?' The messages are peppered with lots of laughing emojis and hearts.

Cleanfluencing cultures actively embrace images of happy house-wives at work. By doing so, cleanfluencers engage in an act of possibly unwitting rebellion against feminist orthodoxies that have long posited that the mass exploitation of women's domestic labour is a core form of collective unhappiness. As the interview with the woman from the WITH campaign earlier on in the chapter also demonstrates, from the 1980s, popular images of the housewife began to be reoriented specifically towards a thinly veiled attack on feminists and women who refuse narrow definitions of themselves as housewives. This never opens up wider collective discussions about how best to challenge inequalities. Sara Ahmed cites Darla Shine's book *Happy Housewives* as a pre-social media example of embracing 'domestic privilege' and a simultaneous rejection of feminist interventions: 'Being home in a warm, comfy house floating around in your pyjamas and furry slippers while sipping coffee as your babies play on the floor and your hubby works to pay for it all is not desperation. Grow up! Shut up! Count your blessings!'[42]

Shine's demand that women shut up and suck it up, presum-ably by rejecting feminist articulations of the injustices and wide exploitation of women's unpaid labour, written almost twenty years ago, appear to have been not only met but penetrated on a previously unthinkably wide scale within popular narratives of housework. Counting your blessings, not complaining, cracking on with the chores in the most efficient and instrumental way possible are part of the fabric of cleanfluencing culture and today run almost completely unchallenged. As we have seen, public declarations of happiness, gratitude and pride are key to being a successful cleanfluencer. In 2023, expressions of housework that explicitly *reject* the unhappy housewife, dissatisfied with her lot, are commonplace. Take, for example, the well-used cleanfluencing quotes, 'I am grateful for: house to clean = safe place to live; laundry = clothes to wear; dirty dishes = food to eat', and 'this home has endless love and laundry.' I may have a never-ending pile of laundry but how can I complain about that when I am surrounded by love?

In other words, the existence of housework is reframed as a privilege – that it exists at all is presented as evidence of one's success and worth as a neoliberal citizen. Repeated expressions of gratitude, counting ones blessings, giving and receiving love, etc., mean that there is no need to either mourn losses or imagine alternatives. By adjusting to the unequal world and conditions that have been offered and indeed the conditions to which we often become accustomed, we lose, as Sara Ahmed argues, a sense of 'other possible ways of living'. The painful reality of recognising and mourning these alternative ways of living means that, in order to remain well adjusted, 'it can be easier to avoid recognition' at all.[43]

The enthusiastic embracing of domestic orthodoxies that is so notable in cleanfluencing cultures effectively silences feminist claims around the happy housewife fantasy and the collective suffering that lingers in the impossible, contradictory and exploitative demands on women within the domestic sphere. Today, the digital housewife has an additional burden. Not only must she enthusiastically embrace housework as a route to personal and familial betterment but, in addition, she must also carefully cultivate, curate and reproduce this image. In today's social media world where people often create their own content, the reproduction of the popular image of the content housewife falls to women themselves. What we see then, in place of the backlash against rigid gendered norms of domestic labour that came earlier, is a freshly glamorised version of housework that rejects the desires reflected in a feminism of alternatives – such as the 'overthinking' described in Chapter 4 that will only make you unhappy – instead embracing the domestic load and inequity, ultimately adjusting her public, digital image to fit with this ortho-doxy. Cleanfluencing does offer a type of solidarity – one where you can laugh, complain, cry and even sometimes say no – but only at carefully considered, appropriate intervals. Rather than building on collective experiences to open up possibilities and imagine radical alternatives, cleanfluencing offers its followers a glaringly narrow set of possibilities and a reluctance to imagine what might lie beyond the familiarity of the traditional, heavily gendered division of domestic labour.

Feminists have long emphasised the dual repercussions of the domestic load as it simultaneously helps to support the continuing functioning of capitalist market economies while also hindering women's ability to actively participate in radical politics. They recognised that the solution to the exhausting domestic burden for women had to be collective. And it is this recognition of the impera-tive of collective solutions to the 'housework problem', alongside the increasingly intensive, individualistic nature of cleanfluencing, and the endless promise of commercial solutions (as discussed in Chapter 1), that has meant that the idea of collective solutions to addressing domestic disparity has all but disappeared from popular discourse.

And yet there are some green shoots. Drawing on the television makeover trend of which cleanfluencing is a more contemporary (and digital) example, Micki McGee imagines that the desire for self-improvement might ultimately be 'appropriated for embracing progressive ends'.[44] Lynne Segal, meanwhile, advocates a move to reclaim the revolutionary power of the collective which has been curtailed by the rapid expansion of 'commercial values and interests' that have pulled apart collectives, as people increasingly seek individual and commercial, rather than collective, solutions for social problems.[45] As any cursory glance at the second-wave women's movement reminds us, there is great joy, happiness and *relief* to be had from collective agendas. Segal notes the 'revolutionary power' of collective joy and the relief to be had from realising that unhap-piness, exhaustion, anxiety, etc. are not simply individual pathologies or personal inefficiencies and failings but also the result of a highly unequal society where the odds are stacked against you.

Conclusion

In this chapter, I have shown how cleanfluencing neatly embodies neoliberal feminist principles of choice and empowerment by facilitating a sense of agency over choices combined with personal desire and centuries-old normative principles of the happy and willing housewife as synonymous with respectable feminine virtues. Increased attempts to 'diversify' cleanfluencing culture do not cancel out the ways that excessive cleaning and tidying and the impossible demands of the immaculate, effortlessly clean and tidy home are ruthlessly promoted alongside seemingly unlimited opportunities to purchase mass-produced consumer goods. High-profile cleanfluencing success stories sell an aspirational dream of happiness, fame, fortune and popular success and the repeated promise to lighten the domestic load. This is all deemed possible from within the rigid confines of a freshly reworked, glamorous digital housewife persona.

The priority must be to uncouple, finally, housework from entrenched ideals of normative 'respectable' femininity and the idea that worthiness has its roots in the ubiquitous display of the perfectly ordered, clean home. Cleanfluencing culture, for all its rhetoric around cleaning 'communities', stands in the way of a radical, alternative and *collective* response to the prevailing inequalities and injustices of domestic labour. Such resistance might help to reduce the domestic burden and impossible standards. A meaningful challenge to current gender inequality would need to oscillate around, first, a loosening of expectations and, second, rather than continuing to *oblige* certain norms, a need to subject them to scrutiny and deliberation. This would ensure that it is norms and expectations that are under the spotlight and subject to surveillance and scrutiny rather than homes and bodies, as remains the case on popular social media.

Conclusion: Killing housework

There can even be joy in killing joy. And kill joy, we must and we do.[1]

You have made this working mummy feel so much better that the housework and mummy duties are enough, that I don't need to chase anything other than a smile on my little girl's face.[2]

The 'domestic perfection' requisite

There can be no doubt that cleanfluencing has intensified the demands on women to ensure a well-ordered, clean and tidy home and to work towards achieving this without complaint, with a smile, while demonstrating superhuman levels of resilience. Against the backdrop of crisis capitalism and advanced neoliberal society, these demands are likely to be felt more acutely than ever. This is especially the case given that they are situated within a broader climate of less support from the state – financially or otherwise – fewer community support networks and initiatives, an advanced cost-of-living crisis, the increased necessity of a dual-income household and the compounding of expectations of the ideal, 'perfect' home, represented in the most ubiquitous way via impossible-to-escape social media channels. Cleanfluencers make cleaning and housework look effortless, for the most part without noting the privileged context within which their own cleaning occurs: in a financially secure environment undertaken by able-bodied, youthful people with familial support and the possibility of paid help, with the space and time to store objects, to declutter and to create order.

Cleanfluencers regularly allude to the fact that trying to recreate in real life the 'perfect' Instagram aesthetic is impossible, but cleanfluencing nevertheless offers endless reminders to women of the importance of housework and the necessity of at least trying to make it happen. Implicit in cleanfluencing is a heavily competitive message: 'I can make it work so why can't you?' There is sometimes empathy ('Just do what you can!'), but ultimately, cleanfluencing is a highly competitive business with the 'best', the most resilient, the most hard working rising to the top, radiant in perfectly ordered homes, shiny, happy children, gleaming surfaces and calm, cosy order. Meanwhile, social media housework discussion groups are increasingly populated with women seeking advice on how to cope with the overwhelm; with balancing a multitude of demands – such as night shifts, single-motherhood, lack of space or a job that insists on movement trackers on the computer – with the housework.

Women (and virtually never men) increasingly use social media to articulate intense feelings of guilt, shame, overwhelm and anxiety when the reality of housework hits home. Responses from others are often empathetic and compassionate, but the solutions offered are to get a cleaner, plan more carefully, batch cook, write a list, take a holiday, carve out some 'me' time or to allocate tasks to other family members, and never to challenge the digital cultures that continue to perpetuate the myth that cleaning is effortless and good for the soul. There is no resistance to the endless representations of domestic perfection nor of the perpetual imagery of women frantically cleaning their homes to achieve this.

Many of the most successful cleanfluencers and their followers are younger women. There is a real risk that the dubious promise that housework brings satisfaction, happiness and personal fulfilment that feminists have railed against for decades will not only come back to haunt us but might also provide a blueprint for young women and girls as they enter adulthood. The highly conservative, at times anti-feminist, message that housework is the natural preserve of women, and that done correctly can bring about wellbeing and empowerment, is concerning. In this book I have argued that it is crucial that we begin to challenge the fresh resurgence of the myth that women are naturally more competent at and find personal fulfilment in housework. This is important not least because these myths have continued to infiltrate every aspect of social life, including within the workplace, where women continue to be seen as more naturally skilled at emotional work, administration and organising. Debate often focuses on the psychological harm of diet culture; today the same concerns might extend to online cleaning cultures too. It offers a new version of the same regressive messaging, this time around impossible-to-attain standards of domestic perfection.

For all the contemporary visibility of women describing their experiences of stress, anxiety and overwhelm, there is little reassurance that the problem does not lie with women themselves or with something that they might be doing 'wrong'. There is surprisingly little reassurance that there is, of course, no way to balance housework in addition to all other caring and paid work responsibilities without exhaustion and overwhelm. In the latter chapters of this book, I have argued that the real, *radical* solution to guilt and shame is to move away from cleanfluencing cultures that, in tandem with the popular representations of housework that came before, compound feelings of inadequacy and intensify and foster competition between individual women. An alternative would be to challenge together the deep-rooted, sexist assumptions and expectations that housework is women's work and that those who cannot manage must be lacking in resilience and fortitude. The recent digital trade in endless glossy images of happy, slim, idealised housewives and mothers frantically but effortlessly cleaning amplifies feelings of guilt and shame in those for whom time, money and a plethora of other constraints mean that this simply isn't possible for anyone save a privileged few. The diversification of inequalities, seen via the integration of 'failure' narratives, serve to amplify rather than ease guilt and shame. The message is that success – the domestic ideal – is all the more impressive when we can see how it has been achieved 'against the odds'. We are witnessing a new type of 'superwoman' syndrome that turns failure into resilience, success and self-worth, simultaneously fostering competition between individual women. Those who make it leave behind their less fortunate sisters trapped in never-ending, undervalued domestic labour, suffering guilt and shame at their individual 'failings'.

'Failure', imperfection and the positive-thinking mindset

I literally do it when I have time. Having a toddler at home makes it ten times harder ... I feel like I spend my life at this sink ... tidying up and putting things away. It's just a repetitive circle. But do you know what? I wouldn't change it for the world. Being a mum is my first job. It is my most important job and it's a job I love doing. I've learnt so much from being a mum ... Parents, we have got this![3]

On one level, cleanfluencing is a retro, highly traditional and conservative version of the happy and willing housewife. Cleanfluencing in this regard might easily be framed as offering merely a glamorous retelling of a particularly regressive version of femininity; one where women are positioned as the natural arbiters of the domestic space, their wellbeing and happiness bound to a fruitless search for the perfect home.

And yet, cleanfluencers present their labour in ways that both articulate *and* reject the requirement to be perfect. As this book has described, trading on the imperfect has become part of the imperative of neoliberal feminist subjects. Confessing to one's failures, often in the most omnipresent way, is not only expected, but in addition, so long as failure is ultimately resolved then it is celebrated. In the quote above, Shannon Tomkins, otherwise known as @lifewiththetomkins, a popular cleanfluencing Instagram account with 75,700 followers and multiple links to paid partnership deals, including Morphy Richards and Kleeneze, describes the drudgery, repetitiveness and overwhelm of housework but quickly gives this a positive spin: 'I wouldn't change it for the world.' Positive self-help movements actively promote the failure-to-success narratives where personal salvation and survival even from the most difficult of situations are rendered possible with just a few learnable skills from the self-help toolkit. These include thinking with a positive mindset, exercising, staying hydrated, 'me time', meditation or of course, as we have seen, cleaning and tidying. All of which offer a temporary reprieve from the demands, stresses and strains that permeate late capitalist societies in ever new, often brutal ways.

The most celebrated cleanfluencers are notably imperfect and regularly confess to feelings of stress and anxiety, sometimes around the pressures to keep on top of the housework but ultimately insisting, perhaps contradictorily, that housework also eases anxiety. In response to a question from a follower, 'Why do you clean so much?', Shannon Tomkins replies, 'I just do! A clean home = a happy Shannon.' Responsibility for coping and surviving is firmly placed at the door, not only of individuals who must take personal responsibility for their misery, but also at the door of individual *women* whose supposed natal responsibility to care, clean, mop up and organise the domestic mess and fallout of highly unequal societies remain steadfastly unchanged. Within cleanfluencing cultures, we see the seamless merging of two powerful cultural narratives. On the one hand, the all-powerful positive-thinking movement, emerging off the back of three decades of unfettered neoliberalism, combined with a historically entrenched focus on women as housewives.

That cleanfluencers tend to reject the 'housewife' label entirely is highly significant, yet it is unsurprising given the brutally low status attached to housework. In today's liberal, individualised societies, women are endlessly assured that they have choice, equal opportunities and agency *and* that they are entitled to personal joy, happiness and time for self-care. 'Housewifery' is today widely seen as bound up with the opposite: oppression, misery, exploitation, drudgery and boredom, as the popular 'grumpy housewife' Mrs Hinch filter discussed in Chapter 2 reminds us. Housework within cleanfluencing is thus reinvented in ways that shake off these labels. Domestic chores are rewritten as relaxing, comforting, joyful, fun, satisfying and an act of meaningful self-care. I have argued in this book that this fantasy is particularly lucrative, enabling big business to reap serious financial profits and society more broadly to continue to benefit from the unpaid labour of women. It is a fantasy bolstered by what Jenny Huberman describes as the 'spirit of digital capitalism', within which all are seemingly complicit, even those who are never likely to benefit from the vast profits it elicits.[4] Every share, 'like', hashtag and comment provides free marketing and advertising for corporate giants.

Cleanfluencing has thus become the latest trend in so-called self-help strategies. It appears to offer a compromise between the conflicting divisions between the public sphere of economic capital and the private sphere of domestic reproduction. The particular representation of housework that is reproduced in cleanfluencing culture is one that is developed within postfeminist cultures of choice, empowerment, confidence and the myth of equality. Cleanfluencing accounts are thus peppered with discourses of 'doing it for myself': planning ahead, creating order and buying fun new cleaning products *for you*.

The diversification of domestic inequality is demonstrated in other ways too and has increasingly made cleanfluencing culture difficult to challenge. The increased presence of men in cleanfluencing videos as well as in advertising for household cleaning products more generally is notable. Yet men are almost always appendages to the housework; only exceptionally rarely are they the protagonists of the cleaning journey and cleanfluencing accounts. The repertoire is all too familiar: women being sold the mirage of a type of happy housewifery, women taking almost sole responsibility for the domestic load, women being persuaded that housework can lead to personal and familial betterment, women being sold an indeterminable list of products, devices, plans, guides, workbooks and endless advice, all promising to lighten the domestic load. The job *is* possible if only you learn how to do it properly. The repertoire is not new and its alarming resurgence sets back previous advances towards equality around domestic labour, and especially notions of women as the natural arbiters of the domestic sphere, in dangerously regressive new ways.

This time, though, the repertoire comes with a twist. Inequalities stay fundamentally the same but are repackaged to appear more palatable. In this book I have shown how one notable way in which cleanfluencers achieve this is by vocally recognising the strain of domestic labour, including references to feminist ideas around the mental load, the double shift and even – ironically – the psychological pressures of ubiquitous social media images of home and bodily perfection. As Chapter 3 showed, today this also extends to new confessional cultures around mental health, although the association between feminist critiques of domestic labour and psychological distress is never acknowledged. Instead, housework is posed as the solution, with the structural causes of poor mental health left ignored. Certain phrases are often used that emphasise the central role and responsibility of individual women to haul themselves out of crisis – 'Just be you!', 'You've got this!' – a colourful, romanticised, twenty-first-century version of the same mopping up of the 'rags and bones' – the same shitty residue of capitalism that Sheila Rowbotham described in the 1970s. This time, though, women's crisis management skills are celebrated, and 'failure' – so long as it is ultimately overcome – becomes central to the cleanfluencing narrative.

As I have explored, particularly in Chapter 1, *relatability* and 'authenticity' are core to the cleanfluencer's appeal. Often cleanfluencers present their stories in a deadpan, exhausted voice: 'Today hasn't been easy if I'm honest', 'I've got to get the baby down to nap so I can get some chores done', 'The kitchen is like a bomb site', etc. But then invariably she sweeps into action. At the time of writing, cleanfluencers are in the process of 'undecorating' after Christmas. Reels are dominated by frantic post-Christmas clean-ups and decluttering stories. The hashtag #cleanuary is in full swing, and the most popular cleanfluencers have produced their own guided clean-ups, tick-off lists and cleaning challenge templates to help get the job done.

The unflinching message running throughout all of cleanfluencing culture is the importance of working on self-improvement and particularly on your own relationship with housework rather than challenging the unequal structures into which women continue to be locked. And of course, the unpaid and uneven system of domestic labour remains untouched and unchallenged. Relatability in this regard, as it underpins cleanfluencing culture, ultimately excuses patriarchy and lets it off the hook.

Postfeminist housewives? The impossible burden of domestic inequalities

Cleanfluencing accounts regularly adopt the vocabulary of feminist activism, even the slogans and iconography of the Women's Liberation Movement. However, this is always reappropriated to signal ways that women themselves via their *personal* attitudes towards housework are individually responsible for change. It is of course an impossible burden, whereby women are tasked with finding ways of personally resolving what are in fact deeply entrenched historical structures built into the very fabric of capitalism. Today's 'confidence culture' mantra is embedded in cleanfluencing,[5] with individual women seeking neoliberal, personal and commercial solutions to what are in fact complex structural inequalities deeply rooted within late capitalism. For all the discussion of the mental load, flexible working and anxieties around not being able to create the perfect home, the solution is resolutely personal.

Social media favours the exposure of those who harness inequalities and injustice, making unequal structures work for them. In Chapter 2, I described this as a new process of 'turning inward', where a privileged few 'make it' while everyone else struggles along within the same systems of inequality. Thus, cleanfluencers are often adept at identifying the strain, exhaustion and anxiety at the domestic load but revert back to personal solutions to resolve this. Discussions of the mental load, calls for policy changes around flexible working and content challenging current workplace orthodoxies that are still broadly organised around the long-established assumption that there will be someone at home performing the cleaning, tidying, caring and administration are increasingly visible on social media. Yet representations of housework remain stubbornly normative, with the deep gendered inequalities of housework barely acknowledged. In this book, I have shown how cleanfluencers in the main accept the load, acknowledge the anxieties around doing it well, but ultimately take personal responsibility for their struggles. The lack of male participation in the housework is brushed aside with either jokes, 'he makes the bed wrong!', or justifications, 'he does the DIY', 'he works really hard for us through the week'; or men are simply included as occasional appendages to cleanfluencing videos: 'teamwork makes the dream work!' Inequalities are thus broadly justified and remain decoupled from feelings of anxiety and overwhelm that have become a cornerstone of cleanfluencing culture.

Nevertheless, cleanfluencing can be seen as a real and meaningful response to the injustices of housework. It represents a genuine attempt to manage the ravages of economic and social crises by finding ways to make the job easier and more palatable, perhaps even building up your own feelings of self-worth in the process. Individuals have long sought ways of making systems of entrenched injustices work for them and, as we have seen, cleanfluencing is no exception. It is little surprise that women have long sought ways to find value in their hitherto invisible labour, nor that they have looked for ways of making money from it. This is particularly true within an economic climate where adequately paid work that sufficiently complements domestic life is almost impossible to find.

I have argued throughout this book that it is crucial to make sense of housework against a backdrop of feminist activism that has long railed against the rigid expectations of women and their unpaid labour. Cleanfluencing exists within a culture whereby unpaid labour is chronically devalued. By rejecting the 'housewife' label and instead repositioning housework so that it becomes tantamount to sparking joy, easing anxiety and promoting self-care, this dilemma appears to be temporarily resolved.

And yet, working as they are within the logics of capitalism, with its focus on individual ownership, means that there is only space for a few people to truly benefit from cleanfluencing. In common with other types of influencer culture, the focus is on showering individuals with praise and credit rather than promoting collective action that might benefit the lives of all. Thus, lines of separation between humans deepen even where their shared experiences – in this case the complex demands of domestic labour – might be very similar. Cleanfluencing culture thus ensures that relations between people become about commodities, competition and ownership rather than a shared commitment to change. This is the case even where accounts are dedicated to helping to address serious economic realities. @MoneyMumOfficial, for example (discussed in Chapter 1), is an Instagram account dedicated to saving followers money and helping families to budget. The popularity of this account and similar money-saving and household-budgeting social media content is unsurprising given the recent cost-of-living crisis in the UK, yet this account and others offer opportunities to purchase goods and services in almost every post. The goods on offer are generally cheap, but ultimately the focus is on *buying* one's way out of a crisis.

In our post-Covid world, compounded by the cost-of-living crisis, everyday experiences of precarity and uncertainty make it difficult for many to feel optimistic about their futures.[6] The sheer accessibility of cleanfluencing – in terms of both the relatability of cleanfluencers who position themselves as a type of digital 'family' and the entrepreneurial promise of turning what you must do anyway into a commercial opportunity that is, we are assured, accessible to all – was discussed in Chapter 1. It is an opportunity seized on by many as evidenced by the sheer volume of cleanfluencing accounts mimicking the hugely successful format popularised by Mrs Hinch. It is endlessly aspirational, future-oriented and cheerily optimistic – perhaps cruelly so given how few cleanfluencers are able to make a living from their endeavours.

In cleanfluencing cultures, then, women compete in a literal but also in an attention-seeking economy. Cleanfluencing draws attention to and gives visibility to housework, opening up an opportunity for women to demonstrate their prowess and ability to seamlessly navigate the conflicting demands of home, work and family. It facilitates a hugely seductive fantasy that pertains to ideals of hyper-efficient superwoman syndrome. It is an example of 'leaning in' par excellence,[7] perpetuating the myth that personal strength, resilience and positivity are all it takes to thrive across all the conflicting spheres of home and work.

Consumerism is the lynchpin of late capitalist economies and today, housework is as heavily commodified as ever. As we have seen, particularly in Chapter 1, cleanfluencers fit neatly into these wider economic structures by, first, *becoming* the commodity itself and, second, by tapping into new forms of selling, marketing and advertising, all while making it appear as if they aren't selling anything at all, since recommendations are made out of kindness or altruism and come 'from the heart'.

I have argued throughout this book that cleanfluencing operates as a cog in a highly lucrative industry that in turn exists within a capitalist system that profits from fostering envy and competition between individuals for scarce resources, praise, value and status, and which thrives on creating division and separation between women. Instagram gives the impression of 'community' but in fact it separates women, physically but also emotionally, as anxieties are transformed into something commodifiable rather than offering the potential for collective protest and resistance.

Sara Ahmed's call to arms in the quote at the beginning of this chapter – 'kill joy we must' – is the first step in developing a much needed counter narrative to the prevailing orthodox approach of the cleanfluencers. Women are told time and again that saying no, seeking out and articulating alternatives, rebelling against the mainstream will inevitably lead to unhappiness. They learn not to be difficult, to keep the peace, to keep their surroundings clean, calm and ordered, especially in moments of crisis.

Cleanfluencers offer a soft, friendly and relatable front behind which lurks an all too familiar consumer capitalist enterprise. This enterprise centres around the celebration of some of the most conservative and normative narratives of women as housewives, domestic servants and wives. Today the same commercial celebration of housework continues, this time with women creating their own content, without the need for a man in a shiny suit compering or a starchy educator explaining the rules of domestic science. The hyper-organisation, efficiency and superhuman ability to hold it all together within unforgiving economic circumstances are celebrated and venerated, yet these traits are highly gendered and inequalities go stubbornly unchallenged. The old adage of women mopping up the mess and stains left by crisis capitalism remains.

Dismantling the 'happy housewife'

Betty Friedan's landmark study *The Feminine Mystique* appeared to shatter the fantasy of the 'happy housewife'. And yet, as this book shows, her power endures, the endless reproduction of the fantasy continuing to conceal and distort unhappiness. The repeated sentiments of happiness that are so readily shared throughout cleanfluencing culture have a twofold effect. They work to remind women to be satisfied with their lot; to accept the chores with a smile because, after all, contemporary notions of happiness are so closely entwined with a cosy, warm, clean and well-ordered home. To challenge the domestic orthodoxy, it is implied, is to be unhappy, dissatisfied, an overthinker, a killjoy – a *feminist*. Second, they open up space for the promise of a better, happier you that is within reach to those of us willing to play by the rules. In cleanfluencing culture, the promise is one of a renewed self that is a perfect, hyper-efficient, super-organised, imagined version of one's true self. Cleanfluencers, with their endless supply of images of domestic perfection, serve as a constant reminder of the possibility of an ideal domestic self that is always just out of reach, and of course they sell us the products that we are promised will bring us one step closer to a blissfully happy domestic nirvana. 'Dream-high', 'I'm living the dream' and 'make the dream a reality' stand as hugely popular sentiments used regularly in cleanfluencing discourses. The 'dream' is exactly that – an out-of-reach longing for an imagined domestic bliss. As Sara Ahmed suggests, the 'promise' often made by corporations trying to sell us stuff is one of a *feeling* of happiness and contentment: 'we might speculate that what is unequally distributed is the feeling that you have what should make you happy, a *distribution of the promise of a feeling*, or the feeling of a promise rather than the distribution of happiness as such'.[8]

Earlier, 1970s feminist accounts of housework brought to the fore the capitalist exploitation of women: the ways in which inequalities of domestic labour and its centuries-old devaluation not only curtails women's wider potential and expansion of self but also locks poorer and working-class women into some of the most low-status and badly paid jobs globally. The continued positioning – still firmly entrenched and reproduced in contemporary digital cultures – of housework as women's work, bound up with obligations to care, love and to hold together the multiple loose strings of capitalism, means that the very systems of exploitation, and in particular the intersections of gender, race and class, remain firmly and stubbornly unchallenged.

Radicalism and radical solutions are thus curtailed, particularly within crisis capitalism, where isolated individuals move further away from the sort of collectivity that is required to provoke meaningful change and the dismantling of exploitative power structures around domestic labour. Women in contemporary, highly digitised societies increasingly seek out individualised solutions to crisis. For working-class women, cleanfluencing offers a means of making visible some of the previously unseen detail of housework, and presents an attempt to revalue it, not only via its cultural visibility but also via its economic possibilities, as paid digital labour or digital entrepreneurship.

The increased individualisation of care and domestic labour leaves earlier calls for collective and radical feminist alternatives abandoned. We see instead a type of 'defanged' feminism,[9] whereby the battle for domestic equality has morphed into a postfeminist response that has contradictorily intensified the division between women and their experiences of domestic labour. Solutions to the domestic burden habitually take the form of outsourcing – passing the domestic load to others. If feminism means avoiding the privileging of one group of women over another, then the ritual outsourcing of domestic labour to very low-paid women must be seen to be problematic, drawing a circle around one's privilege. Advances to feminist activism could benefit from oscillating around domestic labour, as it is so pivotal to the structures of capitalist and patriarchal society. The sheer volume of low and unpaid domestic labour that women are routinely expected to perform keeps women from finding collective solutions and men from having to take an equal share of the domestic burden. One of the conclusions of this book is that the popularity of cleanfluencing unwittingly justifies the low-status, low-paid nature of housework, by endlessly positioning it as 'women's work' which should be performed out of duty, love and pride.

Under the guise of 'collectivity' and 'community', social media in fact divides, reframing frustrations, anger and resentment as hyper-individualised pathologies that are up to the individual to solve. Consumers, followers and purveyors of digital media thus become unwittingly complicit in unequal structures, bound up in the highly seductive lure of social media that at once stirs up endless feelings of competition, judgement, envy and impossible standards of clean and tidy, and simultaneously promises that a salve to those feelings can be found within the very same social media accounts and products.

Without radical, collective solutions, misogynistic assumptions around domestic labour, who does what, the positioning of housework as a natural extension to the fair nature of women that is fundamentally 'women's work', are likely to prevail and run unchallenged. Part of the solution requires a cultural shift, but it also reflects a social and economic moment. Wherever we see moments of crisis, the popular image of the happy housewife resurges as fresh attempts are made to ensure women's willing participation in unpaid labour. Today, the economic demands of contemporary capitalism mean that the strive towards the perfect home is either outsourced or facilitated by the double shift and capitalism remains held together as it has long been by the low and unpaid labour of women.

Furthermore, the discourse of *choice* has become all powerful and often used as a critique of feminism. Whether it is in the 1980s WITH campaign discussed in Chapter 6 or contemporary cleanfluencers framing 'choice' as central to their decisions to make their housework hyper-visible, feminism is regularly batted away as curtailing choice, adding to stress and anxieties and being judgemental. Today, there is a strong recognition and articulation of the double shift – the burden of balancing too much. The solution – often articulated as a critique of the perceived judgement of other women and of the problems with feminism – is rarely one that lies in a more equal distribution of labour between men and women. Rather, men are still broadly exempt from the debate – it is still women having the domestic labour debate between themselves. Women are still constantly treading a careful balance between acceptable domestic femininity, sexual acceptability and participation in high-status paid work, all the while making it look as if they are in control.

The solution, of course, is not to try and 'have it all', nor is it about making judgements around choice or relinquishing women's hard-won rights within paid work. Furthermore, the solution does not lie in abandoning feminist activism and debate, which has long held inequalities of domestic labour at its core. Rather, the solution lies in a reframing of debates pertaining to equalities around domestic labour that recognise its necessity, value and importance, and in doing so offers up radical opportunities for new equal divisions of housework.

Neoliberalism twists human relationships, emotions and feelings into something entirely commodifiable and venerates those who can demonstrate that they are self-managing, autonomous and enterprising neoliberal subjects.[10] It creates forms of culture that become almost impossible to critique because they rely so heavily on individual social media celebrities to spread the message; critiques sound like unkindness, expressions of envy or just being mean. It is a watertight system of capitalist reproduction and ultimately this is what makes cleanfluencing cultures and their rigid reproduction of feminine stereotypes of the willing and happy housewife increasingly difficult to challenge.

For years, companies, especially supermarkets, have looked for new and increasingly innovative ways of tracking and predicting shopping practices, choices and buying habits. This taps into a wider point that I have tried to make in this book, namely that women are all too aware of the ways in which consumer capitalism often cynically attempts to gain their approval. Women understand the wastefulness inherent in unnecessary consumption, and they are tuned in to the ways in which global industries compete for their attention and money. The extent to which choice is overwhelming rather than liberating is a theme often reported by women consumers as they attempt to navigate their ways through the burgeoning range of available yet fundamentally very similar products.

Like housework, the shopping that accompanies it is arduous, time-consuming and thankless.

Yet, as this book has demonstrated, consumer capitalism is also adept at flexibly responding to this recognition, by endlessly reinventing and reglamourising the products that it produces. This is of course nothing new, but the digitisation of cleaning cultures entwined with hyper-commercialisation and underpinned by the promise of self-betterment, personal joy, happiness and 'confidence culture' are recent transformations that have been galvanised in the last few years within popular cleanfluencing cultures.

Global companies and corporations have for decades been intent on developing new ways of both tracking and predicting women's shopping habits, from watching and drawing maps of the routes taken by shoppers in supermarkets, to the introduction of store cards, to algorithmically tracking online activity. Consumers were persuaded that these technological advances would help them save money, benefit from targeted promotions and generally make shopping easier, but in fact they have ended up facilitating a new and highly effective way of collecting individualised data on shopping habits, practices and routines, which in turn are used for targeted promotions and ultimately the creation of new desires.[11] Today, the new digital consumers as influencers are doing this lucrative profit-generating labour for free. Every tag, share, comment and like – every carefully curated photo montage or video reel of the perfect home that makes use of increasingly sophisticated, self-taught media production techniques – provides free advertising, marketing and algorithmic information around practices, desires and anxieties, offering a type of free, digital housewifery that the early market researchers could only have dreamt of.

In this book, I have shown how cleanfluencing culture has helped to create an ideal scenario for unfettered capitalist production and the ongoing stability of gendered inequalities of domestic labour; one where women are seemingly willing and able to invest much of their own time, money and effort, not only into creating the perfect home but also in doing the digital labour essential for the promotion, advertising and marketing of the products and the aspirational lure of the promised lifestyles that are associated with it. It is little wonder that the biggest conglomerates have targeted one or two influencers for special attention, transforming them into super-wealthy, prestigious celebrities. These high-profile, celebrated cleanfluencers, who have achieved mass fandom, provide good value in terms of racking up trade, as they constantly persuade their legions of followers that cleaning must happen alongside the purchase of endless cheap, mass-produced homeware and constant engagement with digital content and the promise of similar financial rewards, happiness and security to those who willingly conform. The seeming mass willingness of women to enter into this predominantly unpaid digital labour, which has become key to capitalist supply chains, is a far cry from the early days of women as consumers. Women have long borne the brunt of the unpaid labour of cleaning, tidying and domestic consumption, and have become increasingly responsible for promoting products themselves. The Tupperware parties of the 1950s, more recently followed by Pippa Dee clothing parties and Body Shop 'reps', offered women flexible work and an opportunity to earn money and embody a type of 'entrepreneurial' spirit, yet the scale on which women are now invested in providing free digital labour, ultimately creating enormous profits for global enterprises, is unprecedented. Today, women are increasingly enmeshed in clean-fluencing cultures, carefully curating images of their own homes, endorsing products and brands and reproducing aspirational desires for lifestyles that incorporate happiness, joy and personal satisfaction, perhaps unwittingly doing the work that market researchers, shopping psychologists, advertisers and corporate giants would once have done themselves.

This represents a shift in control from consumers as mindless automations, passively responding to the marketed goods on offer – the 'zombie housewife'[12] who is unable to resist goods forced upon her by increasingly sophisticated marketing techniques. In the age of the consumer-as-computer, consumers are reimagined as acquiring a type of 'individual agency', using their 'user-friendly, hands-on personal machines' as they flexibly move between the myriad products on offer, skilfully coordinating and navigating their way through different moods and needs. The new regimes of consumer choice and the shopper's role as decision maker within them is thus repositioned as a form of empowerment rather than automation or brainwashing. As this book has shown, the powerful reinvention of the image of the 'empowered' and confident consumer is a mirage, with global digital platforms and industry giants using these new forms of highly sophisticated exploitation to cash in.

The anxieties that the precarious and unattainable desires of neoliberalism instils in us are played out in the rhythms of everyday life, in popular culture and in our consumption practices. I have previously written about how low-income, working-class women, whose lives rode on a wave of gnawing everyday anxieties and stresses around money, turned to lottery tickets as a glimpse of a life that was not dominated by painful, relentless thoughts about not having enough money.[13] Neoliberalism thrives within a context where individuals are pressured by endless reminders that they are not measuring up and by warnings regarding the consequences for those who don't; of the transformative potential of the self, of thinking, longing and cleaning your home to a point where, it is promised, you will find happiness and personal fulfilment. Contemporary individuals who exist within the confines of a deeply enhanced and ubiquitous digital age live out their imagined lives against the often gritty reality of life as it actually is. A key feature of life in contemporary digital societies is the constant search for ways to bridge that gap.

In the early decades of the twenty-first century, domestic life has become steadily more commodified, most recently with the meteoric rise of digital media offering up a range of self-help strategies that present individualised solutions to what are often structural problems. Nowhere is this more evident than in the online digital cleanfluencer, who posts positive affirmations and tips for self-care and wellbeing while simultaneously offering multiple opportunities to buy a never-ending range of consumer products. The use of the language and vocabulary of the 1970s movement – words such as 'empowerment', 'liberating' and 'freedom' – are common but they almost completely strip away the political demands for change that characterised this movement. In this new digital age, change is down to *you*.

In declaring that 'the personal is political', the Women's Liberation Movement was making the radical claim that domestic life and the work that women do within it matter. Some fifty years later, it seems more important than ever that we shout loudly that housework *is* political. I have argued in this book that a radical politics of housework can help to combat burgeoning gender inequalities. Crucially, we need to build a resistance to the ongoing decoupling of housework and politics and to emphasise the ways in which the white woman housewife is entangled within the social relations of global capitalism. Her whiteness, her Britishness and her location within the domestic is embedded in a highly exploitative global process, where products made in sweatshops and factories in the Global South, often causing significant ecological damage in the process, are fetishised and given a veneer of shiny, mass appeal and respectability.

Women in postcolonial, capitalist and patriarchal societies often find themselves caught in a double bind of heavy scrutiny: first, for their participation (or not) in paid work; and second, for their ability to be 'good' wives, mothers and homemakers. 'Value' is closely associated with being the 'right' type of stay-at-home mother who is hardworking, respectable, aspirational and does not ask for help; particularly not for state support. At the same time, she demonstrates exceptional homemaking skills. Online cleanfluencing offers an ideal solution to this impossible double bind, whereby women can utilise online social media platforms to establish themselves as domestic entrepreneurs.

The impossibly high standards of cleanliness, order and domestic bliss that we see represented on social media are growing in popularity and are setting women up to fail again and again. Yet it is harder than ever to step away from the relentless demands of today's hyper-visible forms of housework. In today's neoliberal model of capitalism, women are seen as responsible for their own successes and failures and are encouraged to be avid consumers. This is particularly true for contemporary representations of the housewife.

The fandom and huge following that surrounds the most popular cleanfluencers demonstrates how fans not only self-identify with the celebrity housewife in a way that they never have before but also enter into a new type of consumer relationship.

Followers are fans and consumers. Selling is reframed as 'gifting', as an act of generosity and kindness, and as women supporting one another. We see a move away from the 'cold' money and marketing of cleaning products, with the business and corporate side of selling masked by a deepening of narratives around friendship, kindness and gratitude towards the consumer. *I love you guys!* No one does this better than the cleanfluencer, who is particularly effective at couching the corporate reality of their accounts with platitudes of friendship, positivity and generosity. This specific business model is highly effective and lucrative. Most big-name global cleaning corporations, such as Procter & Gamble, now work extensively with online cleanfluencers to market their products.

Housework is positioned by cleanfluencing culture as pleasurable, exhilarating, fun, joyful and inextricably linked to desire. At the beginning of the book, I discussed Simone de Beauvoir's account of the temporal joy and satisfaction of 'shining stoves',[14] which ultimately extinguishes desire, anger and regret at a life half-lived. The contemporary happiness industry thrives on these same temporal, personal pleasures afforded by mass-produced products and fantasies. This is especially the case for the twenty-first-century cleanfluencer whose online content promises reprieve from the intense demands and expectations of crisis capitalism. Women have the impossible task of carving out a space for the expression of selfhood within the confines of a rigid patriarchal and capitalist order. I argue that cleanfluencing diffuses the potential for meaningful dialogue about the collective and structural transformations required to bring about equality by twisting feminist concerns about the stifling expectations of domestic labour into an intensely personal project of the self. Personal flaws, such as the often used exclamation 'I need to get my shit together!', are celebrated but only when they are juxtaposed with stories of personal redemption, efficacy, success and order.

The return of the housewife

For a long time, popular discussions around female emancipation have tended to focus on women's ability or not to participate in capitalist production, with only very scant reflection on inequalities in the domestic sphere. The fact that cleanfluencing offers such a seductive lure towards the ubiquitous reproduction of women frantically cleaning and tidying their homes, seemingly effortlessly achieving domestic perfection, should concern us all. Cultural perceptions and stereotypes of women as natural arbiters of the domestic space have always been accompanied by the persistence of gendered inequalities in other spheres of social life, including the outsourcing of low-value domestic labour to poorer women, a lack of flexibility in the workplace and an expectation that women will pick up the slack at work as well as at home. The real 'value' of housework, despite the promises of cleanfluencing culture, continues to be pitifully low. At its core is the familiar language of liberal individualism, with its boundless promises of personal satisfaction and pleasure. As this book has shown, cleanfluencing continues to compound the old expectation that women should willingly and happily perform domestic labour for free, out of love, duty and gratitude.

Figures

Acknowledgements

I am very grateful to the many people who have supported me in a variety of ways throughout the writing process.

I am privileged to work in the Department of Sociology at the University of York alongside the most brilliant colleagues and students anyone could wish for, and whose daily intellectual generosity, encouragement and enthusiasm has been invaluable. In particular, thanks to Dave Beer and Raphael Nowak, my co-lecturers on the Popular Culture, Media and Society module, who share my scholarly delight in all things popular. Thanks also to colleagues at the York Centre for Women's Studies, especially Clare Bielby, who kindly hosted an event where I was able to present an early version of my work. Laura Schwartz's rigorous and thought-provoking chairing of the event and her work on twentieth-century domestic servants helped to inspire fresh directions in my writing.

Thanks to Diane Negra, who invited me to University College Dublin in 2022 to present my research at the Irish Influencers symposium. I am grateful to her and to the symposium participants for their enthusiasm and helpful suggestions, particularly around marking out the potential for feminist resistance to some of the depressingly familiar domestic tropes described in this book.

An anonymous reviewer offered helpful feedback on an early version of the manuscript and introduced me to the 1975 slow cinema feminist classic *Jeanne Dielman*. I was also privileged to receive correspondence from Marsha Rowe, a co-founder of *Spare Rib* magazine. Marsha kindly granted permission to reproduce the image of the Women's Liberation Movement tea towel and sent words of encouragement.

Laura Swift and Shannon Kneis at Manchester University Press offered support and guidance at every stage of the publication process and Tom Dark (now at Edinburgh University Press) championed the book from its conception, for which I am hugely grateful.

I am indebted to many wonderful academic colleagues whose friendship, feminism and scholarly brilliance have sustained me over many years. In particular Gerda Reith, Lydia Martens, Kate Bedford, Fiona Nicoll and Jo Littler, whose care and guidance helped me to reverse my research out of a particularly sticky cul-de-sac.

My aunt, Dr Mari Williams, and her pioneering research into women and science have been an inspiration since childhood. My mum, Hilary Casey, dedicated much of her time to helping me with childcare, housework and practical support without which I simply would not have been able to write.

Simon distracted me with big skies, music and nature. And my wonderful sons Alfie and Joe brought and continue always to bring boundless love, inspiration and joy.

Notes

Introduction: Why are women still cleaning up?

1 Mrs Hinch is the popular British social media cleaning influencer Sophie Hinchliffe.
2 Casey, E. and Huq, R. (2022) 'Biscuits and Unicorns: Shifting Meanings of Domestic Space in a Post-Lockdown World', *Journal for Cultural Research*, 26(1), 24–38.
3 Mahdawi, A. (2019) 'Meet the Online Cleanfluencers', *The Guardian*, 29 March, www.theguardian.com/lifeandstyle/2019/jan/29/meet-the-cleanfluencers-the-online-gurus-who-like-things-nice-and-tidy (all URLs accessed September 2024).
4 McClintock, A. (1995) *Imperial Leather: Race, Gender, and Sexuality in the Colonial Contest*. New York: Routledge.
5 *Ibid.*, 209.
6 *Ibid.*
7 Mies, M. (1986) *Patriarchy and Accumulation on a Global Scale*. London: Zed Books.
8 Wallace Collection (2023) *The Virtuous Woman* https://wallacelive.wallacecollection.org/eMP/eMuseumPlus?service=ExternalInterface&module=collection&objectId=65173&viewType=detailView.
9 Mies (1986: 100).
10 Mies (1986: 110).
11 Bhattacharyya, G. (2018) *Rethinking Racial Capitalism: Questions of Reproduction and Survival*. London: Rowman and Littlefield.
12 Davis, A. (1981) *Woman, Race and Class*. New York: Penguin.
13 *Ibid.*, 39.
14 Boston Globe (1975) 'Iceland Women's Strike Cripples Nation', https://maydayrooms.org/wp-content/uploads/2014/06/WfHw.SF_Media5.jpg.
15 Federici, S. (1974) *Wages against Housework*. London: Power of Women Collective.

16 James, S. (1973) 'Women, the Unions and Work, Or ... What Is Not to Be Done', *Radical America*, 7(4–5).

17 See, for example, Women's Budget Group (2020) *Crises Collide: Women and Covid-19*. WBG; The Fawcett Society (2020) *Coronavirus: Impact on BAME women*. The Fawcett Society.

18 Bryant, M. (2021). 'A Kick in the Teeth: British Mothers and Pregnant Women Fear Return to Workplace', *The Guardian*, 4 September, www.theguardian.com/business/2021/sep/04/a-kick-in-the-teeth-british-mothers-and-pregnant-women-fear-return-to-workplace; Topping, A. (2021) 'Covid-19 Crisis Could Set Women Back Decades Experts Fear', *The Guardian*, 29 May.

19 Orgad, S. (2019) *Heading Home*. New York: Columbia University Press.

20 Monica Geller is a character from the popular American television sitcom *Friends* known for her stringent attitude to cleaning and tidying.

21 The full title of the film is *Jeanne Dielman, 23 Quai de Commerce 1080 Bruxelles* (1975).

22 Andrew, A., Catan, S., Dias, M. C., Farquharson, C., Kraftman, L. and Krutikova, S. (2020) 'Parents, Especially Mothers, Paying Heavy Price for Lockdown', Institute for Fiscal Studies, 27 May.

23 Segal, L. (2017) *Radical Happiness: Moments of Collective Joy*. London: Verso.

24 See, for example, Casey, E. and Martens, L. (eds) (2007) *Gender and Consumption: Material Culture and the Commercialisation of Everyday Life*. Farnham: Ashgate; Giles, J. (2004) *The Parlour and the Suburb: Domestic Identities, Class, Femininity and Modernity*. Oxford: Berg.

25 Martens, L. and Scott, S. (2006) 'Under the Kitchen Surface: Domestic Products and Conflicting Constructions of Home', *Home Cultures*, 3(1), 39–62.

26 Friedan, B. (1964) *The Feminist Mystique*. London: Penguin.

27 Giles (2004).

28 Engels, F. (2010) *The Origin of the Family, Private Property and the State*. London: Penguin.

29 Marcel, K. (2016) *Who Cooked Adam Smith's Dinner? A Story about Women and Economics*. London: Granta.

30 For example, in December 2022, the businessman and *The Apprentice* star Alan Sugar remarked that he was 'sick of this working from home culture ... The people who benefitted the most from Covid are a bunch of lazy layabouts.' Hines, D. (2022) 'Alan Sugar Slams People Who Work from Home as a "Bunch of Lazy Layabouts"', *The Standard*, 14 December, www.standard.co.uk/showbiz/alan-sugar-work-from-home-lazy-layabouts-b1047169.html.

31 Pregnant then Screwed is a British charity founded in 2015 with the aim of ending the 'motherhood penalty' in the workplace.

32 Women's Budget Group (2020).

33 Ang, I. (1990) *Desperately Seeking the Audience*. London: Edward Arnold.

34 Shields, C. (2003) *The Republic of Love*. London: 4th Estate.

1 'I really wanted to share this with you all!': The commercial success of the cleanfluencer

1 From @lauracleanaholic Instagram account 2023.

2 The Ideal Home Show is an event held annually at Olympia in London. The show was created in 1908 by the *Daily Mail* newspaper. It was sold to Media 10 in 2009.

3 The Clean & Tidy Home Show, October 2022, www.cleanandtidyhomeshow.com/ news/home-influencer-community-sparkles.

4 For example, TV interior designer Lawrence Llewelyn-Bowen, TV dinner party etiquette advisor Rosemary Sharger and Kate Hardcastle, also known as 'The Customer Whisperer'.

5 From the Clean & Tidy Home Show website, www.cleanandtidyhomeshow.com/.

6 The Clean & Tidy Home Show, September 2022, www.cleanandtidyhomeshow. com/news/lauras-shine-squad-story.

7 Casey, E., Childs, S. and Huq, R. (2022) 'A Gendered Pandemic: Editors' Introduction', *Journal for Cultural Research*, 26(1), 1–5.

8 Stacey Solomon is an *X Factor* finalist and television presenter who also has a very successful cleaning and tidying Instagram account with 5.9 million followers at the time of writing.

9 Turner, G. (2010) *Ordinary People and the Media: The Demotic Turn.* London: Sage.

10 Mrs Hinch (2019) *Hinch Yourself Happy: All the Best Cleaning to Shine Your Sink and Soothe Your Soul.* London: Penguin, p.9, emphasis added.

11 Comment from a Mrs Hinch follower 2022.

12 Lefebvre, H. (1947) *Critique of Everyday Life.* Paris: Grasset.

13 See Beer, D. (2022) *The Tensions of Algorithmic Thinking: Automation, Intelligence and the Politics of Knowing.* Bristol: Bristol University Press, for a detailed summary of the relationship between everyday life and algorithmic thinking.

14 Casey, E. (2023) 'Welcome to the Shopping Revolution! Commodifying Selfhood and Rearticulating Consumer Capitalism at the Metro Centre Gateshead', *The Sociological Review*, 72(2), https://doi.org/10.1177/00380261231194504. Here I explore the shifting consumption practices in the 1980s. I note the rise of the hyper-individual consumer during this time alongside a new hyper-real reflection of community.

15 Littler, J. (2017) *Against Meritocracy: Culture, Power and Myths of Mobility.* London: Routledge.

16 Berlant, L. (2011) *Cruel Optimism.* Durham, NC: Duke University Press.

17 Turner, G. (2010) *Ordinary People and the Media: The Demotic Turn.* London: Sage.

18 *Ibid.*, p.155.

19 Rojek, C. and S. Baker (2020) *Lifestyle Gurus: Constructing Authority and Influence Online.* Cambridge: Polity.

20 @_ellenokeeffee Instagram account, August 2018.

21 Bauman, Z. (2007) *Consuming Life.* Cambridge: Polity Press.

22 *Ibid.*, p.13.

23 For example Ang (1990) and Brunsdon, C. (2000) *The Feminist, the Housewife, and the Soap Opera*. Oxford: Oxford Television Studies.

24 Rettberg, J. W. (2018) *Snapchat: Phatic Communication and Ephemeral Social Media*. Ann Arbor: University of Michigan Press.

25 Leaver, T., Highfield, T. and Abidin, C. (2020) *Instagram*. Cambridge: Polity, p.1.

26 Asda 2013 Christmas advert, www.youtube.com/watch?v=7cWkG7Fffno.

27 Sweney, M. (2013) 'Asda Cleared over "Sexist" Christmas Ad Despite More Than 600 Complaints', *The Guardian*, 30 January, www.theguardian.com/media/2013/jan/30/asda-christmas-ad.

28 Jarrett, K. (2016) *Feminism, Labour and Digital media: The Digital Housewife*. London: Routledge.

29 See Littler (2017) for a discussion of 'mumpreneurs'.

30 Clarke, A. (2001) *Tupperware: The Promise of Plastic in 1950s America*. New York: Random House.

31 See Giles (2004), who argues that responses to the modern are often played out in the most private and even intimate of domestic spaces.

32 Martens and Scott (2006: 58).

33 For example DeVault, N. M. (1991) *Feeding the Family: The Social Organisation of Caring as Gendered Work*. Chicago: University of Chicago Press; Charles, N. and Kerr, M. (1988) *Women, Food and Families*. Manchester: Manchester University Press.

34 Pahl, J. (1989) *Money and Marriage*. London: Macmillan.

35 BeRo recipe book, 17th edition, emphasis added. The booklets were free but contained advertising for BeRo self-raising flour.

36 Martens, L. and Scott, S. (2006) 'Under the Kitchen Surface: Domestic Products and Conflicting Constructions of Home', *Home Cultures*, 3(1), 39–62.

37 Negra, D. (2009) *What a Girl Wants: Fantasizing the Reclamation of Self in Postfeminism*. London: Routledge.

38 Skeggs, B., Thumin, N., and Wood, H. (2008) '"Oh Goodness, I Am Watching Reality TV": How Methods Make Class in Audience Research', *European Journal of Cultural Studies*, 11(1), 5–24.

39 See also Turner (2010).

40 See, for example, Paula Akpan, the director of the Black Girl Festival, www.bbc.co.uk/news/newsbeat-44686074 .

41 Bauman (2007).

42 Bauman (2007: 6).

43 Bauman (2007).

44 @moneymumofficial Instagram account October 2022.

2 Housework turned inwards: Cleanfluencing and the self

1 From the blurb from Greedy, C. (2023) *You Do You! An Inspirational Guide to Getting the Life You Want*. London: Penguin (@missgreedyshome on Instagram).

Notes

2 Friedan, B. (1964) *The Feminist Mystique*. New York: Penguin.
3 Jones, L. (2023) *Matrescence: On the Metamorphosis of Pregnancy, Childbirth and Motherhood*. London: Allen Lane.
4 *Ibid.*, p.259, emphasis added.
5 De Beauvoir, S. (2006) *Memoirs of a Dutiful Daughter*. London: Penguin.
6 De Beauvoir, S. (1949) *The Second Sex*. London: Penguin, p.470.
7 *Ibid.*, p.471.
8 Mies (1986).
9 De Beauvoir (1949: 471).
10 Rowbotham, S. (1973) *Women's Consciousness, Man's World*. London: Verso, p.74.
11 *Ibid.*
12 I have argued elsewhere that the National Lottery offered a temporary escape from the bleak inequalities and austerity capitalism that had routinely failed them. Casey, E. (2007) *Women, Pleasure and the Gambling Experience*. London: Routledge.
13 Rowbotham (1973: 77).
14 Rowbotham (1973: 78).
15 Oakley (1974).
16 Oakley, A. (2018) *Sociology of Housework*. Bristol: Policy Press.
17 Oakley in a new introduction to the *Sociology of Housework*, *ibid.*, p. 10, emphasis added.
18 In an article for *The Observer*, McVeigh draws on Institute for Public Policy Research showing that 80 per cent of married women do more housework than their husbands. This rises to 90 per cent when it is narrowed down to cleaning and washing. McVeigh, T. (2012) 'Forty Years of Feminism – but Women Still Do Most of the Housework', *The Observer*, 10 March, www.theguardian.com/society/2012/mar/10/housework-gender-equality-women.
19 Jarrett (2016).
20 Oakley, A. (1974) *Housewife*. London: Penguin, p.196.
21 *Ibid.*
22 From *The Minimalists* website, www.theminimalists.com/minimalism/.
23 Woodward, S. (2021) 'Clutter in Domestic Spaces: Material Vibrancy, and Competing Moralities', *The Sociological Review*, 69(6), 1214–28.
24 See also Holmes, H. (2019) 'Unpicking Contemporary Thrift: Getting on and Getting by in Everyday Life', *The Sociological Review*, 67(1), 126–42.
25 Winship, J. (1987) *Inside Women's Magazines*. Lewes: Rivers Oram Press, p.157.
26 Gilroy, P. (2006) *Postcolonial Melancholia*. New York: Columbia University Press.
27 Freeman, H. (2020) 'Tradwives: The New Trend for Submissive Women Has a Dark Heart and History', *The Guardian*, 27 January, www.theguardian.com/fashion/2020/jan/27/tradwives-new-trend-submissive-women-dark-heart-history.

28 Nicholas, S. (2020) 'Darling, I'll Do Anything to Make You Happy! How the Tradwives Sacrifice Their Own Careers to Satisfy Their Husbands' Every Whim ... and Insist It's the Secret of Marital Bliss', *Daily Mail*, 24 January.

29 *Ibid.*

30 Orgad (2019).

31 *Ibid.*, p.216.

32 *Ibid.*

33 From *Good Housekeeping* 1971; cited in Martens, L. and Scott, S. (2005) '"The Unbearable Lightness of Cleaning": Representations of Domestic Practice and Products in "Good Housekeeping" Magazine (UK): 1951–2001', *Consumption, Markets and Culture*, 8(4), 379–401.

34 'Hoover for Happier Homes' commercial, www.youtube.com/watch?v=WVhJx8Hf4gc.

35 For example, Williamson, J. (1986) *Consuming Passions: The Dynamics of Popular Culture*. London: Marion Boyars.

36 Martens and Scott (2005: 382).

37 Casey (2023).

38 Lyrics included in the 1996 'Chuck out Your Chintz' Ikea commercial.

39 Greedy (2023).

40 Skeggs, B. (1997) *Formations of Class and Gender*. London: Sage; Lawler, S. (2005) 'Disgusted Subjects: The Making of Middle-Class Identities', *The Sociological Review*, 53(3), 429–46.

41 Solomon, S. (2021) *Tap to Tidy: Organising, Crafting and Creating Happiness in a Messy World*. London: Ebury Press.

42 Lawler (2005).

43 Skeggs (1997).

44 Schwartz, L. (2019) *Feminism and the Servant Problem: Class and Domestic Labour in the Women's Suffrage Movement*. Cambridge: Cambridge University Press.

45 *Ibid.*, p.99.

46 *Ibid.*, p.106, emphasis added.

47 Cited in Schwartz (2019).

48 *Ibid.*, p.102.

49 *Ibid.*, pp.102–3.

50 *Ibid.*, p.109.

51 See Caroline Walker's paintings of the 'invisible' female workers of London.

52 In the midst of the 2020 COVID-19 'lockdown', Prime Minister Boris Johnson announced that it was nevertheless 'safe' for nannies, cleaners and tradespeople to continue to work in other people's homes.

53 Howard, S. (2020) 'Sorry but It Is Selfish to Hire a Cleaner, Even If That's Difficult to Admit', *Huffington Post*, 15 May, www.huffingtonpost.co.uk/entry/cleaner-domestic-work_uk_5ebe742ac5b6500cdf66bcc8.

54 Some 93 per cent of domestic cleaners in the UK are women, the majority of whom are also migrants (*Ibid.*).

55 *Ibid.*

56 Written in summer 1981. 'Sally' is possibly the historian Sally Alexander. Rowbotham (1973: 129).
57 Hochschild, A. (1989) *The Second Shift.* London: Penguin.

3 'I'm broken and it's beautiful': Digital housework and the promise of happiness

1 Kondo, M. (2014) *The Life-Changing Magic of Tidying Up: The Japanese Art of Decluttering and Organizing.* New York: Penguin, p.7.
2 Brodesser-Akner (2016).
3 McClaren (2014).
4 Kondo (2014).
5 *Ibid.*
6 *Ibid.*, p.5, emphasis added.
7 Orgad, S. and Gill, R. (2022) *Confidence Culture.* Durham, NC: Duke University Press.
8 Sandlin, J. and Wallin, J. (2022) 'Decluttering the Pandemic: Marie Kondo, Minimalism, and the "Joy" of Waste', *Cultural Studies*, 22(1), 96–102. Note the increased popularity of Marie Kondo's minimalist decluttering method during the COVID-19 pandemic.
9 Casey, E. and Littler, J. (2022) 'Mrs Hinch, the Rise of the "Cleanfluencer" and the Digital Domestication of Neoliberal Anxiety: Scouring Away the Crisis', *Sociological Review*, 70(3), 489–505.
10 Nathanson, E. (2013) *Television and Post-feminist Housekeeping: No Time for Mother.* New York: Routledge, p.25.
11 From the online KonMari shop, https://shop.konmari.com/.
12 *The Guardian* (2019) 'Pass Notes', 19 November.
13 Dotsikas, K. et al. (2023) 'The Gender Dimensions of Mental Health During the Covid-19 Pandemic: A Path Analysis', *PLOS One*, 18(5), e0283514, https://doi.org/10.1371/journal.pone.0283514.
14 Orgad and Gill (2022: 69).
15 Team Happy Place (2023) '100 Million Downloads of the Happy Place Podcast', happyplaceofficial.co.uk, 13 July, www.happyplaceofficial.co.uk/discover/100-million-downloads-of-the-happy-place-podcast/.
16 Cotton, F. (2017) *Happy: Finding Joy in Every Day and Letting Go of Perfect.* London: Orion Spring, p.4.
17 Cotton, F. (2021) *Speak Your Truth: Connecting with Your Inner Truth and Learning to Find Your Voice.* London: Orion Spring, pp.15–16. See also Orgad and Gill (2022: 75).
18 Hatterstone, S. (2022) 'People Underestimate Me: Stacey Solomon on Snobbery, the X Factor and Her Plan to Sort Britain Out', *The Guardian*, 29 September, www.theguardian.com/lifeandstyle/2022/sep/29/people-underestimate-me-stacey-solomon-on-snobbery-the-x-factor-and-her-plan-to-sort-britain-out.
19 Solomon (2021: 11–12), emphasis in original.
20 Woodward (2015).

21 Ouellette, L. and Hay, J. (2008) *Better Living through Reality TV: Television and Post-welfare Citizenship*. London: Wiley-Blackwell, p.30.

4 'Laughter can get you through the hard days': The cultural politics of housework

1 This is a quote regularly repeated throughout cleanfluencing social media. It is generally originally attributed to the author A. A. Milne.
2 Rowbotham (1973: 67).
3 See also Orgad and Gill (2022).
4 Brossard, B. and Chandler, A. (2022) *Explaining Mental Illness: Sociological Perspectives*. Bristol: Bristol University Press.
5 Elsewhere, I have critiqued the 'personal responsibility' mantra inherent in the discussion of gambling-related harms. See Casey (2007).
6 From the Clean & Tidy Home Show website, www.cleanandtidyhomeshow.com/news/shine-not-shame.
7 Jarrett (2016).
8 The Instagram account @lifewiththetomkins was originally called @lifewiththeszoltyseks and changed to reflect Shannon Tomkins' married name.
9 McRobbie, A. (2020) *Feminism and the Politics of Resilience*. Cambridge: Polity.
10 Rottenberg, C. (2022). 'Disavowing Dependency: On Angela McRobbie's Feminism and the Politics of Resilience', *European Journal of Cultural Studies*, 25(1), 335–7, 335, https://doi.org/10.1177/13675494211032972.
11 Friedan (1964: 58).
12 Gavron, H. (1966) *The Captive Wife: Conflicts of Housebound Mothers*. London: Pelican, p.149.
13 From the Clean & Tidy Home Show Instagram account, 16 June 2023.
14 The new shopping malls in the 1980s similarly promised 'community'. See Casey (2023).
15 Winship (1987: 149).
16 See McStravick, S. (2020) 'Meet Northern Ireland's Very Own Mrs Hinch Who Is Using Her Instagram Platform to Speak out about Mental Health', *Belfast Live*, 7 October, www.belfastlive.co.uk/whats-on/be/meet-northern-irelands-very-mrs-19063111.
17 The British mental health charity Mind likens anxiety to the feeling of nervous anticipation when you are sitting on a chair that is teetering backwards.
18 Orgad and Gill (2022).
19 Capetta, A. (2019) 'How Spring Cleaning Can Help Manage Stress, According to Psychologists', *Good Housekeeping*, 21 March.
20 Marks, C. (2018) 'Drudgery? No Cleaning's Glamorous and Helps You Bear Anxiety, Say Social Media Stars Who Have Vast Armies of Fans Tuning in … to Watch Them Scrub the Sink', *Daily Mail*, 21 October.

21 Oxford CBT (2022) 'Stress Management: Clutter, Cleaning and Mental Health', 4 March, www.oxfordcbt.co.uk/stress-management-cleaning/.

22 Mountford, L. (2023) *Live, Laugh, Laundry: A Calming Guide to Keeping Your Clothes Clean – and You Happy*. London: Penguin.

5 The return of the housewife: Housework in the aftermath of crisis

1 Bates, L. (2020) 'How the Coronavirus Sent Women Back to the 1950s', *The Telegraph*, 15 December.

2 World Book Day was established in 1998. It is a UK charity event held annually in March. Every school-aged child is provided with a book voucher.

3 Salter, J. (2023) 'What's behind the Success of the "Cleanfluencers"?' *Financial Times*, 17 March, www.ft.com/content/d79a3deo-bc91-46c6-864 1-52002d1f6f78.

4 Gill, R. (2020) *Changing the Perfect Picture: Smartphones, Social Media and Appearance Pressures*. London: City, University of London, p.1.

5 *Ibid.*, p.4.

6 Hester, H. and Srnicek, N. (2023) *After Work: A History of the Home and the Fight for Free Time*. London: Verso.

7 Aitkenhead, D. (2019) 'The Interview: Russell Brand on His Hedonistic Past, Marriages and Becoming a Father', *The Times*, 20 January, www.thetimes.co.uk/article/the-interview-russell-brand-on-his-hedonistic-past-marriages-and-becoming-a-father-wn6gjkwzd.

8 Easton, M. (2023) 'Women Still Do More Housework, Survey Suggests', BBC News, 21 September, www.bbc.co.uk/news/uk-66866879.

9 Marcel (2016: 30).

10 Department of the Taoiseach (2023) 'Government Approves Proposals for Referendums on Family and Care', gov.ie, 7 December, www.gov.ie/en/press-release/c9193-government-approves-proposals-for-referendums-on-family-and-care/.

11 Laird, H. and Penney, E. (2023) 'Goodbye to Ireland's ""Women in the Home" Constitution Clause?', *RTE*, 5 December, www.rte.ie/brainstorm/2023/1205/1201586-ireland-article-41-women-in-the-home-constitution-clause-1937-referendum/.

12 Daly, M. (1989) *Women and Poverty*. London: Attic Press.

13 Hill, S., McTighe, T. and Carney, G. (2023) 'More than "Lovely Girls": Revisiting Ireland's Housewife of the Year Competition', *RTE*, 4 July, www.rte.ie/brainstorm/2023/0717/1394891-housewife-of-the-year-competition-archive-history-irish-woman-feminism/.

14 See www.rte.ie/archives/2020/1216/1184868-women-in-the-home/ for an interview with Nora Gilligan, who established the Women in the Home campaign.

15 Martens and Scott (2006).

16 Birmingham Live (2013) 'At Home with the Iron Lady: Margaret Thatcher's Exclusive 1978 Interview with the Mail', 9 April, www.birminghammail.co.uk/news/local-news/home-iron-lady—margaret-2572517.

Notes

17 Quote from the 1978 Thatcher interview in the *Daily Mail*. See *Ibid*.

18 Skeggs (1997: 90).

19 Campbell, B. (1987) *Iron Ladies: Why Do Women Vote Tory?* London: Virago, p.237.

20 *Ibid.*, p.234.

21 Bray, G. (2019) *The Organised Mum Method*. London: Piatkus, p.14.

22 *Ibid*.

23 Fury, P. (2023) *How Does She Do It? The Kids, Tyson and Me*. London: Hodder & Stoughton.

24 Hester, H. and Srnicek, N. (2023) *After Work: A History of the Home and the Fight for Free Time*. London: Verso.

25 Gordon, T. (1990) *Feminist Mothers*. London: Palgrave, p.15.

26 For example, the popular feminist comic by 'Emma' called *Mental Load* and an increase in TikTok and Instagram reels about the strain of the mental load.

27 Sims, C. (2023) 'The One Phrase that Saved My Marriage and Helped Me to Ease the Mental Load', *Good To Know*, www.goodto.com/family/the-one-phrase-that-saved-my-marriage-and-helped-me-to-ease-the-mental-load.

28 Berlant, L. (2008) *The Female Complaint: The Unfinished Business of Sentimentality in American Culture*. Durham, NC: Duke University Press.

29 Orgad and Gill (2022: 159).

30 *Ibid*.

31 For example, Campbell (1986); Hall, S. (1988) *The Hard Road to Renewal: Thatcherism and the Crisis of the Left*. London: Verso.

32 Orgad (2019).

33 Criado Perez, C. (2019) *Invisible Women: Exposing Data Bias in a World Designed for Men*. London: Random House.

34 Ehrenreich, B. and English, D. (1979) *For Her Own Good: 150 Years of the Experts' Advice to Women*. London: Pluto, p.59.

35 See interviews with both Rowbotham and Wainwright in Littler, J. (2023) *Left Feminisms*. London: Lawrence Wishart.

36 Arruzza, C., Bhattacharya, T. and Fraser, N. (2019) *Feminism for the 99%: A Manifesto*. London: Verso, p.11.

37 *Ibid*.

38 Clarke, K. (2016) 'Willful Knitting? Contemporary Australian Craftivism and Feminist Histories', *Journal of Media and Cultural Studies*, 30(3), 298–306.

39 Orgad and Gill (2022) describe the 'girl powering' of culture. This term is borrowed from them.

40 Berlant (2011).

41 Rottenberg (2022).

42 Ahmed, S. (2010) *The Promise of Happiness*. Durham, NC: Duke University Press, p.51.

43 *Ibid.*, p.79.

44 McGee, M. (2012) 'From Makeover Media to Remaking Culture', *Sociology Compass*, 6(9), 685–93.

45 Segal (2017).

Notes

Conclusion: Killing housework

1 Ahmed (2010: 87).
2 Follower comment on a Mrs Hinch Instagram post, 2023.
3 @lifewiththetomkins, January 2024.
4 Huberman, J. (2022) *The Spirit of Digital Capitalism*. Cambridge: Polity.
5 Orgad and Gill (2022).
6 Huebner, C. and Arya, D. (2020) 'The New Pessimism: How COVID-19 Has Made Young People Lose Faith in Their Own Agency', LSE Blog, 11 September, https://blogs.lse.ac.uk/covid19/2020/09/11/the-new-pessimism-how-covid-19-has-made-young-people-lose-faith-in-their-own-agency/.
7 The idea of 'leaning in' was popularised by Sheryl Sandberg in her 2013 book of the same name.
8 Ahmed (2010: 51).
9 Rottenberg (2022) describing Angels McRobbie's account of feminism and resilience culture.
10 Gill, R. and Scharff, R. (eds) (2011) *New Femininities: Postfeminism, Neoliberalism, and Subjectivity*. London: Palgrave Macmillan.
11 Bowlby, R. (2000) *Carried Away: The Invention of Modern Shopping*. New York: Columbia University Press.
12 *Ibid.*, p.246.
13 Casey (2007).
14 De Beauvoir (1949).

Bibliography

Abidin, C. (2018) *Internet Celebrity*. Leeds: Emerald.

Ahmed, S. (2010) *The Promise of Happiness*. Durham, NC: Duke University Press.

Anderson, B. (2000) *Doing the Dirty Work: The Global Politics of Domestic Labour*. London: Zed Books.

Andrew, A., Catan, S., Dias, M. C., Farquharson, C., Kraftman, L. and Krutikova, S. (2020) 'Parents, Especially Mothers, Paying Heavy Price for Lockdown'. Institute for Fiscal Studies, 27 May.

Ang, I. (1990) *Desperately Seeking the Audience*. London: Edward Arnold.

Arruzza, C., Bhattacharya, T. and Fraser, N. (2019) *Feminism for the 99%: A Manifesto*. London: Verso.

Banet-Weiser, S. (2018) *Empowered: Popular Feminism and Popular Misogyny*. Durham, NC: Duke University Press.

Bates, L. (2020) 'How the Coronavirus Sent Women Back to the 1950s', *The Telegraph*, 15 December.

Bauman, Z. (2007) *Consuming Life*. Cambridge: Polity Press.

Beer, D. (2022) *The Tensions of Algorithmic Thinking: Automation, Intelligence and the Politics of Knowing*. Bristol: Bristol University Press.

Berlant, L. (2008) *The Female Complaint: The Unfinished Business of Sentimentality in American Culture*. Durham, NC: Duke University Press.

Berlant, L. (2011) *Cruel Optimism*. Durham, NC: Duke University Press.

Bhattacharya, T. (2017) *Social Reproduction Theory*. London: Pluto.

Bhattacharyya, G. (2018) *Rethinking Racial Capitalism: Questions of Reproduction and Survival*. London: Rowman and Littlefield.

Boston Globe (1975) 'Iceland Women's Strike Cripples Nation', https://maydayrooms.org/wp-content/uploads/2014/06/WfHw.SF_Media5.jpg.

Bowlby, R. (2000) *Carried Away: The Invention of Modern Shopping*. New York: Columbia University Press.

Bramall, R. (2019) *The Cultural Politics of Austerity*. London: Palgrave.

Bray, G. (2019) *The Organised Mum Method*. London: Piatkus.

Brodesser-Akner, T. (2016) 'Marie Kondo, Tidying Up and the Ruthless War on Stuff', *New York Times*, 6 July.

Bibliography

Brossard, B. and Chandler, A. (2022) *Explaining Mental Illness: Sociological Perspectives.* Bristol: Bristol University Press.

Brunsdon, C. (2000) *The Feminist, the Housewife, and the Soap Opera.* Oxford: Oxford Television Studies.

Bryant, M. (2021) 'A Kick in the Teeth: British Mothers and Pregnant Women Fear Return to Workplace', *The Guardian*, 4 September, www.theguardian.com/business/2021/sep/04/a-kick-in-the-teeth-british-mothers-and-pregnant-women-fear-return-to-workplace

Campbell, B. (1987) *Iron Ladies: Why Do Women Vote Tory?* London: Virago.

Capetta, A. (2019) 'How Spring Cleaning Can Help Manage Stress, According to Psychologists', *Good Housekeeping*, 21 March.

Care Collective (2020) *The Care Manifesto.* London: Verso.

Casey, E. (2007) *Women, Pleasure and the Gambling Experience.* London: Routledge.

Casey, E. (2023) 'Welcome to the Shopping Revolution! Commodifying Selfhood and Rearticulating Consumer Capitalism at the Metro Centre Gateshead', *The Sociological Review*, 72(2), https://doi.org/10.1177/00380261231194504.

Casey, E., Childs, S. and Huq, R. (2022) 'A Gendered Pandemic: Editors' Introduction', *Journal for Cultural Research*, 26(1), 1–5.

Casey, E. and Huq, R. (2022) 'Biscuits and Unicorns: Shifting Meanings of Domestic Space in a Post-lockdown World', *Journal for Cultural Research*, 26(1), 24–38.

Casey, E. and Littler, J. (2022) 'Mrs Hinch, the Rise of the "Cleanfluencer" and the Digital Domestication of Neoliberal Anxiety: Scouring Away the Crisis', *Sociological Review*, 70(3), 489–505.

Casey, E. and Martens, L. (eds) (2007) *Gender and Consumption: Material Culture and the Commercialisation of Everyday Life.* Farnham: Ashgate.

Charles, N. and Kerr, M. (1988) *Women, Food and Families.* Manchester: Manchester University Press.

Clarke, A. (2001) *Tupperware: The Promise of Plastic in 1950s America.* New York: Random House.

Clarke, K. (2016) 'Willful Knitting? Contemporary Australian Craftivism and Feminist Histories', *Journal of Media and Cultural Studies*, 30(3), 298–306.

Craig, L. (2007) 'Is there Really a Second Shift and if So Who Does It? A Time-Diary Investigation', *Feminist Review*, 86, 149–70.

Criado Perez, C. (2019) *Invisible Women: Exposing Data Bias in a World Designed for Men.* London: Random House.

Daly, M. (1989) *Women and Poverty.* London: Attic Press.

Davies, W. (2016) *The Happiness Industry.* London: Verso.

Davis, A. (1981) *Woman, Race and Class.* New York: Penguin.

De Beauvoir, S. (1949) *The Second Sex.* London: Penguin.

De Beauvoir, S. (2006) *Memoirs of a Dutiful Daughter.* London: Penguin.

De Benedictis, S. and Orgad, S. (2017) 'The Escalating Price of Motherhood: Aesthetic Labour in Popular Representations of "Stay-at-Home" Mothers', in *Aesthetic Labour: Rethinking Beauty Politics in Neoliberalism*, edited by A. Sofia Elias, R. Gill and C. Scharff (pp.101–16). London: Palgrave.

Bibliography

Delphy, C. (1984) *Close to Home: A Materialist Analysis of Women's Oppression*. London: Verso.

DeVault, N. M. (1991) *Feeding the Family: The Social Organisation of Caring as Gendered Work*. Chicago: University of Chicago Press.

Dobson, A. S. (2015) *Postfeminist Digital Cultures: Femininity, Social Media and Self-representation*. London: Palgrave.

Dotsikas, K. et al. (2023) 'The Gender Dimensions of Mental Health During the Covid-19 Pandemic: A Path Analysis', *PLOS One*, 18(5), e0283514, https://doi.org/10.1371/journal.pone.0283514.

Duffy, B. E. (2019) *Not Getting Paid to Do What You Love: Gender, Social Media and Aspirational Work*. Newhaven, CT: Yale University Press.

Ehrenreich, B. and English, D. (1979) *For Her Own Good: 150 Years of the Experts' Advice to Women*. London: Pluto.

Engels, F. (2010) *The Origin of the Family, Private Property and the State*. London: Penguin.

Evans, M. (2016) *The Persistence of Gender Inequality*. London: Polity.

Fawcett Society (2020) *Coronavirus: Impact on BAME women*. London: The Fawcett Society.

Federici, S. (1974) *Wages against Housework*. London: Power of Women Collective.

Federici, S. (2012) *Revolution at Point Zero: Housework, Reproduction, and Feminist Struggle*. London: Verso.

Freeman, H. (2020) 'Tradwives: The New Trend for Submissive Women Has a Dark Heart and History', *The Guardian*, 27 January, www.theguardian.com/fashion/2020/jan/27/tradwives-new-trend-submissive-women-dark-heart-history.

Friedan, B. (1964) *The Feminist Mystique*. New York: Penguin.

Fury, P. (2023) *How Does She Do It? The Kids, Tyson and Me*. London: Hodder & Stoughton.

Gavron, H. (1966) *The Captive Wife: Conflicts of Housebound Mothers*. London: Pelican.

Giles, J. (2004) *The Parlour and the Suburb: Domestic Identities, Class, Femininity and Modernity*. Oxford: Berg.

Gill, R. (2020) *Changing the Perfect Picture: Smartphones, Social Media and Appearance Pressures*. London: City, University of London.

Gill, R. and Scharff, R. (eds) (2011) *New Femininities: Postfeminism, Neoliberalism, and Subjectivity*. London: Palgrave Macmillan.

Gilroy, P. (2006) *Postcolonial Melancholia*. New York: Columbia University Press.

Girard, A. (1958) 'Le budget-temps de la femme mariée dans les agglomérations urbaines', *Population*, 13(4), 591–618.

Gordon, T. (1990) *Feminist Mothers*. London: Palgrave.

Greedy, C. (2023) *You Do You! An Inspirational Guide to Getting the Life You Want*. London: Penguin.

Hall, S. (1988) *The Hard Road to Renewal: Thatcherism and the Crisis of the Left*. London: Verso.

Hatterstone, S. (2022) 'People Underestimate Me: Stacey Solomon on Snobbery, the X Factor and Her Plan to Sort Britain Out', *The Guardian*, 29 September, www.theguardian.com/lifeandstyle/2022/sep/29/people-underestimate-me-stacey-solomon-on-snobbery-the-x-factor-and-her-plan-to-sort-britain-out.

Hearn, A. (2017) 'Witches and Bitches: Reality Television, Housewifization and the New Hidden Abode of Production', *European Journal of Cultural Studies*, 20(1), 10–24.

Hester, H. and Srnicek, N. (2023) *After Work: A History of the Home and the Fight for Free Time*. London: Verso.

Hill, S., McTighe, T. and Carney, G. (2023) 'More than "lovely girls": Revisiting Ireland's Housewife of the Year Competition', *RTE*, 4 July, www.rte.ie/brainstorm/2023/0717/1394891-housewife-of-the-year-competition-archive-history-irish-woman-feminism/.

Hochschild, A. (1989) *The Second Shift*. London: Penguin.

Hochschild, A. (2012) *The Managed Heart: Commercialisation of Human Feeling*, 3rd ed. Berkeley: University of California Press.

Holmes, H. (2019) 'Unpicking Contemporary Thrift: Getting on and Getting by in Everyday Life', *The Sociological Review*, 67(1), 126–42.

Hook, J. (2007) 'Women's Housework: New Tests of Time and Money', *Journal of Marriage and Family*, 79, 179–98.

Hooks, B. (1984) *Feminist Theory: From Margin to Center*. London: Taylor & Francis.

Howard, S. (2020) 'Sorry but It Is Selfish to Hire a Cleaner, Even If That's Difficult to Admit', *Huffington Post*, 15 May, www.huffingtonpost.co.uk/entry/cleaner-domestic-work_uk_5ebe742ac5b6500cdf66bcc8.

Huberman, J. (2022) *The Spirit of Digital Capitalism*. Cambridge: Polity.

Huebner, C. and Arya, D. (2020) 'The New Pessimism: How COVID-19 Has Made Young People Lose Faith in Their Own Agency', LSE Blog, 11 September, https://blogs.lse.ac.uk/covid19/2020/09/11/the-new-pessimism-how-covid-19-has-made-young-people-lose-faith-in-their-own-agency/.

James, S. (1973) *Women, the Unions and Work, Or ... What Is Not to Be Done*. London: Crest Press.

Jarrett, K. (2016) *Feminism, Labour and Digital Media: The Digital Housewife*. London: Routledge.

Jensen, T. (2018) *Parenting the Crisis*. Cambridge: Policy.

Jones, L. (2023) *Matrescence: On the Metamorphosis of Pregnancy, Childbirth and Motherhood*. London: Allen Lane.

Kondo, M. (2014) *The Life-Changing Magic of Tidying Up: The Japanese Art of Decluttering and Organizing*. New York: Penguin.

Kondo, M. (2016) *Spark Joy: An Illustrated Master Class on the Art of Organizing and Tidying Up*. New York: Penguin.

Laird, H. and Penney, E. (2023) 'Goodbye to Ireland's "Women in the Home" Constitution Clause?', *RTE*, 5 December, www.rte.ie/brainstorm/2023/1205/1201586-ireland-article-41-women-in-the-home-constitution-clause-1937-referendum/.

Lawler, S. (2005) 'Disgusted Subjects: The Making of Middle-Class Identities', *The Sociological Review*, 53(3), 429–46.

Bibliography

Leaver, T., Highfield, T. and Abidin, C. (2020) *Instagram*. Cambridge: Polity.

Lefebvre, H. (1947) *Critique of Everyday Life*. Paris: Grasset.

Littler, J. (2023) *Left Feminisms*. London: Lawrence Wishart.

Littler, J. (2017) *Against Meritocracy: Culture, Power and Myths of Mobility*. London: Routledge.

Lungumbu, S. and Butterly, A. (2020) 'Coronavirus and Gender: More Chores for Women Set Back Gains in Equality', *The Guardian*, 20 November.

McClaren, L. (2014) 'Japan's "Queen of Clean" Promotes Benefits of a Tidy Home', *Globe and Mail*, 24 April.

McClintock, A. (1995) *Imperial Leather: Race, Gender, and Sexuality in the Colonial Contest*. New York: Routledge.

McGee, M. (2012) 'From Makeover Media to Remaking Culture', *Sociology Compass*, 6(9), 685–93.

McRobbie, A. (2020) *Feminism and the Politics of Resilience*. Cambridge: Polity.

McVeigh, T. (2012) 'Forty Years of Feminism – but Women Still Do Most of the Housework', *The Observer*, 10 March, www.theguardian.com/society/2012/mar/10/housework-gender-equality-women.

Mahdawi, A. (2019) 'Meet the "Cleanfluencers", the Online Gurus Who Like Things Nice and Tidy', *The Guardian*, 29 January, www.theguardian.com/lifeandstyle/2019/jan/29/meet-the-cleanfluencers-the-online-gurus-who-like-things-nice-and-tidy.

Mahdawi, A. (2019) 'Meet the Online Cleanfluencers', *The Guardian*, 29 March, www.theguardian.com/lifeandstyle/2019/jan/29/meet-the-cleanfluencers-the-online-gurus-who-like-things-nice-and-tidy.

Marcel, K. (2016) *Who Cooked Adam Smith's Dinner? A Story about Women and Economics*. London: Granta.

Marks, C. (2018) 'Drudgery? No, Cleaning's Glamorous and Helps You Beat Anxiety, Say Social Media Stars Who Have Vast Armies of Fans Tuning in ... to Watch Them Scrub the Sink', *Daily Mail*, 21 October.

Martens, L. and Scott, S. (2005) '"The Unbearable Lightness of Cleaning": Representations of Domestic Practice and Products in "Good Housekeeping" Magazine (UK): 1951–2001', *Consumption, Markets and Culture*, 8(4), 379–401.

Martens, L. and Scott, S. (2006) 'Under the Kitchen Surface: Domestic Products and Conflicting Constructions of Home', *Home Cultures*, 3(1), 39–62.

Mies, M. (1986) *Patriarchy and Accumulation on a Global Scale*. London: Zed Books.

Mountford, L. (2023) *Live, Laugh, Laundry: A Calming Guide to Keeping Your Clothes Clean – and You Happy*. London: Penguin.

Mrs Hinch (2019) *Hinch Yourself Happy: All the Best Cleaning to Shine Your Sink and Soothe Your Soul*. London: Penguin.

Mrs Hinch (2020) *The Little Book of Lists*. London: Michael Joseph.

Mrs Hinch (2020) *This Is Me: A Memoir*. London: Penguin.

Nathanson, E. (2013) *Television and Post-feminist Housekeeping: No Time for Mother*. New York: Routledge.

Negra, D. (2009) *What a Girl Wants: Fantasizing the Reclamation of Self in Postfeminism*. London: Routledge.

Bibliography

Nicholas, S. (2020) 'Darling, I'll Do Anything to Make You Happy! How the Tradwives Sacrifice Their Own Careers to Satisfy Their Husbands' Every Whim ... and Insist It's the Secret of Marital Bliss', *Daily Mail*, 24 January.

Oakley, A. (1974) *Housewife*. London: Penguin.

Oakley, A. (2018) *Sociology of Housework*. Bristol: Policy Press.

Orgad, S. (2019) *Heading Home*. New York: Columbia University Press.

Orgad, S. and de Benedictis, S. (2015) 'The Stay at Home Mother, Postfeminism and Neoliberalism: Content Analysis of News Coverage', *European Journal of Communication*, 30(4), 418–36.

Orgad, S. and Gill, R. (2022) *Confidence Culture*. Durham, NC: Duke University Press.

Ouellette, L. (2019) 'Spark Joy? Compulsory Happiness and the Feminist Politics of Decluttering', *Culture Unbound*, 11(3–4), 534–50.

Ouellette, L. and Hay, J. (2008) *Better Living through Reality TV: Television and Post-welfare Citizenship*. London: Wiley-Blackwell.

Oxford CBT (2021) Stress Management: Clutter, Cleaning and Mental Health, www.oxfordcbt.co.uk/stress-management-cleaning/, accessed November 2021.

Pahl, J. (1989) *Money and Marriage*. London: Macmillan.

Pink, S. (2004) *Home Truths: Gender, Domestic Objects and Everyday Life*. London: Palgrave.

Raun, T. (2018) 'Capitalizing Intimacy: New Subcultural Forms of Micro-Celebrity Strategies and Affective Labour on YouTube', *Convergence* 24(1), 99–113.

Rettberg, J. W. (2018) *Snapchat: Phatic Communication and Ephemeral Social Media*. Ann Arbor: University of Michigan Press.

Rojek, C. and Baker, S. (2020) *Lifestyle Gurus: Constructing Authority and Influence Online*. Cambridge: Polity.

Rottenberg, C. (2022) 'Disavowing Dependency: On Angela McRobbie's Feminism and the Politics of Resilience', *European Journal of Cultural Studies*, 25(1), 335–7, https://doi.org/10.1177/13675494211032972.

Rowbotham, S. (1973) *Women's Consciousness, Man's World*. London: Verso.

Salter, J. (2023) 'What's Behind the Success of the "Cleanfluencers"?' *Financial Times*, 17 March, www.ft.com/content/d79a3deo-bc91-46c6-8641-52002d1f6f78.

Sandberg, S. (2013) *Lean in: Women, Work, and the Will to Lead*. New York: Random House.

Sandlin, J. and Wallin, J. (2022) 'Decluttering the Pandemic: Marie Kondo, Minimalism, and the "Joy" of Waste', *Cultural Studies*, 22(1), 96–102.

Schwartz L. (2019) *Feminism and the Servant Problem: Class and Domestic Labour in the Women's Suffrage Movement*. Cambridge: Cambridge University Press.

Segal, L. (2017) *Radical Happiness: Moments of Collective Joy*. London: Verso.

Shields, C. (2003) *The Republic of Love*. London: 4th Estate.

Sims, C. (2023) 'The One Phrase that Saved My Marriage and Helped Me to Ease the Mental Load', *Good To Know*, www.goodto.com/family/the-one-phrase-that-saved-my-marriage-and-helped-me-to-ease-the-mental-load.

Skeggs, B. (1997) *Formations of Class and Gender*. London: Sage.

Bibliography

Skeggs, B., Thumin, N., and Wood, H. (2008) '"Oh Goodness, I Am Watching Reality TV": How Methods Make Class in Audience Research', *European Journal of Cultural Studies*, 11(1), 5–24.

Sobande, F. (2020) *The Digital Lives of Black Women in Britain*. London: Palgrave.

Solomon, S. (2021) *Tap to Tidy: Organising, Crafting and Creating Happiness in a Messy World*. London: Ebury Press.

Sweney, M. (2013) 'Asda Cleared over "Sexist" Christmas Ad Despite More Than 600 Complaints', *The Guardian*, 30 January, www.theguardian.com/media/2013/jan/30/asda-christmas-ad.

Tait, A. (2020) 'Influencers Are Being Taken Advantage of: The Social Media Stars Turning to Unions', *The Guardian*, 10 October www.theguardian.com/media/2020/oct/10/influencers-are-being-taken-advantage-of-the-social-media-stars-turning-to-unions.

Thorarensen, T. (1975) 'Iceland Women's Strike Cripples Nation', *Boston Globe*, 25 October.

Topping, A. (2021) 'Covid-19 Crisis Could Set Women Back Decades Experts Fear', *The Guardian*, 29 May.

TUC (2021) 'Working Mums Paying the Price', www.tuc.org.uk/workingparents.

Turner, G. (2010) *Ordinary People and the Media: The Demotic Turn*. London: Sage.

Walby, S. (1990) *Theorizing Patriarchy*. London: Wiley.

Walby, S. (2015) *Crisis*. Cambridge: Polity.

Wallace Collection (2023) The Virtuous Woman, https://wallacelive.wallacecollection.org/eMP/eMuseumPlus?service=ExternalInterface&module=collection&objectId=65173&viewType=detailView.

Williamson, J. (1986) *Consuming Passions: The Dynamics of Popular Culture*. London: Marion Boyars.

Wilson, J. (2016) *Neoliberalism*. London: Routledge.

Wilson, J. and Chivers Yochim, E. (2017) *Mothering Through Precarity*. Durham, CA: Duke.

Winship, J. (1987) *Inside Women's Magazines*. Lewes: Rivers Oram Press.

Women's Budget Group (2020) *Crises Collide: Women and Covid-19*. London: WBG.

Woodward, S. (2015) 'The Hidden Lives of Domestic Things: Accumulations in Cupboards, Lofts, and Shelves', in *Intimacies, Critical Consumption and Diverse Economies*, edited by E. Casey and Y. Taylor. London: Palgrave.

Woodward, S. (2021) 'Clutter in Domestic Spaces: Material Vibrancy, and Competing Moralities', *The Sociological Review*, 69(6), 1214–28.

Index

EU authorised representative for GPSR:
Easy Access System Europe, Mustamäe tee 50,
10621 Tallinn, Estonia
gpsr.requests@easproject.com

www.ingramcontent.com/pod-product-compliance
Lightning Source LLC
Chambersburg PA
CBHW011537260326
41914CB00036B/1977/J